# HOGAN'S HEROES

# HOGAN'S HEROES
## BEHIND THE SCENES AT STALAG 13

Brenda Scott Royce

**BOOKS**

RENAISSANCE BOOKS
Los Angeles

*To the unsung hero of our family,*
*Helena Mete*
*Code Name: Gramma*

Library of Congress Cataloging-in-Publication Data

Royce, Brenda Scott.
   Hogan's heroes : behind the scenes at Stalag 13 / Brenda Scott Royce.
     p. cm.
   Originally published: Jefferson, N.C. : McFarland, c1993.
   Includes bibliographical references and index.
   ISBN 1-58063-031-6 (alk. paper)
   1. Hogan's heroes.  I. Title.
   PN1992.77.H56R49 1998
   791.45'72—dc21                                         98-39326
                                                            CIP

10 9 8 7 6 5 4 3 2 1
Manufactured in the United States
Distributed by St. Martin's Press

Design by Tanya Maiboroda

Portions of this book were previously published
in the McFarland & Co. 1993 hardcover edition,
*Hogan's Heroes: A Comprehensive Reference.*

# ACKNOWLEDGMENTS

The most important assistance I received on this book came from the individuals who worked on *Hogan's Heroes* and who generously gave of their time over the years to share their memories with me. For them, my special thanks: Werner Klemperer, Robert Clary, Larry Hovis, Leon Askin, Howard Caine, Bernard Fox, Kenneth Washington, Jerry London, Laurence Marks, Howard Morris, Richard M. Powell, Gene Reynolds, Albert S. Ruddy, Kay Fein Pattison, Mary Feldman, Chris Anders, Lee Bergere, Victoria Carroll, William Christopher, Henry Corden, Eddie Firestone, Bert Freed, Harold Gould, Tom Hatten, Robert Hogan, Sandy Kenyon, Leonid Kinskey, Paul Lambert, Ruta Lee, Gavin MacLeod, Laurie Main, Frank Marth, Marlyn Mason, Dave Morick, Stewart Moss, Paul Picerni, and Vito Scotti. Thanks also to Judy Jeffers of Bing Crosby Productions and Randy Ragland of Rysher Entertainment.

The following individuals and organizations have each contributed time, information, or materials to the preparation of this book and my appreciation cannot be overstated: Kathy Bartels, Mark Batira, Howard Berlin, Roger Christman, Stephen Cox, Gary Crane, Jim Davidson, Chris Finkbeiner, Otto Franklin, Paul Grieshop Jr., Matthias Hamann, Marilyn Hering, Lanette Hohl, Kathleen Jacobs, Linda Kay, Richard Laban, Paul Lichota, Vicki

Linde, Robbin Love, David Martindale, Madeline McGrail, Norman Pomeroy, John Reese, Dale Roberts, Jim and Melody Rondeau, Mark Smeby, Vince Waldron, David Wojtowicz, Stefan Worbs, Johnnie J. Young, Todd Zaganiacz, Gayla Raul of Film Favorites, Jonathan Rosenthal of the Museum of Television and Radio, Diane and Stephen Albert of the *TV Collector*, Bill Morgan of TV Toys, Katharine Loughney and the Library of Congress, Janet Lorenz and the Academy of Motion Picture Arts and Sciences, the Theater Collection at the New York Public Library, Robert Franklin and Rhonda Herman of McFarland and Company, and Donna Malone of Bernie Ilson Public Relations.

Thanks to everyone at Renaissance Books, particularly Joe McNeely for making this paperback edition possible, and Bill Hartley, Michael Dougherty, Kimbria Hays, Paula Leto, Kathryn Mills, and Jim Parish.

As always, my deepest appreciation goes to my family and friends for their support and encouragement.

# CONTENTS

# FOREWORD

When I was asked to write the foreword for this book, I gladly accepted the opportunity to relate how important *Hogan's Heroes* has been to my work. The six years of *Hogan's Heroes* were some of the most enjoyable years of my career, and it was particularly exciting to work with such a group of talented and professional peers on a continuing basis, something I had not experienced before.

*Hogan's Heroes* is now considered a "classic," much like *M*A*S*H* or *The Mary Tyler Moore Show*. It is obviously a series that can be seen again and again and it seems to continually find new fans every year. I have been told that more people see the program now (because of its wide syndication) than did when it was on the CBS television network. Many stations now play it five times a week (some stations even twice a day), giving it continuing exposure. I know the show still "works," because I get letters from fans all over the country telling me how much they enjoy it.

In recent years, I have been active on Broadway and in regional theaters and concert halls all over the world. Wherever I go, not a day goes by without some fans stopping me in the street or at a restaurant or an airport to express how much they still enjoy the show. I am proud to have portrayed Colonel Klink and to have been recognized by my peers with two Emmys and five consecutive nominations.

Finally, I must take the opportunity to compliment Brenda Scott Royce on this outstanding book. Her research is remarkably accurate, her style makes for easy reading, and I am sure everyone who owns this book will get as much enjoyment out of it as I did.

—Werner Klemperer

# INTRODUCTION

In the *New York Daily News's* "TV Review" column on December 20, 1965, reviewer John Horn compared *Hogan's Heroes* to Buster Keaton's 1927 film *The General,* in an attempt to illustrate his opinion that the standards of comedy had grossly declined if *Hogan's* was considered good comedy. He implied that the "cerebral" comedy of *Hogan's* was inferior to the "physical" comedy of the silent era. His closing remark in the column renders his expertise questionable. He wrote, "We don't think *Hogan's Heroes* will be playing on TV, even as a curio, a generation from now."

More than thirty years after Mr. Horn's column appeared in print, *Hogan's Heroes* is indeed airing, in hundreds of markets worldwide. Its popularity in syndication has given rise to generations of younger fans.

When the series premiered in 1965, critics' reactions ran from one extreme to the other. *Variety* gave the pilot episode an excellent review, calling it "genuinely creative farce comedy, well conceived, written, directed and played." However, much negative press was generated, mainly from those who mistakenly believed the comedy was set in a concentration camp.

When the American public was first exposed to the premise of *Hogan's Heroes,* many were outraged. A prisoner-of-war camp in World War II Germany was an inauspicious choice of settings for a TV sitcom. War is not funny, and yet a number of successful film and television comedies set in wartime had already been produced. Jack Benny's classic black comedy *To Be or Not to Be* parodied the Nazi regime as early as 1942. A POW camp was untried territory in television situation comedy, and it seemed inappropriate to laugh at such a harsh reality as prisoners of war. Therefore *Hogan's Heroes* incited more than its fair share of criticism.

To further aggravate the situation, many people confused prisoner-of-war camps with concentration camps, where millions of inmates were starved, treated inhumanely, and murdered. In a *TV Guide* interview, John Banner explained: "People get upset when they think we are making fun of a concentration camp. You can't make fun of a concentration camp." No one would know that better than cast mate Robert Clary. In 1942, Clary was deported from France and taken to Germany, where he suffered three years of savage treatment in concentration camps. At the end of the war, Clary learned that of the thirteen members of his family who were sent to concentration camps, he alone survived.

POWs, on the other hand, are protected by the Geneva Prisoner of War Convention regulations for the ethical treatment of prisoners. Though confinement in a prisoner-of-war camp does not in reality make for fun and frolics, *Hogan's Heroes* was not based in reality. It was a parody, an escapist form of comedy. The fictional Stalag 13 was never meant to be representative of a real POW camp.

The comedy of *Hogan's Heroes* rose not out of the setting, but out of the characters—a bunch of guys outwitting authority. It was a familiar formula in a setting that was unfamiliar to most TV viewers and therefore caused a great deal of uneasiness. The controversy was heightened by a radio promo produced by humorist Stan Freberg, which had Bob Crane chirping, "If you liked World War II, you'll love *Hogan's Heroes*." The reaction, of course, was that people did not "like" the war, and that the commercial was in poor taste. The spot was yanked from the airwaves. Crane later admitted that he had reservations about doing the ad but did not heed his better judgment. Barring that blunder, everyone involved with *Hogan's* did all they could to minimize the controversy by concentrating instead on producing a unique, top-quality comedy. If A. C. Nielsen is the judge, they succeeded. *Hogan's Heroes* was the highest rated new show of the 1965–66 season, ranking #9 among all network shows. It was an unqualified hit.

A few of the performers who appeared on *Hogan's Heroes* cast their votes with the series' opposers. Leonid Kinskey portrayed a Russian POW in the pilot episode and said that during the shooting he could not escape the image

**The first season cast of *Hogan's Heroes*. From left to right: Werner Klemperer, John Banner, Cynthia Lynn, Bob Crane, Larry Hovis, Robert Clary, Ivan Dixon, Richard Dawson.** © Bing Crosby Productions, Inc. Reprinted with permission.

of the Nazi regime. He filmed the pilot, but says he turned down the offer to be a regular on the series. Actor Paul Lambert, an Army Air Corps lieutenant in World War II, appeared in four episodes of the series, but says his motive was strictly monetary. "I always felt a little queasy about doing this show about 'funny Nazis.' If it weren't for the money, I wouldn't have done *Hogan's*."

The cast of *Hogan's Heroes* are all outspoken on the controversy. Most echo the opinion of co-creator Al Ruddy: "In these United States, we have so many varied types and personalities. You cannot do anything without offending certain people. The morality is more important than pleasing everybody. I had no moral problem at all doing *Hogan's*. It was about how these prisoners survived and prevailed over the Germans. Comedy has no boundaries. You can't put a hard line parameter around comedy."

Once the dust settled, *Hogan's Heroes* was seen for what it was: a satire never meant to be taken seriously. Each episode saw the resourceful prisoners accomplishing impossible tasks, making fools of their captors, and forgoing the opportunity to escape so they could continue to aid the Allies. The ridiculous twists and preposterous situations abundant in each script gave evidence to the fact that *Hogan's Heroes* was a harmless farce. As Larry Hovis puts it, "It was really about the ingenuity of the GIs. Hopefully, if anything, it makes war seem ridiculous."

To enjoy *Hogan's Heroes* was to suspend disbelief for thirty minutes a week, to root for the Allies, to see goodness prevail amid a series of absurd situations.

The premise of *Hogan's Heroes* was as follows: Hogan's "heroes" were not actually prisoners, but volunteers on a mission. Their mission was to assist escaping Allied prisoners and to use every means at their disposal to sabotage and harass the enemy. Colonel Robert Hogan commanded the 504th Bomb Squadron before he was recruited to lead an espionage and sabotage group operating against the enemy from behind their own lines. Hogan's team of experts included Kinchloe ("Kinch"), an electronics and radio expert; Carter, an explosives specialist; Newkirk, a safecracker and pickpocket; and LeBeau, whose talents ranged from gourmet cooking to tailoring.

When we first met the heroes in the pilot episode, they had already set up an extensive tunnel system, radio network, and counterfeiting and manufacturing factories, and had taken over virtual control of the camp from its unsuspecting kommandant, Colonel Wilhelm Klink. It is not explained how the prisoners managed to construct such an incredible underground operation, but the ineptness of their German captors suggested that it hadn't been too difficult.

Both Colonel Klink and Sergeant Schultz were immediately criticized in the press as being "lovable Nazis," a being incomprehensible to most people. That label was inaccurate as neither character was a Nazi, and despite their sometimes willing cooperation with Hogan, they were never wholly on the side of the Allies—never part of the "heroes."

Colonel Klink and Sergeant Schultz were members of the Luftwaffe—the German Air Force, not the Gestapo (the Nazi secret police), or the murderous SS (the German "elite guard" in charge of the concentration camps). Neither was in favor of the war; they were merely soldiers performing their duty—Klink doing as much of his duty as might help him gain a promotion, and Schultz doing as much of his duty as possible without harming anyone—especially himself.

Colonel Wilhelm Klink was a man who did not agree with Hitler's ideals, but was terrified of admitting that fact. He followed orders and ran his stalag, but would have preferred to hide under a rock somewhere until the war was over. In constant fear of the Gestapo and the threat of a combat position, Klink was easily manipulated by Hogan.

The relationship between Klink and Hogan was one of the mainstays of the series. Though their roles of war pitted them against one another, each needed the other to survive. A more rigid kommandant would have made Hogan's operation impossible. And without Hogan's assistance, Klink could have been ousted to the Russian front on several occasions. A large number of Hogan's missions dealt with trying to save either Klink or Schultz from such a fate. As time went on, Hogan and Klink developed an unconscious, guarded partnership.

Also essential to most of the heroes' plots was the dim-witted sergeant of the guards, Hans Schultz. Sergeant Schultz, who wanted nothing more from the war than to survive it, so frequently looked the other way when the heroes were up to "monkey business" that "I know nothing, I see *nothing!*" quickly became his catch phrase.

The real villains in *Hogan's Heroes* were represented by Klink's superior, General Burkhalter, and the nasty Gestapo agent, Major Hochstetter. While Klink and Schultz were no match for the clever Colonel Hogan, Burkhalter and Hochstetter provided more of a challenge. General Burkhalter occasionally showed his weaknesses—pretty fräuleins, greed—which Hogan took full advantage of. Due to these weaknesses, Burkhalter appeared to be more human than monster. On the other hand, Major Hochstetter, the Gestapo personified, never faltered in his depiction of the evil madman driven by a desire to serve the Führer and destroy the enemy.

Writer Richard M. Powell explained his approach to writing for these characters: "On the shows I did, I tried to show the Nazis and the Gestapo in a highly unfavorable light, even though it was comedic. I tried to show that the whole Nazi regime was based on fear. In a lot of my scripts I would have the Gestapo come in and throw the fear of God into everybody. And of course Hogan would use that for his own purposes. I had no compunctions about doing this show. I wasn't trivializing the Nazis at all." In one Powell script, "A

Tiger Hunt in Paris" (#42), a Gestapo officer threatens Hogan: "If you have lied to me, I have every legal right to shoot you now. If you have told me the truth, I have every legal right to shoot you—now." This kind of dialogue was typical of the Gestapo on the series.

The makers of *Hogan's Heroes* were not claiming to present a documentary of life in World War II Germany. The characters were extreme, the situations preposterous. Subjects such as concentration camps and gas chambers were taboo. The protests died out a few months after the series premiered.

*Hogan's Heroes* weathered the storm of harsh criticism. It lasted for six seasons on CBS—which in the precarious television industry is no modest achievement—and it remains one of the most popular syndicated shows in the 1990s.

# CREATION

hen *Hogan's Heroes* first aired on September 17, 1965, it marked the beginning of a six-year success story. The cast and crew, some of whom were just getting their feet wet in television, were beginning a long and prosperous association. But the airing of the pilot marked the end of the process for its two creators, Bernie Fein and Al Ruddy. Both men were involved with the show from that day forth financially, and Fein even stayed with the show as associate producer for one year, but the all-important, magical creation process had ended. *Hogan's Heroes* was out of their hands and into the hands of the producer, actors, directors, and writers—and the public.

## Bernard Fein and Albert S. Ruddy, Creators

Before *Hogan's Heroes* changed their lives, Bernard Fein was an actor who wanted to write and Albert S. Ruddy was an architect who wanted a career change. They met in the early sixties through a mutual friend, film director Brian Hutton *(First Deadly Sin, Kelly's Heroes)*. The two men, both in their early thirties, became fast friends. They decided to team up and try writing for television. Ruddy had no previous experience in TV. Fein, as an actor, had costarred on Phil Silvers' *Sergeant Bilko* series and guest-starred in such series as *The Twilight Zone, 77 Sunset Strip,* and *The Untouchables.* Neither had done any writing. Dauntlessly, the two set out to write a television pilot.

In retrospect, Ruddy realizes that their expectations were unrealistic. In fact, he attributes their success to luck and ignorance. "If someone were to ask me today what their chances of selling a television pilot are I would say you might as well go to Vegas," a more seasoned Ruddy asserts. "Writing a television pilot is like playing the lottery. It's a one-in-a-million shot." But at the time, the two men were full of wide-eyed optimism and ignored the admonitions of skeptical friends.

The result of their collaboration was a sitcom based in a minimum security prison, where the ingenious prisoners coordinated escape activities and had virtual control of the prison, always outsmarting the warden. Despite a genuinely funny script, they could not sell the project. Ruddy reflects, "We couldn't find a sponsor for the series, because no one wanted to sponsor 'a night in the slam.'" American television audiences were not ready to accept inmates as protagonists, and in order for the idea to sell, the characters had to be made more sympathetic.

[Ten years after *Hogan's Heroes'* debut, a sitcom set in a minimum security prison did make it to the air. *On the Rocks* starred Mel Stewart and Tom Poston as a hard-nosed corrections officer and his mild-mannered guard (think Klink and Schultz), and concerned a bunch of multiethnic inmates who used every opportunity to one-up their captors. The series debuted in September 1975 and was canceled after one season. Despite the similarities, *On the Rocks* was not derived from *Hogan's Heroes,* but was based on a British television series, *Porridge.*]

The transformation of the setting from American prison to prisoner-of-war camp was exactly what was needed to take the edge off and make the audience side with the prisoners. Conflicting stories have been printed concerning how the change was brought about. A popular version is one that co-creator Bernie Fein was fond of telling. He contended that he was on a plane to New York—he was leaving Los Angeles and giving up his writing career—when he sat next to someone who was reading *Von Ryan's Express.* As he told the story in the *Hollywood Citizen-News* in 1965, "I just saw the cover. I had never read the book...but something clicked. I knew what I had to do—change the locale to a wartime prison camp. You may not believe this, but the only thing I could think of was what if [the plane] should crash before I could rewrite the show."

This story has been repeated in books about television history, but it does not reflect the actual course of events. Bernie's widow, Kay Fein Pattison,

**Co creator Albert S. Ruddy.**
Photo courtesy Al Ruddy.

explains, "Bernie did tell that story about *Von Ryan's Express,* but that is all it was—a story. Bernie liked to make history/life a bit more colorful or interesting than it was in reality. He was highly imaginative and entertaining and told amusing stories." A pleasant side effect for the Feins was that they became acquainted with the author of *Von Ryan's Express,* David Westheimer, as a direct result of the story.

In actuality, a rumor that one of the other networks was using a POW camp setting prompted the change. NBC was putting together *Campo 44,* a series about Americans held in an Italian prisoner-of-war camp. (Coincidentally, *Campo 44* was written by David Westheimer, the author of *Von Ryan's Express.*) At *Campo 44,* the Italian captors had very little interest in fighting the war. The kommandant was more interested in tending to his garden than his prisoners, and the second in command was a dim-witted sort, Capitano Barracutti, played by veteran character actor Vito Scotti. Scotti recalled, "Barracutti's feeling was 'Let's have war, but not spill blood. Especially my blood!'"

Scotti, whose most memorable roles include Dr. Balinkoff on *Gilligan's Island,* Sam Picasso on *The Addams Family,* and Captain Fomento on *The Flying Nun,* believed that while the *Campo 44* pilot was being filmed, someone got hold of a script and it was quickly converted into *Hogan's Heroes.* "And so from *Campo 44* came *Hogan's Heroes.* Identical thing. And we were out." Scotti held no grudges, though, and later guest-starred on *Hogan's Heroes* as the war-hating Major Bonacelli.

Al Ruddy admits that *Campo 44* provided the inspiration for *Hogan's Heroes'* change of locale, but not in such a direct manner as a bootlegged script. "We read in the paper that another network was doing a sitcom set in an Italian prisoner of war camp and we thought *perfect*. We rewrote our script and set it in a German POW camp in about two days."

Kay Fein Pattison recalls that her husband Bernie overheard in an office at CBS that the network was considering an hour-long drama about a POW camp and that prompted the rewrite. It is likely that CBS was shopping for a project to compete against *Campo 44* and was considering an hour-length project. Vito Scotti felt that the controversy that surrounded *Hogan's Heroes* would not have been a problem with *Campo 44,* because the Italians were not in favor of the war, whereas Germany and America were direct adversaries in the conflict. Scotti explained, "The Italians were against war, so there was no after-war animosity, whereas the German situation was something people had a difficult time laughing at." Bernard Fox, who played Colonel Crittendon on *Hogan's Heroes,* would have played a recurring role on *Campo 44,* had it been picked up as a series. He, too, thinks the Italian setting would have made more sense.

**Co-creator Bernie Fein.**
Photo courtesy Kay Fein Pattison.

Ironically, the unsold *Campo 44* pilot did not make it on the air until September 9, 1967. The similarities between it and *Hogan's Heroes* were obvious, and *Campo 44* was called a cheap rip-off of *Hogan's* by those who did not know it had actually preceded the CBS hit. *Variety* called *Campo 44* "*Gomer Pyle*-ish" and blasted NBC for even considering putting it on the air.

Once inspired by hearing about the *Campo 44* locale, Fein and Ruddy sprang into action and rewrote their pilot in record time. Though the setting and characters were changed, the basic plot remained the same. In the original, the government plants a spy among the convicts in the prison. Once the spy is accepted by the other prisoners, they show him their covert operations. Instead of making license plates, they are manufacturing cigarette lighters and are providing escaping prisoners with money. When they discover the spy's identity, the prisoners turn the situation around and implicate the spy in an escape attempt. This formula, using different settings and characters, is identical to the structure of the pilot which finally made it on the air in September of 1965. The claim that Ruddy and Fein plagiarized from either *Campo 44* or *Stalag 17* (as was later charged in a lawsuit) is clearly false.

After their hasty revision, Bernie Fein and Al Ruddy pitched their new script to the networks. According to a story printed in *Canned Laughter: The Best Stories from Radio and Television,* the pilot was first pitched to NBC, but the peacock network declined after its executives queried, "If the pilot is this good, how could they sustain it week after week?" At CBS, there was definite interest. A meeting was set up with Mike Levy (of Artists' Agency), Hunt Stromberg (head of CBS West Coast programming), William S. Paley (founder-president of CBS), Mike Dann (vice president of programming for CBS), Al Ruddy, and Bernie Fein. Levy outlined the premise of the series for the assembled VIPs. When the pitch was over, William Paley announced, "I find the idea of doing a comedy set in a Nazi prisoner-of-war camp reprehensible." Al Ruddy recalls of that fateful moment: "Mike Levy's mouth dropped open. Then I proceeded to explain to him [Paley] the premise of the show. I literally acted out a half-hour of the show—the barking dogs, the machine-gun sound effects, the works. It was hilarious! At the end of it, Paley said it was the best presentation he had ever heard."

After closing the deal with CBS and Bing Crosby Productions, Bernie Fein and Al Ruddy chose to follow separate career paths. Each earned over $40,000 for the script, plus "substantial royalties." No longer struggling writers, the two gained a reputation as "bright young men" practically overnight. Ruddy used this leverage to move into producing films. It was based on the success of *Hogan's Heroes* that he produced *The Longest Yard* and *Little Fauss and Big Halsey.* CBS had approached Ruddy with an offer to produce *Hogan's,* but he turned it down. He asserts, "I wanted to go into films and producing for television just didn't appeal to me." People thought he was insane for turning down a lucrative career as a television producer, but Ruddy stuck with his plan. His decision proved to be a wise one, as he went on to a very successful film producing career. His films include *The Godfather* (which won the Academy Award for Best Picture in 1972), *Megaforce,* *Lassiter,* and *Cannonball Run* and its sequels. His company, Ruddy-Morgan Productions, most recently produced *Bad Girls* (1994), a western starring

## STALAG 13 OR 17?

A popular misconception is that *Hogan's Heroes* was adapted from the 1953 film *Stalag 17*. Though there were slight similarities between the two, *Stalag 17* was no more a precursor to *Hogan's* than were *Sergeant Bilko* or *McHale's Navy*. The authors of the play on which the film was based were so convinced that *Hogan's* was plagiarized from their work that they filed a lawsuit against CBS. Playwrights Donald Bevan and Edmund Trzcinski wrote the Broadway play, *Stalag 17*, which was adapted for the screen by Billy Wilder and Edwin Blum. The film version was a tremendous success, and its star, William Holden, won an Academy Award for his performance.

    *Stalag 17* concerned the activities of a group of American prisoners-of-war held in a German camp. Unlike the blatant comedy of *Hogan's Heroes*, *Stalag 17* was a serious, stirring drama with comic undertones. *Stalag 17's* plot centered around the prisoners' discovery that there is a spy among them who has been informing the Germans of escape plans. The story bears a likeness to the initial episode of *Hogan's Heroes*, which had the men discrediting a German spy who was planted among the prisoners.

    Bob Crane said that his character was based on James Garner's role in the 1963 film *The Great Escape,* which recounted the mass escape of seventy-six Allied prisoners from Stalag Luft III in March 1944.

    One striking similarity between *Hogan's Heroes* and *Stalag 17* is that the main guard in both pieces was named Sergeant Schultz. In Bernie Fein and Al Ruddy's script, there was no character named Schultz. Richard M. Powell, who rewrote the pilot, said that he created the Schultz character. "I didn't read or see *Stalag 17*," he attests. "Sergeant Schultz was a character I invented. I took the name from the Jack Benny film *To Be or Not to Be*. The Schultz character was important to the sitcom because I felt some sort of go-between was necessary between the prisoners and Klink."

Drew Barrymore and Andie MacDowell, and *Heaven's Prisoners* (1996), a mystery-thriller with Alec Baldwin and Teri Hatcher.

    Unlike Ruddy, Bernie Fein wanted to remain with *Hogan's Heroes* after the sale of the pilot. He signed on as associate producer of the series. He worked closely on the day-to-day production for the first season, but his option was not renewed by Bing Crosby Productions the following season. Executive producer Ed Feldman often did not agree with Fein's suggestions and the two were not a compatible production team. "Feldman did not care for Bernie, although I don't know what caused the tension between them," recalls Kay Fein Pattison.

Though Sergeant Schultz proved to be an immensely popular character in the series, naming him "Schultz" may not have been a wise choice. Kay Fein Pattison says, "Bernie and Al did not steal the idea, but the producers changed some things—like naming one of the Germans Schultz—that created similarities."

The authors of *Stalag 17* filed a lawsuit in January 1967 against CBS and Bing Crosby Productions. They charged that in 1963, they submitted a one-hour script to CBS which was based on their play and the network turned it down. Bevan and Trzcinski claimed that rather than buy their series, CBS sought out two unknown writers to write the same thing, thereby costing the network less money.

*Hogan's* co-creator Albert S. Ruddy calls the charge "ridiculous." The playwrights asked for an injunction against the broadcast of the series until the case was settled, but were denied. The case did not go to trial until after the series ended its original run. Producer Ed Feldman, creators Al Ruddy and Bernie Fein, and writer Richard M. Powell were subpoenaed as witnesses. Mary Feldman recalls, "They kept asking Ed if he had read *Stalag 17* and he said he had not. Then they asked him where he got the word 'stalag.' But of course 'stalag' was a well-known term."

Ruddy shares his memories of the lawsuit. "The trial was about one year after the show. I was in New York working on *The Godfather* and I had to go downtown to appear as one of the witnesses. The suit was against CBS, but we were involved because they claimed we were in collusion with CBS to cheat them. The outcome of the trial was unbelievable. The jury actually decided in favor of the *Stalag 17* authors. What happened next was a rare occurrence—the judge reversed the jury's decision. It was called a bench reversal. When a judge issues a 'bench reversal' he's saying that the jury did not do their job, that there was not sufficient evidence to justify their decision. The judge in this case thought it was ludicrous. And once a judge issues a bench reversal there is no turning it around, and there was never any appeal." ★

Following his stint as associate producer, Fein continued pursuing his writing career. He optioned *The Prince on Center Street,* a pilot he co-wrote with Ed Adamson, and a project called *Bellingham Group* for Twentieth Century Fox TV. His subsequent projects did not match the success of *Hogan's Heroes.* Bernie Fein passed away in September 1980 after an extended illness.

Although the Ruddy-Fein writing team did not collaborate on any projects after *Hogan's,* they had written a few things prior to that script that garnered some interest from producers. A sitcom with a western setting, *Mingo* was about the "fastest mouth in the West." Screen Gems was interested in it, but they had trouble casting the pilot. "We needed someone who looked like John Wayne, but could be funny. We just couldn't cast it and it didn't go anywhere," Ruddy recalls.

Though they never worked together professionally after *Hogan's*, Fein and Ruddy remained great friends. "There was never a fracture in the relationship," Ruddy says warmly. "We had a marvelous time writing the pilot. It was the turning point in both our lives."

### Edward H. Feldman, Executive Producer

When approached with Bernie Fein and Al Ruddy's script, Basil Grillo (then head of Bing Crosby Productions) gave it to Ed Feldman and several other producers to elicit their opinions. According to Feldman's widow, Mary, Ed did not think the original script was in very good form and did not want to be involved with it. After discussing it further, he decided that the idea had promise and could make an interesting series if some changes were made. Of all the producers queried, only Feldman came up with creative ideas. Feldman was hired by Grillo to produce the series on behalf of Bing Crosby Productions.

Over the next six years, Feldman sat quietly behind the scenes at *Hogan's Heroes* and was the person most singularly responsible for the series' success. Not a "star producer," in the words of one of the actors, his name was not often found in media headlines. His friends and colleagues describe him as a gentle man who exerted total control over his productions while maintaining a friendly atmosphere.

In a 1966 *TV Week* interview, Bob Crane said, "I don't mean to take anything away from myself or Werner or John, but the real secret is Ed Feldman, the producer. It's the man in the front office that makes the program. There are different writers, different directors, but Ed Feldman pulls it all together. He's the Sheldon Leonard, the Paul Henning, the man with the touch."

Werner Klemperer says, "I would say that without Ed Feldman, I really don't think the six years could have been the way it was and could have been as successful. Because his control was total. And he had good taste. He was a very gentle, sweet guy. He was very good to me during the entire run, and I admired and respected him. He was wonderful."

Robert Clary echoes those sentiments. "Ed Feldman was the best. The reason *Hogan's Heroes* was so successful is because of him. In a television series, if you don't have a good producer, it's not going to work. He hires the writers, the directors, the cutters, the actors—he oversees everything. And he was very, very good. Not mean, never. Nobody could say anything bad about

**Executive producer Ed Feldman on the set with John Banner and Werner Klemperer.** Photo courtesy Mary Feldman. © Bing Crosby Productions, Inc. Reprinted with permission.

him. He was gentle to everybody. But he did hold the reins. And he knew what he was doing, because *Hogan's Heroes* was his baby, and he made it what it was."

Richard M. Powell, one of the series' primary writers, says, "Ed Feldman has to be given the major credit, because he was very capable and very well liked by everybody. And he directed quite a few of the episodes. I always liked it when he directed mine because he did them better than any of the other directors did. And he was able to laugh with them, and at the same time be enough of a producer and a boss so that things didn't get completely out of line."

Howard Caine recalled, "He was the one who made the show. He had so much humanity. Eddie Feldman knew that if you wanted to do a good show you had to pay money for it. You had to pay more to hire better writers. You had to pay the writer to do his own script changes. You had to pay more to the actors, more money to get better actors. And if you went into overtime for whatever reason, you paid overtime instead of rushing it. Whatever it took to get a good show, to get a quality show, took more time, took more money. He was a perfectionist. What was important was the quality, the result."

A native of New York, Feldman studied advertising at Columbia and Yale Universities. His first job was with the Buchanan Ad Agency in New York City. His promising career as an ad man was interrupted by the outbreak of World War II. He served with the 313th Bombardment Wing of the 20th Air Force, achieving the rank of first lieutenant.

After the war, Feldman resumed his career in advertising, with stints at the Biow Company and North Advertising. He then moved into radio, producing and directing the Milton Berle, Eddie Cantor, and Garry Moore radio shows. His television career began with assignments on *I Love Lucy* and *My Little Margie*. In 1955, Feldman joined Desilu Productions as a vice president. In 1956 he produced his first television series for Desilu, *The Brothers*. The brothers in the title were played by Gale Gordon (best known as *The Lucy Show*'s Mr. Mooney) and Bob Sweeney (who later became one of *Hogan's* regular directors). *The Brothers* was canceled at the end of its first season.

Feldman's next assignment was producing *Angel*, a comedy about a French newlywed trying to cope with American lifestyles. The series lasted for one year, after which Feldman produced *Here's Hollywood,* an interview show focusing on the lives of celebrities. In 1962, *Here's Hollywood* was off the air and Feldman's fourth series, *Fair Exchange,* was on.

*Fair Exchange* concerned the families of two World War II buddies, one in New York City and the other in London. Both men had teenage daughters. The daughter living in New York wanted to attend the Royal Academy of Dramatic Arts in London. The teenager in London wanted to live in New York and learn the American way of life. The two families agreed to exchange the girls for one year to give each the opportunity to fulfill her dreams.

Feldman spoke of his experience with *Fair Exchange* in a 1965 *TV Guide* article. "Everybody predicted it would be a hit. When it hit the air, the reviews were all raves—I still have them. Even today people tell me how great it was. They just didn't watch it." *Fair Exchange* began as an experimental hour-long sitcom and was canceled after only three months. CBS was flooded with letters from viewers who loved the show and *Fair Exchange* was given a second chance. It reappeared in March 1963 in a new half-hour format and after thirteen more episodes was once again canceled.

Feldman's next producing assignment was Glynis Johns's short-lived series, *Glynis*. Next, he helped launch the top-ten hit *Gomer Pyle, U.S.M.C.*, by producing the first thirteen episodes. He moved from *Gomer Pyle* right into *Hogan's Heroes*.

Feldman served as producer of *Hogan's Heroes* from its debut in September 1965 until early 1969, when William A. Calihan took over as producer and Feldman's title changed to executive producer. At that time Feldman took on another series' challenge. *The Queen and I* starred Larry Storch and Billy DeWolfe, with *Hogan's Heroes* frequent guest star Dave Morick in a small role. Feldman produced the series, about a decrepit ocean liner and its ship's purser's attempts to save it. *The Queen and I* aired from January to May 1969 for a total of thirteen episodes.

The family atmosphere on the *Hogan's Heroes* set has been exalted by most of those involved with the series. Ed Feldman can be named as the person most responsible for breeding the friendly environment. He had the ability to joke around with the cast and crew and at the same time keep a firm handle on all aspects of the production. Several years after *Hogan's Heroes*, Feldman told an interviewer: "Even though I was running the show, I could not behave as a tyrant. I had to cajole and do it with humor so as not to give the impression that I was authority. But that only served to help us all work together so beautifully. I don't think I'll ever have the kind of relationship in this business that I had with the guys on that show." In addition to his producing responsibilities on *Hogan's*, Feldman also directed a total of twenty-six episodes.

After *Hogan's Heroes*, Feldman remained very active in television—producing and directing. In 1977, he teamed up once again with Bob Sweeney to produce a new series, *The Andros Targets*. *Variety* rated the series poorly, calling it "nothing new," and it was canceled after thirteen episodes. Feldman also served as a producer on *The Doris Day Show* for a year and the prime-time soap opera *Flamingo Road* from 1980 to 1982. He directed episodes of *Flamingo Road*, *Baker's Dozen*, *At Ease*, *AfterMASH*, *The Lucie Arnaz Show*, and several pilots. Feldman and Richard M. Powell teamed up to write and produce television pilots for MGM. Powell says of the three-year deal, "Unfortunately MGM was in a down period at that time and there were management changes, and we were weren't able to accomplish very much. But we always had fun working together."

Feldman was known in the industry as a top-notch professional and a friendly man. He and his wife Mary remained friends over the years with most of the cast, crew, writers, and directors from *Hogan's Heroes*. His main passion outside of his work was golf. On November 30, 1988, Feldman died of heart disease. His memory lives on in each of the 168 episodes of *Hogan's Heroes*. The average viewer may not be aware of it, but those who worked on the show will attest to the care and devotion Feldman put into each and every episode. "*Hogan's Heroes* was his baby," said Robert Clary. His baby made him proud.

### Richard M. Powell, Writer

Bernie Fein and Al Ruddy conceived a highly imaginative premise for a unique situation comedy. The framework they laid was enough to sell the idea to CBS and Bing Crosby Productions, but as the pair were not experienced scriptwriters, their original script needed some fine-tuning before it would be ready. Richard M. Powell, who later became one of the series' three main writers, relates that he first became involved with *Hogan's Heroes* at this point. "The script was by two people who were not really writers. Ed Feldman recognized that the script was not really shootable as it was and asked if I could rewrite it." With less than two weeks before the pilot was scheduled to begin shooting, Powell worked quickly. He preserved Ruddy and Fein's original story, but rewrote most of the dialogue and created some of the characters, including Schultz and Kinchloe.

Powell and Ed Feldman had worked together when Powell was under contract to write for *The Andy Griffith Show* and *Gomer Pyle, U.S.M.C* and Feldman was an associate producer for Desilu, the studio that produced both series. Powell accepted the task of revising the pilot but didn't think it had much of a chance on the network. "I really forgot about it, because I had done a number of pilots, and very few of them got on. The things I liked usually didn't get on, and I did like this."

*Hogan's Heroes* beat the odds and Powell wrote four out of the first five episodes, helping to establish the pattern the series would follow. He also consulted with Feldman on the casting of the lead characters.

## Casting

Walter Matthau as Colonel Hogan? John Banner as Klink and Werner Klemperer as Schultz? An entirely different series would have been the result of these unlikely casting choices, which were actually considered in the early production stages of the show.

Bob Crane was so natural as Hogan that it seemed the role was written for him. It was not, however, and one of the show's creators had quite another actor in mind when it came time to cast the role. Bernie Fein's widow Kay recalls, "Bernie had suggested Walter Matthau for Colonel Hogan. He had worked with him and liked him. Although Walter was not well known in Hollywood, he was a highly respected New York actor. As soon as Bernie brought up Matthau's name, Ed Feldman said, 'He can't do comedy.' Fortunately no one told Walter or Neil Simon this and Mr. Matthau has gone on to a brilliant comedy career."

Another actor Fein suggested for the role of Robert Hogan was Robert Hogan. Bernie Fein named the starring character after his friend, actor Robert Hogan. But what's in a name? Name alone was not enough to land Hogan the role of his colonel namesake. Hogan was an unknown at the time, and CBS wanted to go with a "name" actor. (Hogan later starred in *Peyton Place*, *Days of Our Lives* and *Operation Petticoat*, among other series.) One of the names CBS offered the part to was Van Johnson, who declined.

While the casting process was going on, Bob Crane was juggling a costarring role on *The Donna Reed Show* with a popular morning talk show on Los Angeles radio station KNX. During his second season with *Donna Reed*, disagreements arose between Crane and Reed's husband and the producer of her show, Tony Owen. Crane's character had become quite popular and his agent bartered for more money for his client. As Owen and Crane traded insults in the media it became clear that Crane would not be continuing with the series. Knowing that he had found his niche in TV comedy, Crane shopped around for a new vehicle. He tested for a pilot, then called *Hogan's Raiders*, on December 22, 1964.

Also considered for the role of Hogan was Richard Dawson. Ed Feldman had seen Dawson in the 1965 film *King Rat* and was impressed with his performance. The producer believed that Dawson had potential as a leading man as well as a comic. After testing both Dawson and Bob Crane, Feldman concluded "Richard still had a very noticeable British accent then and I decided against him. I wanted Hogan to be an all-American, middle-America type. I went with Bob Crane for the part."

Once Crane was set as Hogan, Feldman set out to find the actor to portray the inept Colonel Klink. It was a tough assignment, as not just any actor could convincingly play such a ridiculous character. Feldman's good friend, actor Richard Crenna, was the first to suggest Werner Klemperer. Klemperer relates the story: "They were sitting around in Feldman's office going through the *Player's Directory*, and they came by my name and picture, and Crenna said, 'There's your Klink' and Feldman said, 'That's ridiculous. He does heavies, he does straight stuff, he doesn't do comedy.' And Crenna repeated, 'That's your Klink.' And they called me."

Klemperer tested with Bob Crane and something clicked. Feldman had also tested John Banner and wanted both actors for the series. He was a little uncertain as to which actor should portray Klink and which should play Schultz. Writer Richard M. Powell, who was commissioned to rewrite the pilot, was consulted for his opinion. "I told him I thought John Banner should play Schultz. He probably would have come to that conclusion anyway," Powell reflects. Viewers can get a taste of what the series might have been like if casting had gone the other way by watching "Hogan Goes Hollywood" (#119), in which Klink plays Schultz and Schultz plays Klink in a propaganda film being made at the stalag.

The three main stars signed, a supporting cast was lined up. Feldman had wanted the POWs to be a mix of French, British, and American actors. "Almost like a League of Nations," he later remarked.

Richard Dawson, whom the producer had passed over for the Hogan role, was signed as Cor-

**Werner Klemperer in the mid-1950s, when he was known for playing dramatic roles.**

poral Newkirk, a British prisoner. Godfrey Cambridge was the first actor offered the role of Corporal Kinchloe, but he turned it down. Richard M. Powell suggested Ivan Dixon for the role. He had worked with Dixon as part of a black writers' workshop when the actor was part of a group called Actors for Integration. Dixon took a chance and filmed the *Hogan's Heroes* pilot, never believing it would sell.

While Cambridge was still under consideration for Kinch, his agent, Bill Donohue, met with Feldman and had the foresight to ask what other types he needed for the pilot. Feldman answered, "I need a Frenchman." Donohue also represented singer/actor Robert Clary. Clary was in town and had recently stopped by his agent's office to say hello. Donohue sprang into action. "Robert Clary is in town," he told Feldman. Feldman had seen Clary perform in nightclubs and was instantly sold on the actor. "That's exactly who I want, where is he? Bring him to me." Donohue arranged the interview and Clary was signed without even auditioning.

Two actors were signed for the pilot but did not continue as regulars in the series. Leonid Kinskey portrayed Minsk, a Russian prisoner. Best known for his role as Sascha in *Casablanca,* the veteran character actor performed in the pilot but declined to appear in the series. He explains his change of heart: "The moment we had a dress rehearsal and I saw German SS uniforms, something very ugly rose in me. I visualized millions upon millions of bodies of innocent people murdered by the Nazis. One can hardly, in good taste, joke about it. So in the practical life of the TV industry, I lost thousands of dollars, but I was, and am, at peace with myself concerning my stepping out of the great success *Hogan's Heroes.*"

The pilot episode featured another American POW, Sergeant Olsen. Stewart Moss played Olsen and was originally intended to be one of the regular heroes. The actor did not want to commit to a series contract. Striking a deal with Feldman, he appeared in the pilot, and then as his availability—and the producer's needs—warranted. The pilot established Olsen as the "outside man" of *Hogan's* operation. He stayed on the outside until a prisoner escaped, then he traded places with the man, in order to keep the same number of prisoners in the camp. When the prisoner returned, or another was smuggled in, Olsen returned to the outside. Moss also appeared as characters other than Olsen in three *Hogan's* episodes.

Two of the five heroes from the pilot having escaped from the confinement of a series, Feldman hired Larry Hovis to fill the vacancies and round out the cast. Hovis appeared in the pilot episode as Lieutenant Carter, an escaping POW who is aided by the gang at Stalag 13. Carter escaped at the end of the pilot episode. Believed to be a one-shot deal, Hovis was very effective in the pilot episode and Carter (a sergeant for the series) was drafted as the fourth of *Hogan's Heroes.*

## Production

While at Desilu Productions, Ed Feldman had worked with an apprentice film editor named Jerry London. He recruited London to edit the *Hogan's Heroes* pilot. London recalls that they were under extreme pressure to work fast to complete the pilot. "I worked ninety hours that week, because they had to get it ready so fast. I worked until two in the morning, came back at eight, around the clock. I remember we got the last day's dailies on Saturday, I put it together on Sunday and added the drum music and opening titles. And we showed it to the producers on Monday and Tuesday, and Wednesday the network saw it, and Thursday it was sold. That's how fast it happened."

The pilot episode was filmed in black and white, as color was in its infancy at the time. The remainder of the series was filmed in color at Feldman's insistence. The producer had the foresight to realize that filming in color would make the series more valuable in syndication.

After the series was sold and ready to move into production, Feldman offered Richard M. Powell the job of story editor, but Powell declined. "I said that I would be more inclined to write on a show that didn't have a story editor, because I know story editors rewrite, and all writers have sufficient ego to think that their words are pearls, and they resent very much having excessive rewrites." Feldman took Powell's suggestion, and *Hogan's Heroes* never had a story editor. If any changes or revisions were needed on any script, they were done by that script's original writer.

Jerry London was hired as Feldman's assistant. In addition to overseeing the editing of the episodes, he learned all facets of the production, enabling him to move up, through the series' run, to associate producer and eventually, to director. He says, "Eddie was great because he let me do everything a producer would do. I'd go to script meetings, I worked on the casting, I worked with the art director and the prop man, just about everything there is to do. And any time we had footage of airplanes or explosions or anything, I'd have to go find them somewhere. Sometimes they'd do it before they wrote the script. They'd say, 'Can you get a shot of a train blowing up?' or something and I'd get the shot and they'd write it. I'd go to the military, they had a library and they would loan us material to put in the show."

As London rose through the ranks behind the scenes, he nudged his assistant, Michael Kahn, into taking over as chief editor. At an American Cinema Editors seminar in October 1994, Kahn said that he hadn't been interested in a career in editing when he started working at Bing Crosby Productions. "I had no sense, no feel for it at all," he recalled. But while working on *Hogan's Heroes,* things started to change. "Slowly but surely things evolved and then I caught on and I figured out that what the old editors used to say: 'The film will tell you what to do' wasn't necessarily valid. I started realizing that I could bend the film, change it and tell it what to do. I did different things, took chances, and I started having a command over the medium. I started to feel passionate about editing." After *Hogan's Heroes,* Kahn moved into editing motion pictures, beginning with George C. Scott's *Rage* in 1972. He has been Steven Spielberg's editor since *Close Encounters of the Third Kind* and has received Academy Awards for *Raiders of the Lost Ark* and *Schindler's List.*

The shooting procedure on *Hogan's Heroes* differed from most television series produced during that era. Most filmed TV episodics were done in three days, blocking and rehearsing each scene just before filming it.

("Blocking" refers to the physical direction of a scene, including the actors' movements and the set-up of cameras, lights, and other technical equipment.) On *Hogan's,* the process was stretched out, allowing more rehearsal time. "We had one whole day of rehearsal on the stage, which was unheard of. They don't do them that luxuriously anymore," says Werner Klemperer. Producer Feldman felt that the quality of the finished project was more important than finishing before deadline or coming in under budget.

Another unusual aspect of filming *Hogan's Heroes,* according to Howard Caine, was the fact that scenes were rehearsed in order. This practice is uncommon in film and television, as it is more practical to film all the scenes which take place in a certain setting first and then move on to another setting. Feldman insisted upon rehearsing in script order, a luxury which gave the actors a feeling of continuity. "In other words," said Caine, "you went into the barracks, if that's where it opened, and then you went into Klink's office, and then you went to the brauhaus over on the other stage, and then you came back into Klink's office, then back to the barracks, then over to the other stage to the tunnel underneath, and back to the barracks, and so on."

Director Gene Reynolds explains why he always rehearsed in script order. "It gave everybody a sense of continuity. When you just go onto one set and do scenes 3, 12, 27, and 36 all on that one set, they're all jumping around, you don't have any sense of what came before. And it's extremely important for an actor, and a director, but especially an actor, to know 'where am I coming from, and where am I going to?'"

Klemperer describes a typical shooting schedule for *Hogan's.* "We met around the table on a Thursday, with the director, producers, writers, the cast, and whatever guests were on, and went through the script and read it a couple of times. Everybody put in a couple of cents' worth of brilliance, made a couple of suggestions. On Friday, we were at the studio, on the soundstage, and we rehearsed all the scenes, with the cameraman there walking with us and the director. We rehearsed them all day long, with the scripts in our hands. And that was the end of the week. And over the weekend we studied our roles for Monday's shoot. Often we would get what's called pink pages, with the rewrites, and then on Monday we started shooting. We shot Monday, Tuesday, Wednesday, three days. Usually from seven to seven, but sometimes later—eight, nine, ten."

Two of the three shooting days were spent filming interiors on the set at Desilu Studios (now the site of Paramount Studios) in Hollywood. The third day was devoted to shooting exterior scenes at 40 Acres, the backlot of what was then Desilu-Culver City, where Stalag 13 was set up. Among the other shows which utilized the 40 Acres backlot (located off Ince Street in Culver City) were *Gomer Pyle, U.S.M.C.* and *The Andy Griffith Show.*

On Thursday the process began again with the next script, unless an episode ran over-schedule and the schedule got pushed back a day. This happened more often with Feldman directing than with any of the other directors, according to Caine. "Eddie would go longer than anybody, and it wasn't because he didn't know what he was doing, it was because he was a perfectionist."

On a television set, the actors spend a lot of time waiting. As camera angles, lighting, and other technical details are being worked out, or scenes are being filmed that don't involve a particular actor, that actor has time on his hands. Robert Clary says, "It was done like a movie, which means you do a master, and then you have to re-light the scene to do a two-shot or re-light the scene to do a close-up. And that takes time." The actors spent that time in a variety of ways. On the *Hogan's Heroes* set, the offstage recreation was often as entertaining as the scenes they filmed.

Bob Crane kept a set of drums on the set, and between takes could always be found practicing. Clary says "Bob Crane was a fanatic drum player, he played great drums. On the set at the studio they had his dressing room with his drums and his records so we'd all know where he was. When the set was ready, all they had to do is take five steps and say 'Bob, set is ready, let's go.' I thought that was very clever of the company to do that. He loved to play drums and nobody cared if the music was very loud."

Crane was not the only one with musical talents. During the last few seasons, Howard Caine began bringing his banjo to the set. "When they didn't need me," says Caine, "I'd be in my dressing room picking on my banjo." Werner Klemperer's dressing room was equipped with a "good hi-fi," as he spent his off time listening to classical music.

Most of the offscreen silliness was perpetrated by Larry Hovis and Richard Dawson. Hovis and Dawson were notorious for their prank pulling and card playing. Stewart Moss, who played Sergeant Olsen in several early episodes, relates, "Dickie Dawson won a good percentage of everyone's salary in the nonstop gin game that went on in his dressing room." Frequent guest star Dave Morick says of Dawson and Hovis, "It took me a few episodes of working with them to realize the routine they liked to pull around people. If you were standing near where they were carrying on a conversation and they had the feeling you were eavesdropping, their subject matter would change and you'd hear the funniest dialogue imaginable. Something about 'his or her arm falling out of its socket and being beaten over the head with it' or words to that effect."

In a 1970 *TV Guide* profile on Larry Hovis, writer Dick Hobson tells of an incident when Hovis and Dawson began talking about costar Ivan Dixon's alleged money troubles. "Poor Ivan," they whined, eventually persuading their costars to cough up two hundred dollars to help Dixon out. Cash in hand, they left the room remarking, "It's been a pretty good day!" When he first joined the cast, Howard Caine believed that Hovis and Dawson were a comedy team, "because of their wonderful, crazy closeness."

Hovis recalls, "We would pull some very elaborate pranks that would take us months to develop. Silly things that made us laugh. One day we were in the commissary, and Sally Kellerman was there. So we had one of the guys that worked there take our plastic flower from our table over to her with our compliments, and she kept staring at us like we were nuts. We did tons of stuff like that. We thought it was wonderful, but of course I'm sure we must have bored everybody silly."

When a group of people work together for six years, things go much more smoothly if they enjoy being together. On the *Hogan's Heroes* set the atmosphere was a very friendly one. "There was an immediate camaraderie, that really started during the pilot," declares Werner Klemperer. Robert Clary says, "It was an excellent group. From the prop men to the cinematographers to the gaffer. It was just a pleasure to go to work. We saw to it that nobody would act like a prima donna. It was the most enjoyable six years."

Larry Hovis attributes that camaraderie to Feldman. He explains, "He made us all feel just as important as anyone else. We all felt necessary, and consequently we had a lot of fun."

Howard Caine, recalling his first day's work on *Hogan's*, says, "I was the guest star. I was treated by everybody as though I was a regular and had always been there. When I came back the following season it was like 'long lost buddy.' Somebody who was there for only one day's work was treated like a big guest star. Nobody could ever feel left out. It was wonderful." Leon Askin calls the family atmosphere on *Hogan's* "the secret of the show's success. It was family. Brotherly love."

Character actor Henry Corden worked on five episodes of *Hogan's Heroes,* most memorably as General von Richter, "The Blue Baron," who viewed Klink as his archenemy. Corden explains why he loved working on *Hogan's* more than on other series: "It's one of the toughest things for a stranger to come on to a series set—the series people always loved each other and were kind of by themselves. Or they disliked each other and there was great tension. In this case *(Hogan's Heroes)*, when we came onto the set we were as much of a part of the family as they were. That was always good. It made for better work." Guest star Vito Scotti had worked with some of the cast members prior to his guest appearance and when he arrived on the set "it was like 'Hi, buddy!' It was great to work with them." These sentiments are echoed by nearly every actor who worked on the series.

Dave Morick was a frequent guest star on the series, usually playing a German guard. He says, "I have never worked with a bunch of consistently nice people as the *Hogan's* regular cast and crew. There was never an uptight moment on the set, as many times as I worked on the show."

The family relationship was not confined to the actors on *Hogan's Heroes*, but extended to the technical staff as well. Howard Caine claims that *Hogan's* was unique among most television series in that respect. For example, generally when an actor throws a party, it is a cast party, for the actors only. Caine explains that throwing a party for the *Hogan's* gang became an enormous undertaking. A typical guest list included, in Caine's words, "the cast, of course, and their wives or dates. Then you would start with Teddy, the prop man. Well, I'm sure as hell not going to leave Murph out, his assistant. And the best boy, and the gaffer, and the cameraman . . . Typically, members of a cast don't have the crew to a party. But we did, because we really were that close."

A family in good times as well as bad, the *Hogan's* group suffered two tragedies during the show's run. Cinematographer Gordon Avil died of a heart attack in April 1970, while the series was on hiatus following the fifth season. Caine had picked up a copy of *Variety* that someone had left on a chair and saw Avil's obituary. "I broke out in tears. I couldn't stop. I was just shocked. This was a member of my family." Robert Clary called Avil "the sweetest man," and remembers Avil giving him advice on how to fight for his key lights in a scene "because I was the smallest, you know." Avil was replaced by his assistant Bill Jurgenson for the final season.

Bill Calihan, who started with the show as a production supervisor and later became the producer, had a secretary who visited the set often and became very friendly with the cast. She was killed in a car accident midway through the run. "The news came to us on the set, and we were destroyed by it," remembers Howard Caine.

# 2

# DISSENT AMONG THE RANKS

**J**ust as there is no such thing as a marriage without arguments, life on the *Hogan's Heroes* set was not harmonious 100 percent of the time. A handful of altercations did occur of which jealousy was obviously a recurring theme. But in the words of Howard Caine, "It was a working marriage." Caine recalled an incident that occurred when assistant director Floyd Joyer accused him of holding up the set. Caine, who was having his costume adjusted, angrily responded that he was never late and never held anyone up unless something like that (costume delay) happened. The two resolved the conflict, as Caine explained. "The next day, Floyd came up and put his arm around me, walked with me, and said, "Howard, I couldn't sleep last night, I could cut my tongue out. It's absolutely true that you are the most professional guy I could ask for."

With a cast of seven regulars and a handful of semiregulars, it was inevitable that jealousy would arise from time to time. Robert Clary admits to feeling resentment at the size of his part at times. "It's hard to be objective," he explains, "because we're all self-interested. I'd like to see one person who says, 'I'm not selfish, I don't care how big my part is. It's part of the ensemble.' I think deep down, we all want to shine, constantly." At one time Larry Hovis felt his role was so unimportant that in a *TV Guide* profile in 1970, he called himself "the invisible man."

**John Banner and Werner Klemperer had a "humorous rivalry" offscreen.**
© Bing Crosby Productions, Inc. Reprinted with permission.

Bernard Fox, who portrayed the recurring character of Colonel Crittendon, recalls, "I was chatting with the producer one time, and I had said something about the problems with the stars and all. And he said, 'You know Bernie, my problems are not with the stars. My problems are with the supporting stars.' Because they were all jostling for more dialogue, more scenes, and stuff like that."

One of the more talked about rivalries existed between Werner Klemperer and John Banner. "It was a humorous rivalry of course," observed Richard M. Powell. "Somehow or other if the camera was on Werner, John Banner would be in the background with a quizzical or funny expression on his face." In that way, Banner was able to steal a scene from almost anybody.

Klemperer and Banner had been friends for almost ten years before they began working together on *Hogan's Heroes*. Their friendship continued throughout the seasons, although Klemperer concedes honestly to a few rifts. "There were times when John and I had—how would you put it—little ego trips. Both of us. But in the main, we got along very well. I respected him, and I think he respected me. I think the fact that I was the only one on the show who was nominated for an Emmy five years in a row and won it twice, didn't endear me to John, necessarily and totally. Not that he didn't wish me luck. And I don't think Bob Crane was terribly delighted about that either."

There was also friction between Crane and Richard Dawson, according to Crane's son, Bob Jr., who recalled, "Dawson and my dad didn't get along because of competitive factors, jealousy on Dawson's part. Dawson had tried out for the role of Hogan and had not gotten it . . . but it was that continual 'I lost the starring role' type of ego attitude on Dawson's part that was the basis for a couple of verbal arguments."

Not pretending that the "family" relationship on the set existed twenty-four hours a day, Klemperer admits that he and Crane "weren't particularly friends on a social level, but we had a good working relationship." Crane revealed shades of resentment toward Klemperer in a 1968 *TV Guide* interview in which he called Klemperer "competitive." Robert Clary says that it is true that Klemperer was competitive, but no more than anybody else. "You have to look out for yourself," he says.

Another area of inter-cast conflict was politics. Klemperer and Clary, like the majority of the cast, were liberal, while Bob Crane was a conservative. "Politically we were miles apart," says Clary. "Bob was a very conservative Republican and I'm a very liberal Democrat, so already his way of thinking about life was not the same as mine." Richard M. Powell noted the political disparity. "They were all fairly liberal, had the same liberal frame of reference to politics, except for Bob Crane, who was conservative. And he was subject to quite a bit of ribbing from the others about his conservative politics."

Rumors of behind-the-scenes friction between series stars are abundant in Hollywood. Television history has seen many series marred by battling cast members, salary disputes, and power struggles. Conversely, when speaking with people involved with *Hogan's Heroes*, words such as "family," "enjoyable," and "friendly" pop up frequently. Director Howard Morris puts the family cliché into perspective. "Look, none of us are going to be buried together. We got along very well. There was little or no jealousy on the set, that I was aware of. There was a lot of laughter."

## 3

# THE PEN IS MIGHTIER THAN THE SWAGGER STICK: THE WRITERS

**W**hen a series continues for six years—168 episodes in the case of *Hogan's*—one would think it difficult to come up with fresh ideas without repeating plots. Writer Richard M. Powell penned twenty-nine episodes and reveals that he had no difficulty in finding unique stories to tell. "On the ones I did, I always tried to come up with a dramatic situation. I tried to avoid plots like giving Klink a birthday party or the usual sitcom things that you see, because for me they don't work very well. I'm not particularly a joke writer, I'm a situation comedy writer. What was funny in what I wrote came out of the situation—or hopefully it did! Having spent four years in the army, I had no problem thinking up dramatic situations."

Ed Feldman credited his writers with the series' success. In 1968, he told *Variety,* "If it weren't for the writers we'd be in a bad way and perhaps never gotten as far as we have. They're the stars of the show. Our three main writers—Dick Powell, Larry Marks, and Artie Julian—dig deep in historical accounts of the last world war and in their fertile comedy minds can convert an innocent incident into a raucous situation."

It has been reported that Feldman poured through books such as *The Rise and Fall of the Third Reich* and *Major Mistakes of World War II* for ideas to pass along to the writers. Bob Crane claimed that ex-POWs were some of his biggest fans and often shared stories that were worked into plots. Many of the cast and crew served in the war and may have contributed ideas based on their experiences. In an article for *TV Scout,* Leon Askin related an incident that occurred when he was interred in a French POW camp during World War II. "One day another prisoner and I and a guard were sent on an errand to a nearby village. The guard deserted us, got drunk in a saloon, passed out, and we brought him back to camp in a wheelbarrow." On *Hogan's* when Schultz took Newkirk into town to see the dentist, Newkirk returned to camp pushing a drunken Schultz in a wheelbarrow.

Gene Reynolds, the series' primary director, discussed the series' approach: "What we try to avoid is the trap that has sprung many shows, especially comedies, the ancient art of copying some other show's routines. We try not to document a POW camp and take some liberties, but our scripts, for the most part, are based on actual experiences and given the comedy touch. If it seems ludicrous, we have second thoughts. But we've never been accused of stealing a scene from another show. It must fit our characters or it's no go."

The three primary writers combined wrote over two-thirds of the entire series. According to Feldman, "The ones that hop around from one comedy to another are not for us. They don't get a chance to warm up to the characters." There was no script consultant, and each writer made his own revisions after working with the cast and staff, an arrangement the writers preferred.

Another plus, according to Powell, was that network interference was at a minimum during that time. "Once *Hogan's* got on, the network had a strictly hands-off attitude about it. They read the scripts, but they never made any suggestions for changes as far as I know. Now you've got six or seven people at the networks reading scripts, making pages and pages of suggestions, overseeing every little detail. It really takes all the creativity out of it."

The following writers and writing teams are listed in descending order by the number of episodes each wrote or collaborated on. Background is given for the major contributors.

### Laurence Marks (68 episodes)

The principal writer, Marks penned more than twice as many scripts as any other contributor. He enjoyed working on *Hogan's Heroes,* where "there was no consultant, editor, or rewrite person." He says that producer Ed Feldman contributed ideas occasionally, but left the writing up to the pros. Marks has written for numerous television series and specials, including *The Doris Day Show, Perry Mason,* and *Phyllis.* He was also a writer and story editor on *M\*A\*S\*H.*

### Richard M. Powell (29 episodes)

Powell rewrote the pilot episode and set the tone for the remainder of the series. In later scripts, he created the characters of Marya, Crittendon, and Tiger. Other writing credits include *Gomer Pyle, U.S.M.C., The Andy Griffith Show,* and over twenty-five pilots. He passed away in 1996.

### Arthur Julian (24 episodes)

An accomplished writer and producer, Julian also served as executive producer for the Sherman Hemsley sitcom *Amen.* Other writing credits include

### ALL IN A DAY'S WORK

The *Hogan's Heroes* staff of writers deserves credit for creating an abundance of unusual, distinctive scripts. However, the following frequently used plotlines can be found as the framework for more than one episode:

The Germans have a new weapon that will surely win them the war. The heroes must destroy it, photograph it, discredit it, or all of the above: Episodes 2, 3, 25, 41, 98, 106, 115, 116, 117, 125, and 157

The heroes must save Klink from being transferred and replaced by a tougher, wiser kommandant: Episodes 4, 34, 45, 47, 59, 60, 88, 105, 132, 150, and 162

The heroes must save Schultz from being transferred and replaced by a tougher, wiser guard: Episodes 14, 37, 93, 141, and 150

The heroes must save Stalag 13 from being closed down and the prisoners being sent to different camps: Episodes 14 and 37

The heroes steal back valuable items that Germany has stolen from France, England or another Allied country: Episodes 18, 48, and 89

A spy is planted among the prisoners: Episodes 1, 47, 102, and 152

One of the heroes wants to escape: Episodes 32, 81, and 145

The POWs kidnap a German for a trade or to gain information: Episodes 6, 49, 107, and 123

A high-ranking German or Axis collaborator wants to defect and needs Hogan's help: Episodes 29, 54, 128, and 158

There's a doppelganger in camp and everyone is seeing double: Episodes 26, 54, 67, and 148–49 ★

## OH, MY! YOU'RE NOT A GUY!

In another recurring theme, Hogan is continually surprised when his contact is a woman.

"Hold That Tiger" (Episode #2)—LeBeau is sent to smuggle Tiger into camp, but the plan hits a snag when he learns that Tiger is a woman. Hogan finds housing a woman and outfitting her as a soldier to be a challenge, but there are obvious perks to her presence.

"Hogan and the Lady Doctor" (Episode #52)—Hogan assumes the civilian doctor the underground is sending is a man. Guess again.

"Man's Best Friend Is Not His Dog" (Episode #98)—When two men and a woman from the Swiss Prison Commission arrive at camp, the last person Hogan guesses is his contact is Hanna.

"Who Stole My Copy of Mein Kampf?" (Episode #108)—Hogan assumes that Leslie Smythe-Beddoes, whom he's been ordered to assassinate, is a man. His plan of presenting Smythe-Beddoes with a booby-trapped electric razor won't work, so he must devise an alternate plan of silencing her.

"The Gasoline War" (Episode #122)—Hogan meets Franz and Louisa, and assumes his contact, Eskimo, is the man. When he learns that Louisa is Eskimo, he wants to rub noses with her.

"Rockets or Romance" (Episode #168)—When told his contact is Frankel, Hogan naturally assumes Frankel's a guy. But oh my, it's Lily Frankel, whom Hogan kissed in an earlier episode. ★

*The Flying Nun, F Troop, Fair Exchange, The Doris Day Show, Gimme a Break,* and *Maude.*

### Phil Sharp (16 episodes)

Sharp's writing credits include *The Doris Day Show, Maude, All in the Family, I Married Joan,* and *The Donna Reed Show.*

### Bill Davenport (13 episodes)

*Mr. Ed, Maude, All in the Family, Good Times,* and *Make Room for Daddy* are listed among Davenport's television credits. He passed away in 1989.

### Ray S. Allen and Harvey Bullock (10 episodes)

The team of Bullock and Allen was one of the longest-running writing partnerships in the television industry. Their credits include over three hundred comedy series episodes, including *Gomer Pyle, U.S.M.C., The Dick Van Dyke Show,*

*The Andy Griffith Show, The Doris Day Show, I Spy,* and *Love, American Style.*

## Art Baer and Ben Joelson (4 episodes)

As a team, Baer and Joelson wrote over one hundred scripts for such TV shows as *Get Smart, Gomer Pyle, U.S.M.C., The Odd Couple,* and *The Jeffersons.*

## David Chandler and Jack H. Robinson (3 episodes)

## James Allardice and Tom Adair (1 episode)

## Jack Elinson (1 episode)

## Ben Gershman (1 episode)

# LIGHTS, CAMERA, ACTION: THE DIRECTORS

**R**obert Clary: "We were blessed by great directors. The director's job, in a television series, is to give enough material to the cutter. The next week, the director is not there; he cannot go to the cutting room and say 'now I want this shot to be in it.' He has to give enough material for them to put together a very good show. And the directors on *Hogan's Heroes* were very good."

Eleven directors were responsible for the 168 episodes of *Hogan's Heroes*. They are listed, with brief biographical summaries, in descending order by the total number of episodes each directed.

### Gene Reynolds (34 episodes)

Best known as the executive producer of *M\*A\*S\*H*, Reynolds started out in Hollywood as a child actor. After honing his directing skills in series such as *Peter Gunn My Three Sons*, and *The Andy Griffith Show*, he became the primary director on *Hogan's*. He left *Hogan's Heroes* when he got a contract to produce and direct *The Ghost and Mrs. Muir* for Fox. He went on to helm *Room 222*, *M\*A\*S\*H*, and *Lou Grant*. A multiple Emmy Award winner, he served as president of the Directors Guild of America from 1993 to 1997. His most recent credits include episodes of *Touched by an Angel* and *Promised Land*.

Reynolds explains why *Hogan's* was one of his most enjoyable career experiences. "We'd shoot indoors for two days and then we'd spend one day outside, so you weren't always confined to the studio. The stories had some variety to them, and the experience was closer to making a movie than just being in a studio. You'd have more panorama, more vista, more movement. And also the characters—Richard Powell would bring in these odd characters, so it wasn't just dealing with the running characters, you had some new people to play with. And the actors were not just straight comics, the actors were often dramatic actors who could play some comedy. And the writing—with Powell, Laurence Marks, and Artie Julian—wasn't just the kind of standard, jokey sitcom-type material. It was a very enjoyable and satisfying experience, and I developed some wonderful, lasting friendships as a result of working on that show."

### Edward H. Feldman (28 episodes)

The producer of the series, Feldman enjoyed directing from time to time. Many say that the quality of the shows Feldman directed was higher than those done by most of the other directors because Feldman took more time and put his heart and soul into every scene.

### Bruce Bilson (25 episodes)

One of the primary directors on *Get Smart,* Bilson moved around from comedy to comedy, working on *Get Smart, The Brady Bunch, Please Don't Eat the Daisies,* and others while squeezing in days on *Hogan's Heroes.* Recent television credits include *Touched by an Angel* and *The Sentinel.*

### Marc Daniels (19 episodes)

Marc Daniels' directing credits include *I Married Joan, Star Trek, Gunsmoke, Bonanza, Alice,* and most historically, the first thirty-eight episodes of *I Love Lucy.* With Desi Arnaz and cinematographer Karl Freund, Daniels pioneered the three-camera method of filming live television programs on Lucy. He died of congestive heart failure in 1989.

### Bob Sweeney (17 episodes)

One of Ed Feldman's best friends, Sweeney teamed with the producer on *The Brothers, The Andros Targets,* and other projects before and after *Hogan's.* He boasts an impressive list of directorial credits, including *The Andy Griffith Show, The Courtship of Eddie's Father, Fantasy Island, Flamingo Road, Trapper John, M.D.,* and *Return to Mayberry.*

### Howard Morris (14 episodes)

Prominent actor, director, and voice-over artist Howard Morris calls his experience on *Hogan's Heroes* "a very happy one," and adds that the series and others of its time were far superior to most of the things on television today. "I worked on *The Dick Van Dyke Show, Andy Griffith, Hogan's Heroes.* We don't have stuff like that no more!" Morris served with Werner Klemperer in World War II, performing for troops in the Pacific. Perhaps best known as Ernest T. Bass on *The Andy Griffith Show,* he recently guest-starred on *Baywatch* and currently lends his voice to the Cartoon Network's animated series *Cow and Chicken.*

### Richard Kinon (12 episodes)

Kinon directed Ed Feldman's previous series *Fair Exchange* before joining the gang at *Hogan's* during the fourth season. Other credits include *Bewitched, The Bob Newhart Show, The Partridge Family, Wonder Woman, The Love Boat,* and *Dynasty.*

### Jerry London (10 episodes)

Now a highly successful producer-director, Jerry London's career began on *Hogan's Heroes.* Ed Feldman asked him to edit the pilot episode, then recruited him as editorial supervisor for the series. London later moved up into the associate producer's position, which he called "a great training ground for producing." He had previously had no ambition to direct, and says "Feldman pushed me into it!" After *Hogan's Heroes,* he worked in episodic television for a while, including installments of *The Brady Bunch, The Partridge Family,* and *The Rockford Files.* Chiefly known for directing and producing television movies and miniseries, London earned a Directors Guild of America Award in 1980 for *Shogun.* Other projects include *If Tomorrow Comes, Chiefs, Ellis Island,* and *Get to the Heart: The Barbara Mandrell Story.*

### Robert Butler (5 episodes)

Butler directed the pilot episode and four others in the first season, but did not continue as one of the alternating directors. A Directors Guild Award winner for *The Waltons* and *Hill Street Blues,* his other credits include *Batman, The Dick Van Dyke Show, I Spy, Columbo, Sisters, Moonlighting, Lois & Clark,* and the 1997 feature film *Turbulence.*

### Irving J. Moore (2 episodes)

Moore also directed episodes of *Hawaii Five-0, Gunsmoke, Maverick,* and *Dallas.* He died in 1993.

### John Rich (2 episodes)

A prolific producer-director whose credits include *Our Miss Brooks, Gunsmoke, All in the Family, The Dick Van Dyke Show, Barney Miller,* and *MacGyver.*

# 5

# HEIL NIELSEN: THE RATINGS

**W**hen it premiered, *Hogan's Heroes* was an immediate hit with viewers. It also scored big with reviewers who weren't caught up in the "you can't have fun with Nazis" controversy. The *Variety* reviewer was unreserved in his praise of the pilot, calling Crane "very strong," Banner and Klemperer "excellent," and the show itself "genuinely creative farce comedy." His remarks not confined to the stars, this critic called the supporting members of the group, "excellent down the line—right to the dogs!" Frank Wilson of the *Indianapolis News* called it "wild, completely unbelievable and fun."

At the other extreme, Jack Gould of the *New York Times* criticized the series' depiction of Nazis "as silly old buffoons, hopeless oafs who have more in common with Desilu Studios than Hitler." (The same reviewer called *The Mary Tyler Moore Show*'s premiere episode "a preposterous item about life as an 'associate producer' in a TV newsroom." Both series survived the *Times*' criticism and filmed 168 episodes each.)

When the Nielsen ratings were reported for the two weeks ending September 26, 1965, *Hogan's Heroes* ranked No. 5, ahead of *The Lucy Show* and *The Andy Griffith Show*. While it never reached the No. 1 ranking in the Nielsens, it placed a very respectable No. 9 for its first season, beating out all the other new shows

## AND THE WINNER IS . . .

*Hogan's Heroes* was a frequent contender at the Emmy Awards. Out of a dozen nominations for the series and cast over the years, Werner Klemperer was the only winner, taking home two Emmys for Outstanding Supporting Actor in a Comedy Series. A listing of the nominations and the winners follows.

**1965–66 season:**
Outstanding Comedy Series nomination—lost to *The Dick Van Dyke Show*
Outstanding Continued Performance by an Actor in a Leading Role in a Comedy Series—nominee Bob Crane lost to Dick Van Dyke
Outstanding Performance by an Actor in a Supporting Role in a Comedy Series—nominee Werner Klemperer lost to Don Knotts of *The Andy Griffith Show*

**1966–67 season:**
Outstanding Comedy Series nomination—lost to *The Monkees*
Outstanding Continued Performance by an Actor in a Leading Role in a Comedy Series—nominee Bob Crane lost to Don Adams of *Get Smart*
Outstanding Performance by an Actor in a Supporting Role in a Comedy Series—nominee Werner Klemperer lost to Don Knotts of *The Andy Griffith Show*
(Ivan Dixon was nominated for an unrelated project, *The Final War of Olly Winter*. He lost to Peter Ustinov.)

**1967–68 season:**
Outstanding Comedy Series nomination—*Hogan's Heroes* lost to *Get Smart*
Outstanding Performance by an Actor in a Supporting Role in a Comedy Series—Werner Klemperer won

---

of the 1965–66 season. The same year it was named "Most Unique New Program," by Quigley Publications, which polled television critics for their votes. The following season it was No. 17, still a hit by Nielsen standards.

Beginning with the 1967–68 season, *Hogan's Heroes* fell below the top twenty in the Nielsens and never reclaimed its top-rated status. This drop in ratings points can mainly be attributed to the network moving it out of its successful Friday night time slot. *Hogan's Heroes* enjoyed its two highest-rated seasons at 8:30 to 9:00 P.M. on Friday nights. When it was shifted to Saturday night at 9:00 P.M. it lost a lot of its younger viewers. Against the *Saturday Night Movie* on NBC, *Hogan's Heroes* fell in ratings points each time a feature film with big name stars aired opposite it. Nevertheless, the series held its own in this time slot for two years. Each subsequent season, CBS shuffled the series around, so that eventually even diehard fans got weary of searching for

Outstanding Performance by an Actress in a Supporting Role in a Comedy Series nomination—Nita Talbot was nominated for Episode #77, "The Hostage." She lost to Marion Lorne of *Bewitched*.

**1968–69 season:**
Outstanding Performance by an Actor in a Supporting Role in a Comedy Series—Werner Klemperer won

**1969–70 season:**
Outstanding Performance by an Actor in a Supporting Role in a Comedy Series—nominee Werner Klemperer lost to Michael Constantine of *Room 222*

**Other Awards:**
16th Annual Quigley Publications Awards (1965):
*Hogan's Heroes* was voted Most Unique New Program in a poll of U.S. television critics.

NAACP Image Award (1967):
The Beverly Hills–Hollywood Branch of the NAACP presented this award to Ed Feldman as Executive Producer of *Hogan's Heroes*.

Ward African Methodist Episcopalian Church (1967):
Annual Producers Achievement Award went to Ed Feldman in 1967 for *Hogan's Heroes*.

Screen Producer's Guild nomination (1965):
Ed Feldman was nominated as producer of *Hogan's Heroes* for best–produced television program of 1965. ★

it on the schedule. This was one of the factors that contributed to *Hogan's Heroes's* cancellation in 1971.

## Promotion Commotion

As with any hit series, *Hogan's Heroes* merchandise was on department-store shelves quicker than you could say "royalties." The *Hogan's Heroes* lunch box was a popular item with kids, as were the series of Dell comic books inspired by the series. With the *Hogan's Heroes* periscope kit, kids could become Allied spies with the aid of a *Hogan's Heroes* badge, ID card, and periscope.

Two albums were released based on Hogan's popularity. One featured Bob Crane playing his drums to the tune of TV sitcom theme songs. *Bob*

**Hogan's Heroes made the cover of TV Guide twice.** Photo courtesy Chris Finkbeiner and Paul Lichota. Reprinted with permission from News America Publications, Inc., publisher of TV Guide magazine © 1965, 1966 News America Publications, Inc.

*Crane, His Drums and Orchestra, Play the Funny Side of TV* was the star's only professional recording despite earlier ambitions of a drumming career. The second *Hogan's*-inspired album featured Robert Clary, Richard Dawson, Ivan Dixon, and Larry Hovis singing World War II songs, and was titled *Hogan's Heroes Sing the Best of World War II.* The album was orchestrated by Jerry Fielding, who wrote the theme music for *Hogan's Heroes.* For the album, Fielding added lyrics to the *Hogan's Heroes* theme music.

Fielding composed music for over thirty films, including Oscar-nominated scores for *The Wild Bunch, Straw Dogs,* and *The Outlaw Josey Wales.* He also wrote music for *McMillan and Wife, The Bionic Woman, Star Trek,* and other series. The *Hogan's* opening was praised by *TV Guide* in 1965 as "the best theme song we've heard."

Though it is now a collector's item, the *Hogan's Heroes Sing* album was not a financial success when it was released. Robert Clary feels that the album was very good and could have done better had it been marketed for general release rather than specialized markets. "Larry Hovis and I were singers to begin with, and Ivan Dixon was marvelous. And we had very good orchestration. I thought it was a good album, but I don't think it sold very well." Hovis agrees. "I really loved it; it was a lot of fun," he says.

Many feel that CBS and Bing Crosby Productions were lax in their promotion of *Hogan's Heroes*. While the network was spending hundreds of thousands on merchandise and marketing of its number one hit, *The Beverly Hillbillies, Hogan's Heroes* was given only cursory attention by the publicity department. Werner Klemperer states, "In my opinion we were not exploited nearly enough." Robert Clary agrees. "Shows like *Beverly Hillbillies* and *Gunsmoke* took advantage of their popularity and they went to opening markets and to fairs and everything. We could have done it, because the three times we went to the meetings of the affiliates in Washington and Chicago, we did our act. All the 'Hogan's Heroes' did something, and it was very entertaining. Therefore we could have done more, we could have gone to fairs, but we never did it."

One stunt the network did orchestrate was a weekend press junket for the series at Ocotillo Lodge in Palm Springs in October 1965. The lodge was converted into a POW camp for the occasion, with attendants dressed as guards. A World War II plane flew overhead dropping propaganda leaflets.

## *Hogan's Heroes* Collectibles

The following collectibles were released during the serie's run. Factors that contribute to the estimated values of these items are: rarity, condition of the item, and its desirability to other collectors. If purchasing from a collector or memorabilia dealer, expect to pay somewhere in the range of these estimates. But you may make surprise finds of these items at garage sales and thrift stores.

### Trading Cards

Released by Fleer in 1965, the 66-card set is hard to find today. Complete sets sell for up to $350, and individual cards are usually priced at about $5.

### The *Hogan's Heroes* Bluff Out Game

This board game, released by Transogram in 1966, is valued at approximately $75 today.

### *Hogan's Heroes* Lunchbox and Thermos

The dome-style box and metal thermos were designed by Elmer Lehnhardt, who also designed lunchboxes for *The Beverly Hillbillies, Gomer*

**Bob Crane poses with a *Hogan's Heroes* comic book, lunchbox, and thermos.**
© Bing Crosby Productions, Inc. Reprinted with permission.

*Pyle, U.S.M.C.*, *The Flying Nun*, and many other series. Released by Aladdin Industries in 1966, they sell today for around $75 to $100.

### *Hogan's Heroes* Comic Books

From 1966 to 1969, Dell released a series of nine comic books based on the series. Today, they sell for around $20 to $25 each.

### Hogan's Heroes World War II Jeep

MPC Models manufactured this jeep assembly kit in 1968. Photos of Bob Crane, Werner Klemperer, John Banner, and a World War II jeep are on the box. Approximate value: $150.

### Bob Crane/John Banner School Tablets

Two 8x10 writing tablets were sold in the 1960s, one featuring Colonel Hogan and the other featuring Sergeant Schultz. They were selling recently for $25.

### Hogan's Heroes Sing the Best of World War II

This album, featuring Robert Clary, Richard Dawson, Ivan Dixon, and Larry Hovis, was released by Liberty Records in 1967. Its approximate value today: $30.

A "Periscope, ID and Badge Set" and "Signal Sender and Compass Set" were both released by Harmony in 1977, long after the series ended its original run, but while it was gaining popularity in syndication. Over the years, other *Hogan's Heroes* merchandise has been released, including a recently licensed Sergeant Schultz "I Know Nutzzzing" T-shirt, a new "TV's Coolest Classics" trading card set, and a series of collector's edition videotapes from Columbia House (1-800-538-7766).

# 6

# AUF WIEDERSEHEN, HOGAN: THE CANCELLATION

everal factors contributed to the cancellation of *Hogan's Heroes* in 1971. The network had volleyed it from time slot to time slot, losing viewers with each subsequent move. Bing Crosby Productions was reportedly eager to end the original run and offer it as a syndicated package, where profit potential was higher. (Nowadays series often appear in syndication while original episodes are still being aired on the network.) Perhaps the fatal blow to *Hogan's Heroes* was delivered by CBS, when the network decided to revamp its image.

Costar Howard Caine felt that during its last few seasons the show was bounced around purposely to lose ratings points in an effort to kill it off. He explains, "In order to syndicate, you needed at least five years in the can. In those days you couldn't syndicate while the show was still in prime-time—or at least nobody ever thought of doing it. If they were doing that then, we might have run another four or five years. Unless a show was hugely successful, they wanted to get it off the air as soon as possible because they made their big profit in syndication. In our sixth season, they put us on opposite the first half hour of Disney. Now we were extremely popular with the kids, young people. And that's where they placed us to kill us. And we knew it."

In the 1970–71 season, CBS decided to clean house in what the media termed the "hick purge." The network's demographics revealed that many of their highest rated programs were popular with the wrong types of audiences. Rural and older viewers, who had made shows like *The Beverly Hillbillies* and *Green Acres* so popular, were no longer the prime target of the network. The young, urban, professional viewer was pinpointed as the prime purchaser of advertisers' products, and a new lineup was slated with shows aimed at this audience. A large percentage of *Hogan's Heroes'* viewership was made up of children—who are not consumers themselves—and it was among the casualties of the purge.

Also instrumental in CBS' mass cancellation of its popular series was the FCC's new prime-time access rule, which went into effect in the 1971–72 season. The rule gave local stations access to prime time from 7:30 to 8:00 p.m., Monday through Saturday. Three hours of programming that had previously been considered prime-time was now reserved for local broadcasts. Accordingly, all three networks had to trim their lineups. CBS took the opportunity to completely overhaul their image. The victims of CBS's demographic demolition included: *Hogan's Heroes, The Beverly Hillbillies, Hee Haw, Mayberry R.F.D., Green Acres,* and even *The Ed Sullivan Show.*

*Hogan's Heroes* aired its last original episode on April 4, 1971. Syndication has brought the series to generations of new fans and to viewers in many other countries, including Germany, where the show draws nearly a million viewers a day. Hugely popular on college campuses, *Hogan's Heroes* has garnered almost a "cult" following and has never left the airwaves in major American markets in the nearly thirty years since its last broadcast. In the estimation of co-creator Al Ruddy, the series has earned close to a hundred million dollars to date. The cast members of *Hogan's Heroes,* while they can enjoy the fame and the memories the series gave them, are no longer reaping the profits. Caine laments, "Everybody used to say 'oh you must be getting rich,' when the show went into syndication." However, as per the standard contract of the period, after the eleventh run of each episode, the stars stopped receiving residual payments. Only star Bob Crane had a deal to receive a percentage of the series' profits in perpetuity.

In 1988, Ross Schafer, then host of Fox Broadcasting's late-night talk show, interviewed Werner Klemperer. Schafer had reunited cast members of TV's *Batman* and *Gilligan's Island* on his show and told Klemperer that they had tried to do the same for *Hogan's Heroes.* With Crane and Banner dead and Richard Dawson nixing interviews, a reunion of this sort was impossible. Nor would the cast be reunited for a TV movie, à la *Return to Mayberry, Rescue from Gilligan's Island,* or *Return to Green Acres.* In the words of

Bernard Fox, who portrayed Colonel Crittendon, "Really, can you see a bunch of sixty-year-old men in a prisoner-of-war camp?"

The release of the feature film version of *The Addams Family* in 1991 launched a new trend in filmmaking: reviving old TV shows for the big screen with new actors in the familiar roles. Several other TV-inspired movies quickly followed suit, including *The Brady Bunch Movie, The Fugitive, The Beverly Hillbillies,* and *Mission: Impossible.* In 1994, industry trade papers reported that a feature film version of *Hogan's Heroes* was in development at Warner Bros. with John Hughes at the helm. The project was later dropped and Warner's option lapsed. In June 1998, Paramount Pictures optioned the film rights. Since Paramount produced the film versions of *The Addams Family* and *The Brady Bunch,* chances are good that they will proceed with *Hogan's.*

If *Hogan's Heroes* does make it to the big screen, don't expect to see any of the original actors popping up in cameos. Klemperer says, "*Hogan's Heroes* had to have been with at least the three of us, and two of those are gone. I would not participate in it." Larry Hovis agrees, "It would be fascinating to see, but I'm sure none of us would be involved. I don't think you can go back. All the people that have done those reunion things, that's great. But I would just feel ridiculous."

Whether or not the series ever finds its way to movie theaters, its popularity continues to grow. There are tributes to *Hogan's Heroes* on the Internet, and a collector's edition video series from Columbia House. It is a testament to the series' comedic excellence that it continues to garner fans, all around the world, thirty years after its debut.

## But Will It Play in Potsdam?

The last place the *Hogan's* gang ever expected their series to play was Germany. After all, the Germans in the series are the losers, continually outwitted by the crafty Allies. Besides, Germans could never be expected to laugh at such a grim period of their country's history, right? But to the astonishment of the *Hogan's Heroes* cast and crew, the series is now a cult hit in Germany, attracting nearly a million viewers a day.

The series was first introduced to German viewers in 1992, with a title that translates roughly as *Barbed Wire and Clean Heels.* The program was a ratings flop. Leo Kirch, founder of Germany's leading film distributor, KirchGruppe, decided to retool the series, and hired Rainer Brandt to redo the show's dubbing. Brandt told the *Wall Street Journal* that he thought the

## SPRECHEN SIE DEUTSCH?

The fictional Stalag 13 was located a few miles outside of Hammelburg in Germany. [There is a real Hammelburg, but its geographic location is not the same as in the series. In one episode, a sign reads "Düsseldorf 20km, Berlin 30km," but Düsseldorf is 250 kilometers northwest of the real Hammelburg, and Berlin is over 360 kilometers to the northeast.] For obvious reasons, the use of Germany's mother tongue was limited, but to lend some realism to the setting, the German characters had to speak at least a little bit of German. The actors who played German characters were often asked to ad-lib bits of German dialogue, and in at least two incidents, this created some unexpected humor.

Actor Chris Anders, a native German, recalls an incident that occurred while he was playing a guard in one episode of *Hogan's Heroes*. "I was supposed to ad-lib in German to signal the Army trucks to take off. And the German word for take off is *fahrt los*. And of course *fahrt* and *fart* are very close. And whoever was directing the scene said 'Cut! We can't use that!' And I said 'Oh, my God!' And the whole set broke up laughing."

Another instance where a German phrase stopped a scene occurred during the filming of Episode #112, "Klink's Old Flame." Actor Dave Morick, playing a guard, had to thank Carter and Newkirk for fixing a car he believed he damaged. Morick remembers, "I had to use the word *danke*. So to show-off during the take, I ad-libbed 'Danke! Danke, vielmaus!' (pronounced *veel mouse*), which I thought to be 'Thank you, thank you very much!' And as Larry and Dick left the scene I heard Larry ad-lib to Dick, 'Did you hear that? He called me a field mouse!' Needless to say we had to shoot it again because I burst out laughing. When the episode aired the 'field mouse' line was left in, but they cut before I started laughing."

problem with the show was that it always made the Germans look like fools. But instead of making the Germans the victors, he chose to make them look even *more* foolish, so that it would be clear that they were caricatures and not meant to be representations of actual German soldiers.

Brandt spent a year rewriting portions of the show's dialogue to make it even sillier than originally conceived. In one episode, in which the Germans plan to drop bombs on London, the German-dubbed version has the characters talk of dropping condoms rather than bombs, their plan being to defeat the British by discouraging them from multiplying. The German version even makes references to a new character—Kalinka, Colonel Klink's never-seen maid who performs housework in the nude. The phrase "Heil, Hitler,"

**A Viewer's Guide to German Phrases**
The following is a brief list of German words and phrases frequently used on
*Hogan's Heroes*:

achtung—attention!
auf Wiedersehen—good-bye
bitte—please
danke—thank you
donnerwetter—I don't believe it! By jove! (literal translation: thunderstorm)
dummkopf—blockhead, dummy
frau—woman, lady, wife
Führer—leader
gnädige frau—madam (literal translation: gracious woman)
hauptmann—captain
heil—hail
herr—master, lord, sir
jawohl (ya' vol)—yes; yes, sir!
kamerad—comrade, chum
kommandant—commanding officer
liebchen—sweetheart
Luftwaffe—the German Air Force
mach schnell—be quick! hurry up!
nein—no
oberst—colonel
raus—outside, scram
schnell—quick, speedy
verboten—forbidden
was ist los?—what is the matter? ★

verboten in Germany now, is substituted with a variety of sayings, including
"Heil Schnitzler," "Adios," or "Thanks be to heaven." When Nazi characters
display the stiff-armed salute, they are dubbed as saying, "This is how high
the cornflowers grow." The episode titles for the German-dubbed version
often differ from the originals. For instance, in Germany, "That's No Lady,
That's My Spy" (#161) is *Transvestit vom Dienst* or "Transvestite on Duty."
"The Sergeant's Analyst" (#141), in which Schultz has been unwittingly delivering information hidden in loaves of bread, is *Der Pumpernickelbote* or
"The Pumpernickel Messenger."

The revamped version, titled *Ein Käfig Voller Helden* ("A Cageful of
Heroes"), debuted on Germany's Kabel 1 in 1995 and quickly garnered a

cult following. It far surpasses other American imports, *Friends, Seinfeld,* and *Frasier* in the ratings. Before long, German-language Web sites devoted to the series were finding their way on to the Internet. One webmaster, Matthias Hamann, explains why he thinks the series is so popular, "Many people think it's a silly comedy. But if they don't like it, that's not because of German history. In most American movies and TV shows, because of World War II, the Germans are the bad guys. I have no problem with this . . . Even on German TV shows, Americans are mostly the cool people. It's easy for Hogan to beat the Germans. But the real Germans weren't as silly. *Hogan's Heroes* . . . is not like what we learn in history. It's unreal. That's one of the things that's so appealing about it."

The unlikely hit status of *Hogan's Heroes* in Germany came as a pleasant surprise to those who worked on the series. "I'm amazed!" Larry Hovis avows. "I'm amazed that people *here* still care. That always really surprises me. But I guess it's really an interesting comment on the German people that they can see what we were doing and laugh at that, and I just think it's amazing, and very nice." Werner Klemperer, a native German, adds, "I am delighted that the show is a hit in Germany, because I think Germans should be at a point where they can make fun of themselves. I think it's a good sign. It has to be looked at as a satire, it can't be anything else. You can't take it seriously. So have some laughs!"

Some of the same voice-over artists who were used on *M\*A\*S\*H* were employed to dub the German version of *Hogan's Heroes.* In Germany, Colonel Hogan has the same voice as Captain Hawkeye Pierce, Major Hochstetter has the same voice as Major Charles Emerson Winchester, Carter has the same voice as Radar O'Reilly, and Kinch has the same voice as B. J. Hunnicut. ★

# THE CAST

## BOB CRANE

### *as Colonel Robert E. Hogan*

Hip, glib, cocky, suave. These adjectives have all been applied to both Bob Crane and his TV persona, Colonel Robert Hogan. Hogan was the ideal role for Crane, who had previously turned down several other pilot offers and emcee jobs. Waiting for the right vehicle to showcase his comedic talents was a wise move, and the Crane-Hogan union was a match made in TV heaven.

Crane's flair for comedy was evident early in his life. Terry Romaniello, a classmate of Bob's from Stamford High School, shared several classes with Bob's girlfriend (later wife) Anne Terzian and witnessed many of his schoolboy pranks. "I'll always remember Bob—the clown that he was—coming into our typing class and sitting down at the desk pretending he belonged there. Naturally, the teacher caught on because we were an all girl class!"

Born Robert Edward Crane on July 13, 1929, in Waterbury, Connecticut, Crane's early ambition was to be a professional drummer. He played with a band during his high school years in Stamford, Connecticut, where his parents had moved when Bob was young. He realized his dream of drumming professionally in 1944, when he joined the Connecticut

Symphony Orchestra. He was reportedly dismissed from the orchestra after two years for "cutting up" during a performance. That same year, Crane graduated from Stamford High School. The notation next to his photo in the high school yearbook read "loud ties, drummer, musician of note, home room vice president, wants to be a staff musician in a studio band, voted second most musical in the class."

Crane had been steadily dating Anne Terzian since she was twelve and he fourteen, and they were planning to be married. He began to think that a drumming career wasn't solid enough to support a family on, but he wanted to stay in a music-related field. He chose radio. With his natural comic abilities and love of music, being a disc jockey seemed a perfect career path to follow. Breaking into radio took three years, during which he worked in a jewelry store during the day and played with various dance bands at night. In May of 1949, Crane and Terzian were married. The newlyweds lived with Anne's parents while Crane tried to find work in radio.

Finally, in 1950, he got his foot in the door of the radio business at WLEA in Hornell, New York. Earning only thirty-five dollars a week, Crane lived at the YMCA in Hornell while his bride remained in Stamford with her parents. When Anne announced she was pregnant, Bob decided he must find a job closer to Stamford. He moved to station WBIS in Bristol, Connecticut, but was there only three months before moving again, to WICC in Bridgeport, Connecticut. Bob settled in at WICC for five years, during which time he perfected his radio personality and format. His show in Bridgeport rapidly gained popularity and news of his unique style reached as far as Los Angeles, where radio station KNX was recruiting for a new morning deejay.

KNX offered Crane a five-figure salary to move out to the West Coast and take over the morning spot. Seeing the California job as a possible launching pad for acting jobs, Crane jumped at the offer. He moved his family—wife Anne and son Robert—to Tarzana, a suburb of Los Angeles, in 1956.

Crane's radio show took California by storm. His format was fresh, unique, and unorthodox. A *TV Guide* journalist called it "one of the most frenetic one-man exhibitions in West Coast radio." Crane would splice and insert sound effects and jokes over commercials and interviews, with no topic or celebrity being off limits to his brand of humor. A favorite trick of Crane's was to ask a guest a particularly controversial or embarrassing question and then throw on a record without giving the guest a chance to answer. When the Hollywood payola scandal was at its height, he'd often pull that ploy, asking "When did you start taking payola?" and leaving his startled guest speechless while Crane moved on to something else. One would think a sponsor would be furious at hearing Crane play sound-effects of incessant coughing over their cigarette commercial, or an engine sputtering out of control over an airline's ad. Far from being furious, sponsors and celebrities alike knew the risk involved in doing Crane's show: finding yourself (or your product) as the butt of Crane's jokes. Crane's friend Tom Hatten, a frequent guest on Crane's radio show (and later, a guest star in four *Hogan's Heroes* episodes), recalls, "People in town, big famous people called and wanted to do his show,

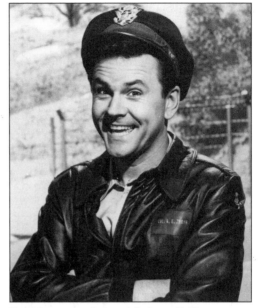

**Bob Crane as Colonel Robert E. Hogan.**
© Bing Crosby Productions, Inc. Reprinted with permission.

because it was a prestigious thing. Everybody listened to it. He had Marvin Gaye on once, and Bob played around with the name Marvin Gaye for ten, fifteen minutes and Gaye didn't know what hit him—but loved it. Nothing was sacred. You knew, if you came on the show, you were going to get it. And everybody loved it."

During his years at KNX, Crane used his time off the air to learn the acting trade. His first step was landing a role in a local theater production of *Tunnel of Love*. The acting bug had bitten Crane, and he changed his long term career plans once more. While mastering his craft in community theater, he began to test the waters in the television industry. Casting directors had a hard time seeing the disc jockey as a serious actor, but Crane persevered. He did guest spots on *The Twilight Zone, General Electric Theater, The Alfred Hitchcock Hour,* and *The Dick Van Dyke Show*. It was the spot on *Van Dyke* that first brought him notice as a comic actor. In the episode, Crane and his wife are a sparring couple whose shouting match at the Petrie's house is clearly heard by the entire group of guests in the other room. The wife demands that Crane leave the party at once. Crane's parting line, as he walks through a roomful of stunned and silent friends, is "Gotta go now. One of the kids is sick!"

Paul West, associate producer for *The Donna Reed Show,* saw Crane on *The Dick Van Dyke Show* and gave him a shot on *Donna Reed.* Crane played Dr. Dave Blevins, a colleague of Alex Stone's. He was so effective in the part that he was brought back for a second episode the next month, and signed as a regular cast member for the 1963–64 season. The character had been renamed Dr. Dave Kelsey by that time, and hastily married off, as *The Donna Reed Show*'s conservative image did not permit a bachelor doctor running around town. Crane was paired with Ann McCrea as his TV wife, Midge Kelsey, and the characters moved in next door to the wholesome Stones of Hilldale.

Crane did not give up his popular morning radio show when he signed on for *Donna Reed.* He told interviewer Art Ronnie in the *Los Angeles Herald-Examiner,* "I'll work something out. I like my radio show too much to give it up and besides it's great exposure." Not to mention the fact that he was earning $75,000 annually at KNX. What he worked out was an exhausting schedule which had him running every day from the KNX studio to Screen Gems down the street where *The Donna Reed Show* was filmed.

Nearly from the start, Crane butted heads with Donna Reed's husband, Tony Owen, the producer of *The Donna Reed Show.* Crane's glib, wisecracking character was somehow incongruous to *The Donna Reed Show* image and Owen often cut out scenes with Crane's character which he felt were too suggestive, causing the actor a great deal of frustration. Still, his character was immensely popular with viewers and even with Miss Reed herself. She told interviewer Hal Humphrey in 1963, "I think we picked up more viewers because we brought in Bob Crane and Ann McCrea as neighbors. I had been brainwashed to think our audience is mostly kids. Now I'd like to run an even wider gamut with our stories."

After two seasons, Crane's *Donna Reed Show* contract ended and a mutual decision was reached by Crane and Owen not to renew for a third season. Owen claimed that he axed Crane when the actor demanded more money. Crane had received several offers to star in series of his own, and was eager to accept if the right vehicle came along. He was no longer happy with his *Donna Reed Show* role, which he described as a "nice type guy who won't make waves." His departure was a nonevent on *The Donna Reed Show.* Ann McCrea remained as Midge Kelsey, and Crane's character Dave was phased out. Midge often mentioned her husband Dave, but he was never shown again.

Many thought Crane was crazy to turn down network offers to emcee game shows or host talk shows, but Crane held out, not wanting to be pigeonholed as an emcee. He was asked to replace Johnny Carson on *Who Do You*

*Trust?* when Carson left the series (he had filled in as guest host during Carson's vacation in the summer of 1962), but declined. Tom Hatten recalls Crane saying, "I don't want to be Johnny Carson, I want to be Johnny Carson's first guest. I want to be the big guest of the night."

Crane himself explained, "Those guys all become typed in their jobs. There's nothing wrong with that, but it's no way to become an actor. When they're looking for someone to play Shylock or Cyrano, the last guy they'd think of would be a host."

The next step on Crane's ladder to success was a starring role on television. Here too he was very selective, turning down several pilot pitches wherein he played inept husbands, inept doctors, or the male costar to an already established female star. When producer Ed Feldman approached him with *Hogan's Raiders,* a comedy set in a World War II prisoner-of-war camp, the actor was intrigued. In a later interview he explained why: "Up until then most of the plots in the pilots that had been offered to me revolved around Janie 'who wants to go to the dance, but oh my God, she hasn't got a boyfriend.'" He tested for the role of Colonel Hogan, the mastermind of the underground operation headquartered in the prisoners' barracks, in December 1964.

Crane was awarded the role of Hogan in the pilot, which was renamed *Hogan's Heroes* during production. When the series was sold and slated for CBS's fall lineup, he left his radio show at KNX. Double duty was manageable when Crane was a supporting character on *Donna Reed,* but would prove difficult now that he was the star and involved in virtually every scene.

*Hogan's Heroes* established Bob Crane as a major television star. He was a popular guest—and guest host—on talk shows, and was featured on the cover of *TV Guide* twice. In 1966 he received his first of two Emmy nominations for Outstanding Actor in a Comedy Series. He lost to one of his mentors, Dick Van Dyke. In 1967 the Emmy eluded him again, this time going to Don Adams of *Get Smart.* Writer Richard M. Powell opined, "I think probably Crane didn't win an award, because everybody considered it a natural part for him. He seemed to be playing himself." Emmy or no Emmy, Crane was immensely popular with viewers. One of his most famous fans was Helen Hayes, who gushed in *TV Guide* "I watch *Hogan's Heroes* regularly...Bob Crane is a wonderful farceur and there are almost none of them around any more. He's habit-forming."

Crane got the opportunity to work with Hayes in a 1969 television production of *Arsenic and Old Lace.* Hayes and Lillian Gish were the two little old ladies who poisoned lonely old gentlemen and Crane played their nephew, Mortimer Brewster. Crane took full advantage of other such opportunities to display his talents outside of his series, either working during his hiatuses or around the *Hogan's* shooting schedule. He put in guest appearances on *Love, American Style, The Smothers Brothers Comedy Hour,* and *The Lucy Show,* among others. In the *Lucy* episode, he played a character very close to himself— Bob Crane, the TV star. In one of her wackiest schemes yet, Lucy is hired as "Iron Man Carmichael," world famous stunt man, on Bob's latest film.

The ambitious Crane wasn't satisfied with stardom on the small screen. He told an interviewer, "I feel the really big stars are in movies, not TV. The problem is to attain star status you can't be the star of a TV series." Crane wasn't anxious to end his role as Hogan, but started planting the seeds of a movie career while still working on the series. Prior to *Hogan's,* Crane had small parts in two movies, *Return to Peyton Place* and *Mantrap.* His TV exposure helped open doors in the movie industry, but he felt that television stars were not given serious consideration for major film roles. He lost roles in *The Courtship of Eddie's Father* and *Never Too Late* to established film actors.

Crane's TV stardom was instrumental in landing him his first starring movie role, but the picture, *The Wicked Dreams of Paula Schultz,* did nothing to further his film career. Producer Edward Small, in an attempt to capitalize on the success of *Hogan's Heroes,* cast his film largely from the stars of *Hogan's,* hoping to ensure big box office sales. His gambit failed and *The Wicked Dreams of Paula Schultz* was a critical—and commercial—failure, proving to Crane that "you've got to quit your television series before they'll consider you in movies." True to his philosophy, Crane stayed away from films until after the cancellation of *Hogan's Heroes.*

During the filming of *Hogan's Heroes,* Crane used his time between takes to practice his drumming. His dressing room was equipped with drums and music equipment. He got the chance to display his drumming talents in Episode #167, "Look at the Pretty Snowflakes," when the prisoners join together for a jam session. Capitalizing on his show's success, Crane released an album, *Bob Crane, His Drums and Orchestra, Play the Funny Side of TV.*

When Crane wasn't playing the drums, or being interviewed, he could be found attending the dailies (the screening of the day's footage). Tom Hatten explains Crane's motives for watching the dailies. "He could be photographed terrifically from certain angles, and like all of us, certain angles didn't work. He was not your typical athlete. While the other guys were out playing football and building themselves up, he was playing drums in Connecticut. He didn't go to the dailies to throw his weight around, but he was shrewd enough to take the time and make sure that he gave it the best he could give and that the show was to his satisfaction." Crane's dedication to giving the show his best resulted in long working hours. Ed Feldman told *TV Guide,* "He's the first one on the set in the morning and the last one to leave. He goes into everything with enthusiasm."

Initially, *Hogan's Heroes* was compared to other sitcoms with military settings—*Gomer Pyle, U.S.M.C., Sergeant Bilko,* and *McHale's Navy. Hogan's* stood out because of Crane's performance. Hogan was a hero in the John Wayne tradition, and Crane assiduously avoided the buffoonish characteristics which marked *Bilko, McHale,* and *Pyle.* Hogan as a clown would have been ineffective. Crane's Hogan was a brash, brave leader who inspired his men to take incredible risks fighting against the enemy. "I'm not Joe Buffoon," Crane told *TV Guide.* "The lines have to mean something. Then if there's any romance, it's believable."

There was plenty of romance. During the run of *Hogan's Heroes,* Hogan was paired with over one hundred lovely ladies. Most were merely trifling affairs, brief flirtations, or methods of gaining information. His most enduring on-screen attachment was with the kommandant's second secretary, Hilda, played by Sigrid Valdis. Offscreen, a real-life romance developed between Crane and Valdis. Crane reportedly also had an affair with Cynthia Lynn, who had played Helga in the show's first season. In 1997, Lynn told *The Globe,* "We used to meet discreetly at our makeup man's house in the Hollywood hills."

To the public, Crane represented the perfect family man. He and wife Anne were married for almost twenty years and had three children—Robert, Deborah, and Karen. Crane even wrote an article for the religious magazine *Guideposts* on how to maintain a harmonious home life. On the surface the Cranes appeared to be a devoted couple.

On May 13, 1969—one week before their twentieth anniversary—Anne Terzian Crane filed for divorce, charging mental cruelty. Bob Crane had moved from the family's home in Tarzana to an apartment in Hollywood one month earlier. He did not contest the divorce, but negotiations for a financial settlement were prolonged and bitter. Shortly after the divorce proceedings were initiated, Bob Crane left town to tour with a summer stock production of *Cactus Flower. Hogan's Heroes* was on hiatus for the summer. Sigrid Valdis also had a role in the production and was going to be on the tour, a fact which led to much conjecture on the nature of their relationship.

Crane's divorce from Anne was finalized in June of 1970, and on October 16, 1970, he married Patricia Annette Olsen, who was known to TV viewers by her stage name—Sigrid Valdis. The series that brought them together was filming what would be its final season. Two months after the last original episode aired on CBS, the couple had a son, Robert Scott. Crane's eldest son, Robert David, was just turning twenty. Valdis had a daughter, Melissa, from a previous marriage.

Bob Crane in the mid-1970s.

Robert Clary says of working with Crane, "He was very nice, he would have a party once a year for the whole cast and he would give good presents during Christmas to the whole cast. He was professional, and he made life easy on the set. Therefore you could not help but like him, even though you may not like the way he's thinking or living his life."

In the years following *Hogan's*, Crane guest-starred on series such as *Quincy, Police Woman,* and *Ellery Queen,* appeared on game shows, and briefly reprised his radio career. When radio personality Dick Whittinghill took a week off in 1972, radio station KMPC recruited Crane—Whittinghill's former rival—to fill in. Between 1956 and 1965, Whittinghill was Crane's major competition during the morning rush hour. In 1972, Crane good-naturedly agreed to take over Whittinghill's show for a week and admitted that after he left radio, he became a fan of his former adversary. In an interview for the *Los Angeles Times,* he spoke of his post-*Hogan* plans. "I'd never go back to radio full time. What I'd eventually like to do is my own TV talk or variety show, but I'll always act." Since he owned a percentage of the *Hogan's Heroes* profits, Crane was not forced to work, but said "I have to plunge into what I want—all the way. I want to go out like Nelson Eddy, you know, die while I'm working."

In 1974, Crane got his second starring role in a film, in Disney's *Superdad.* He played Charlie McCready, an overprotective father who tries to keep his teenage daughter from hanging around with friends he doesn't approve of. Hoping to steer her towards more suitable friends, Charlie begins spending all his time with daughter Wendy. He goes overboard, trying to surf, water-ski, and play football with the young crowd. Despite Charlie's interference, in the end Wendy marries her childhood sweetheart Bart (played by Kurt Russell). Charlie reluctantly gives her away at her wedding, and everybody is happy. The *New York Times* gave *Superdad* a positive review, stating that "some of this generation-gap exercise is quite funny, starting with the performance by Bob Crane."

During Crane's association with Disney, some problems arose due to the actor's habit of frequenting topless bars—certainly an un-Disneylike pursuit. Crane was a nonsmoker and rarely drank, but he regularly made the rounds of various nightclubs and discos. Crane's attitude, as told to an interviewer, was "Look, I love to sit in with small groups and play the drums. What's wrong with that? Of course, I like to look at naked ladies, too." Though Crane was candid about his after-hours activities, they were not common knowledge to his fans—especially the younger ones who made up Disney's audience. In 1976, Crane played a smaller part in *Gus,* another Disney film.

When good film roles were not falling into Crane's path, he considered a return to television—a medium in which he had enjoyed far greater success. A new series was put together which had Crane starring as a forty-two-year-old insurance salesman who quits his job to go to medical school. Plots revolved around the age gap between Crane and his classmates, and his difficulty supporting the family and paying his tuition. Crane played Bob Wilcox, Trisha Hart costarred as his wife Ellie, and supporting roles were played by Todd Susman, Ronny Graham, James Sutorius, and Erica Petal. Originally titled *Second Start,* it premiered on March 6, 1975 under its new title, *The Bob Crane Show.*

Reviewers were not kind to *The Bob Crane Show. Variety* observed that despite being a proven sitcom talent, Crane "appears quite uncomfortable in his absurd role." The series was yanked after airing only fourteen episodes.

Crane had always loved the stage and devoted much of the next few years to touring with a play, *Beginner's Luck.* The play was written especially for him by Norman Barasch and Carroll Moore, authors of *Send Me No Flowers,* in which Crane had performed in Chicago in 1969. In *Beginner's Luck,* Crane played Paul Burnett, a married IBM executive, whose wife discovers his infidelity through a photo in the *New York Times.* His attempts to win his wife back after their separation comprise most of the action.

The play toured cities including San Diego, Long Beach, Tampa, Dallas, Chicago, and Cincinnati before reaching what would be its final engagement, the Windmill Dinner Theater in Scottsdale, Arizona. Australian actress Victoria Berry played Crane's mistress and had been with the tour for several months, while Sandra Giles (as the wife) and Jack Schultz (as Marlowe, the wife's suitor) were new additions to the cast. Bernard Fox, *Hogan's Heroes'* Colonel Crittendon, had played Marlowe in earlier stops on the tour, but was unavailable for the Scottsdale run because he was touring in a French farce with Louis Jourdan and Leslie Caron. Fox says that touring with Crane he found the actor to be somewhat quick tempered, but that "he looked after the actors in his company very well indeed."

*Beginner's Luck* was a hit in Scottsdale, with local critics praising Crane's comedic style. The *Arizona Republic* reviewer noted that "the most remarkable thing about this performance is the way Crane keeps the comedy flowing with his own presence, timing, and added physical business." Crane's stay in town was celebrated by Scottsdale reporters, whose articles focused equally on the play and his impending divorce from Sigrid Valdis. The couple had been separated for months and while Crane was working in Scottsdale, Valdis was vacationing in Seattle with their seven-year-old son, Scotty. Tabloids hinted that a reconciliation was in the air, but Crane told the *Phoenix Gazette,* "I've accepted the idea that my second marriage is ending after seven years." He was served with divorce papers while getting off a plane in Cincinnati, Ohio.

Crane's success in *Beginner's Luck* and his failing second marriage may have been the talk of the town when the star first arrived in Scottsdale, but they were quickly overshadowed by the tragic event which occurred three weeks later.

In the early morning of June 29, 1978, Bob Crane was brutally murdered in his apartment at the Winfield Apartments on East Chaparral Road in Scottsdale. His body was found shortly after two o'clock that afternoon by costar Victoria Berry, who had plans to redub a scene with Crane for a videotape she made to show to casting directors. When Berry arrived, she found the door to his apartment open. She entered calling his name, and then saw a blood-covered body on the bed. Crane's face had been so disfigured that she did not recognize him at first and thought that the bloodied figure might have been a woman. She rushed outside and told a neighbor, "there is someone dead up there in Bob Crane's apartment," then called the police.

When police arrived on the scene they determined that the lifeless body found curled beneath a sheet in the master bedroom was Bob Crane's. His skull had been crushed by a blunt object, possibly a car-jack handle or a heavy pipe. The killer had wiped the blood off the weapon on a sheet corner before removing it from the scene. Dr. Heinz Karnitschnig, the county medical examiner, determined that Crane had been struck at least twice, the first blow being the one that killed him. An electrical cord, taken from a video camera in Crane's room, was tied around Crane's neck after he was dead.

Crane's friends and colleagues were shocked and saddened by the news. Werner Klemperer was on his way to Aspen, Colorado, to perform at the Aspen Music Festival. He says, "We walked into the hotel, and what I always do when I go to a hotel, the first thing I do is turn on the TV set to see if it's working all right. And as I turned it on, there it was: Bob Crane murdered. I almost had a heart attack." Larry Hovis first heard about his friend's death when someone from the *National Enquirer* called to ask him for a quote. He recalls, "I must say, they were very decent, once they realized I didn't even know what they were talking about. Then they became pretty solicitous of my feelings, and we got off the phone. I was stunned."

Bernard Fox, who had not been able to accept Crane's invitation to appear in the play in Scottsdale, says in retrospect, "If I'd been with him, it might have been good, and on the other hand, it might have been bad. Because he always came into the dressing room that we shared before the show, and generally told me where he'd been and what he'd done and who he'd met. And he didn't have anybody with him that he knew on that particular occasion. My part was played by somebody else. And nobody knew who he met or who he was seeing."

Bob Crane was buried on July 5, 1978 in Oakwood Memorial Park in Chatsworth, California. The funeral mass was held at St. Paul the Apostle Catholic Church in Westwood. The pallbearers were Robert Clary, Larry Hovis, Ed Feldman, Crane's oldest son Robert David Crane, actor Eric Braeden (Crane's brother-in-law), and Crane's friend John Thompson. Werner Klemperer was asked to be a pallbearer, but was in Aspen at the time. "I wanted to do it," he states. Among the other two hundred mourners at the funeral mass were Crane's first wife, Anne, with their three children, his widow Patti Olsen with son Robert Scott and daughter Melissa, Crane's mother Rosemary and brother Alfred, Leon Askin, Victoria Berry, John Carpenter, Carroll O'Connor, and John and Patty Duke Astin.

Crane had been signed to star in *Crash,* a television dramatization of the 1972 crash of a jetliner in the Florida Everglades. The TV movie aired in October 1978 with William Shatner, Christopher Connelly, and Adrienne Barbeau in the starring roles. Prior to his death, Crane had taped a segment of a cooking show, *Celebrity Cooks.* The episode was set to air on July 10, 1978, but it was yanked because of offhanded jokes Crane had made about sex and death during the segment. In light of his murder, airing the segment would have seemed in poor taste.

Crane's murder prompted actress Dawn Wells (Mary Ann on *Gilligan's Island*) to campaign for tighter security and protection of actors appearing on the dinner theater circuit. Wells, who also performed in dinner theater productions, felt that Crane's murder showed the vulnerability of actors in such situations. Crane's apartment was rented year round by the Windmill Theater for its guest stars and a spare set of keys were kept at the theater. The spare set turned up missing after the murder and was never located. As there was no sign of forced entry into Crane's apartment, it has been assumed that Crane knew his assailant and had let him into the apartment before going to bed, or that the killer had a key.

Bob Crane's murder remains a mystery to this day. The prime suspect throughout the investigation was Crane's close friend, John Henry Carpenter, who is the last known person to see the actor alive. Crane and Carpenter had been introduced by mutual friend Richard Dawson on the set of *Hogan's Heroes* in 1966. The two formed a friendship based on similar interests: video equipment (Carpenter was a salesman for Sony at the time) and women. On the night before his body was discovered, Crane and Carpenter (not to be confused with horror movie director John Carpenter) had gone out with two local girls. They went first to a bar and later to the Safari Resort coffee shop. Carpenter told police he left Crane at around 2:45 A.M. and later called him to say good-bye. Carpenter had been in Scottsdale for a few days, and flew back home to Los Angeles on the morning of Crane's murder. A hotel employee told police that Carpenter checked out hurriedly, and investigators found that matched Crane's blood type on the rental car Carpenter had used in Scottsdale. These factors led Scottsdale police to pinpoint Carpenter as their prime suspect.

At odds during the investigation were the Scottsdale police department and the Maricopa County Attorney's office. County Prosecutor Charles Hyder said that the evidence against Carpenter was "grossly insufficient" to press charges. The county further alleged that the Scottsdale police department bungled the investigation by allowing Victoria Berry to answer the phone in Crane's apartment before it had been dusted for fingerprints and failing to follow up on several potential clues. Lieutenant Ron Dean and officer Dennis Borkenhagen led the police department's investigation and tried to get an indictment against Carpenter.

Hyder's office refused to issue a complaint against Carpenter. He maintains, "When you're prosecuting, you deal with facts, you deal with evidence.

And you can't file on people, or charge people or prosecute them on hunches. You have to have evidence, and it has to be beyond a reasonable doubt. And it was not here. Wasn't close to it."

Much of the publicity surrounding Crane's murder concerned the vast collection of pornographic videotapes and photographs found in Crane's apartment. Crane had video cameras and other photographic equipment, including a portable film lab, in his apartment. The photos and videos Crane produced were of himself and various women involved in sexual activities. Friend and costar Victoria Berry said that Crane was very open about his activities. Bernard Fox says, "Whenever we got to a town, Bob used to make a beeline for the local girlie show. And I was amazed. He'd let them take snaps of him with these girls, and I'd say, 'Hey Bob, somebody's going to blackmail you one of these days,' but he wasn't worried."

News of Crane's pornographic exploits were a boon to tabloid sales and a shock to fans. Not surprised was Crane's widow Patti. Sergeant Dennis Borkenhagen told *Entertainment Tonight*, "She mentioned that she was aware of his lifestyle when he was out of town, and that he had similar albums and tapes at his residence in California. So she was aware of his activities." In his book, *The Murder of Bob Crane,* Robert Graysmith reports that Patti had appeared with Crane in one of his homemade sex videos.

The pornography angle suggested several possible motives for Crane's murder: a jealous husband or boyfriend, or a famous actress or socialite who may have been videotaped and wanted to protect her secret. Though it is believed from the angle of the blows and the amount of blood spattered on the ceiling that the murderer was a man, police have not entirely ruled out the possibility of it being a woman. One erotic photo album was reported missing from the scene. It is possible that the album was stolen to protect the identity of someone pictured in it. Investigator Borkenhagen feels that the missing album was a red herring, taken to confuse police.

Police have received hundreds of tips over the years, including a number of absurd suggestions: that Crane was murdered by angry Nazis who were upset by *Hogan's Heroes,* or that he was killed by a man whose wife insisted on watching *Hogan's* when he wanted to watch sports. An investigator hired by the *National Enquirer* concluded that Crane was murdered by two local men as part of a murder-for-hire scheme. The police department put little value on the *Enquirer's* findings.

A new DNA test was developed in 1989 that authorities believed could positively tell whether the blood found on Carpenter's rental car was indeed Bob Crane's. A breakthrough in the case was expected, but the tests were inconclusive because the blood sample was too small and too old for a positive identification.

On June 1, 1992, police arrested John Carpenter, citing new developments in the case. Photographs of the door of Carpenter's rental car showed a speck of what appeared to be human brain tissue. The "speck" itself had been overlooked in the initial investigation and had not been preserved. When the case finally went to trial in 1994, defense experts said it was impossible to prove what the speck was. Carpenter was acquitted of all charges.

Case #78-1243, the murder of Robert Edward Crane, remains unsolved. The murder weapon was never found, nor was the missing photo album. John Henry Carpenter, once the prime suspect in the case, died on September 4, 1998. Though the trail has grown cold, interest in the case has never vanished. In 1998, cable network E! produced an hour-long special, *Bob Crane: The E! True Hollywood Story*, with previously unaired home movies of the star. *Good Morning America, Entertainment Tonight, A Current Affair*, and *Inside Edition* have also done segments on Crane's unsolved murder in the past few years. The family and friends he left behind do not know who killed him or why.

### Bob Crane—Selected Credits

**FILM**

*Return to Peyton Place* (1961) 'Peter White'
*Mantrap* (1963)
*The Wicked Dreams of Paula Schultz* (1968) 'Bill Mason'
*Superdad* (1974) 'Charlie McCready'
*Gus* (1976) 'Pepper'

**TELEVISION**

*The Twilight Zone*, "Static" (CBS, 3/10/61) 'voice of disc jockey'
*General Electric Theater*, "The $200 Parley" (CBS, 10/15/61)
*Who Do You Trust?* (ABC, summer 1962) guest host
*The Dick Van Dyke Show*, "Somebody Has to Play Cleopatra" (CBS, 12/26/62) 'Harry Rogers'
*The Alfred Hitchcock Hour*, "The 31st of February" (CBS, 1/4/63) 'Charlie Lessing'
*The Donna Reed Show*, "The Two Doctor Stones" (ABC, 3/14/63) 'Dr. Dave Blevins'
*The Donna Reed Show*, "Friends and Neighbors" (ABC, 4/4/63) 'Dr. Dave Kelsey'

*The Donna Reed Show* (ABC, 9/26/63–4/8/65) 'Dr. Dave Kelsey'
*Channing,* "Hall Full of Strangers" (ABC, 12/25/63) 'Professor Arlen'
*The Hollywood Palace* (ABC, 12/25/65) 'Bob Crane/Colonel Hogan'
*The Lucy Show,* "Lucy and Bob Crane" (CBS, 2/21/66) 'Bob Crane'
*The Smothers Brothers Comedy Hour* (CBS, 2/26/67)
*Arsenic and Old Lace* (ABC TV Movie, 4/2/69) 'Mortimer Brewster'
*Love, American Style,* "Love and the Modern Wife" (ABC, 10/27/69) 'Howard Melville'
*Love, American Style,* "Love and the Logical Explanation" (ABC, 2/19/71) 'Mark'
*The Doris Day Show,* "And Here's . . . Doris" (CBS, 9/13/71) 'Dick Carter'
*Night Gallery,* "House—With Ghost" (NBC, 11/17/71) 'Ellis'
*Love, American Style,* "Love and the Waitress" (ABC, 12/17/71) 'Paul'
*The Delphi Bureau* (ABC TVM, 3/6/72) 'Charlie Taggart'
*Make Mine Red, White and Blue* (ABC Special, 9/9/72)
*Love, American Style* (ABC, 11/23/73)
*Tenafly,* "Man Running" (NBC, 1/2/74) 'Sid Pierce'
*Police Woman,* "Requiem for Bored Wives" (NBC, 11/29/74) 'Deejay'
*The Bob Crane Show* (NBC, 3/6/75–6/19/75) 'Bob Wilcox'
*Mitzi and a Hundred Guys* (CBS Special, 3/24/75)
*Joe Forrester,* "Hard Core" (NBC, 2/23/76)
*Ellery Queen,* "The Adventure of the Hard-Headed Huckster" (NBC, 3/21/76) 'Jerry Crabtree'
*Spencer's Pilots,* "The Search" (CBS, 10/29/76)
*Gibbsville,* "Trapped" (NBC, 12/9/76)
*Nancy Drew Mysteries,* "A Haunting We Will Go" (ABC, 4/3/77)
*Quincy, M.E.,* "Has Anybody Seen Quincy?" (NBC, 3/18/77) 'Dr. Jamison'
*The Love Boat,* "Family Reunion" (ABC, 1/7/78)

**THEATER**
*Tunnel of Love,* Valley Playhouse, CA
*Who Was That Lady I Saw You With?,* Valley Playhouse, CA
*Send Me No Flowers,* Laguna Beach and U.S. tour
*Cactus Flower,* Kenley Players, Columbus, OH
*Beginner's Luck,* U.S. tour, 1973 and 1978
*Beginner's Luck,* Windmill Dinner Theater, Scottsdale, AZ (June 1978)

**AWARDS AND NOMINATIONS**
Emmy nomination, Best Actor in a Comedy Series, for *Hogan's Heroes,* 1965
Emmy nomination, Best Actor in a Comedy Series, for *Hogan's Heroes,* 1966

# WERNER KLEMPERER

## as Colonel Wilhelm Klink

In a role that won him two Emmy awards out of five nominations for Best Supporting Actor in a Comedy Series, Werner Klemperer played the incompetent kommandant of Stalag 13, the "kraut" viewers loved to hate, Colonel Wilhelm Klink. Monocled Klink believed himself to be a hard-nosed, hard-hearted "iron colonel," feared by his prisoners, admired by his staff, and irresistible to women.

Aside from their German ancestry, Werner Klemperer and his famous character have little in common. Born in Cologne, Germany, on March 20, 1920, Klemperer came to the United States as a child when his family was forced to flee their homeland at the beginning of Hitler's regime. While the fictional Klink commanded a Luftwaffe prison camp in Germany, Klemperer served in the United States Army. Klink was an easily fooled buffoon, afraid of combat, confrontation, and his commanding officers. Klemperer is an acclaimed performer whose diverse talents include acting, conducting, and narrating.

Werner Klemperer's father was the late Otto Klemperer, world-renowned symphony conductor, and his mother was an opera singer. Being Jewish, Otto Klemperer was condemned in Germany once Hitler came into power in 1933. Foreseeing that his life would be in danger, Otto Klemperer fled with his family to Vienna, Austria. Two years later he moved the family to the United States, were he would be free from the artistic restrictions placed on him in Nazi Germany. Werner Klemperer was a young boy when the family arrived in Los Angeles, a setting unlike anything he had ever known.

Through his father, Werner obtained an early appreciation of music. Though music has remained a vital force throughout his life, his primary focus has been acting. In a drama class at University High School in West Los Angeles, Klemperer discovered his love for performing. After graduation, he enrolled at the Pasadena Playhouse, where he studied for two years.

In 1942, he entered the U.S. Army, first assigned to a combat position and later with the military police. While stationed in Hawaii, he auditioned for Maurice Evans' Special Services Group. For the next two years, Klemperer toured the Pacific performing in shows for the troops with Evans, a Shakespearean actor who later found fame as Samantha's father on *Bewitched;* Howard Morris, who later became one of *Hogan's Heroes* staff directors; and Carl Reiner, who would later create *The Dick Van Dyke Show,* among other series. Klemperer sees this assignment as a lucky break. "The next two years I had the greatest theatrical training I could've asked for, free of charge in the United States Army, for which I am very grateful. We did do something that was helpful—we supplied the servicemen with entertainment. It was very exciting."

**Werner Klemperer as Colonel Wilhelm Klink.** © Bing Crosby Productions, Inc. Reprinted with permission.

After his release from the service in December 1945, he moved on to New York City, where he supported himself as an usher, stage manager, and waiter, while trying to find acting work. Starting in little theater, he worked his way up to the Broadway stage, costarring with Tallulah Bankhead in *Dear Charles* in 1954. He played one of three men Bankhead's character was scheming to marry. The *New York Times* praised Bankhead's performance, noting that "Werner Klemperer is also amusing as the temperamental Polish pianist." He toured with the comedy until it reached Los Angeles, where he was met with television and film offers.

Klemperer made his film debut as a lawyer in the crime drama *Death of a Scoundrel*. His list of films is extensive, and includes roles in *Judgment at Nuremberg* (starring Spencer Tracy, whom Klemperer credits as his greatest influence as an actor), *Ship of Fools*, and *Operation Eichmann*. In the latter he played the title role of the murderous Nazi Adolf Eichmann. His acceptance of that role prompted Louella Parsons to call him "Hollywood's Bravest Actor." Klemperer said that any initial hesitation he had about playing Eichmann was dissipated by the opportunity to "hold this man up to the world in all his grossness."

One of Klemperer's first jobs in television was on an episode of *Alfred Hitchcock Presents*, which also featured future *Hogan's Heroes* cast mate John Banner.

Steady work in episodic television followed, with appearances on *My Three Sons,* *Maverick, Gunsmoke,* and *Perry Mason* among others. Klemperer soon became known as a character actor, typically playing dramatic European roles.

It was his reputation as a dramatic actor that nearly caused Klemperer to be passed over for the role of Colonel Klink. Producer Ed Feldman had been having a tough time casting the role when actor Richard Crenna pointed out Klemperer's photo in the *Academy Player's Directory.* Feldman's first reaction was "That's ridiculous. He does straight stuff, he doesn't do comedy." Crenna insisted, and Feldman gave in. He called Klemperer's agent and arranged a meeting with the actor.

When Klemperer went to meet with Feldman to discuss the role of Klink, he was in for a big surprise. His agents had failed to tell him that the project was a comedy. "They just said that there was interest in me for a series to play the kommandant of a World War II prison camp. And of course I said yes, I had done those things before. And when I got there I found out that it was from a comedic standpoint and I was totally stunned. I thought they were out of their minds. But then I read the material and I realized that they weren't out of their minds, because it was a big spoof, it was a parody. That's what *Hogan's Heroes* was, a satirical parody."

After meeting with Feldman and testing with Bob Crane, Klemperer was cast in the role of Colonel Wilhelm Klink. He filmed the pilot episode and was certain the series would sell. He says, "There was an incredible feeling of optimism about the pilot." His optimism proved well founded when *Hogan's Heroes* became the top-rated new hit of the 1965–66 season.

In the early days of *Hogan's Heroes,* many people were upset by the use of a German prisoner-of-war camp as a comedy setting. Klemperer feels that the series was really about human relationships, and says "it could have happened in a factory of General Motors, for God's sake!" Though objections died down shortly after the series' premiere, Klemperer still hears an occasional protest. "The question I still get today is 'How is it possible for an actor who is a refugee from Hitler's Germany to play that kind of a part?' And the answer is very simple. When you're an actor, you commit yourself to play all kinds of parts. People always seem to tie your own personal being up with parts you play."

Much of the criticism of *Hogan's Heroes* stemmed from the portrayal of the German captors as inept, bumbling buffoons. Ironically, this is one of the reasons Klemperer agreed to play Klink—the inevitable loser—"as long as I can be sure to put him in the place he belongs. I wouldn't want to play Klink if he were a hero."

Klemperer described his approach to the role in a 1966 interview: "My role is satisfying because it challenges me to develop new little facets of the character. Here and there I can extend his pomposity while never forgetting that he is, basically, just a scared little man. Or again, I can extend his naïveté, or go further with what he believes is his cunning." His well-crafted character earned Klemperer two Emmy Awards out of five nominations.

**Werner Klemperer.** Photo courtesy Werner Klemperer/Bernie Ilson Public Relations.

After *Hogan's Heroes,* Klemperer faced a danger that imperils many stars of long-running television shows—being typecast in the same kind of role that made him famous and never successfully accomplishing the transition into other roles. That predisposition has caused many stars to consider the role that piloted them to stardom to be their kiss of death. Klemperer dealt with the situation and overcame it, by staying away from roles similar to Klink. "I had a little trouble after *Hogan's* for the first year or two," Klemperer says. "They wanted to type me as the same kind of character. Not necessarily a colonel, but that kind of role. And I avoided it like the plague." But that does not mean he feels any contempt towards Klink. "It took a while to get out from under the identity of Colonel Klink, but the fame of the character will remain always, and there's nothing wrong with that. I really think I did a good job. Klink was a well-conceived character. I'm proud of the show." As for his *Hogan's Heroes* costars, while most of the actors have lost contact with one another, Klemperer remains good friends with Robert Clary.

As *Hogan's Heroes* is very popular in syndication, Klemperer is constantly recognized as Colonel Klink. He still receives fan mail and he enjoys hearing from fans of the show. He understands the series' enduring popularity. "Sometimes while flipping the channels I'll come across *Hogan's Heroes,* and I'll watch it and it's a fun experience because some of those segments are like new to me because I've forgotten them. And it plays very well. The show has an extremely strong staying power. That's why I can understand why so many fans watch the reruns over and over again."

Over the years, Klemperer has made periodic television appearances, including comic roles on *Love, American Style, The Love Boat, Matt Houston,* and *Law and Order.* Though he enjoys this type of work, Klemperer has always preferred working in front of a live audience to performing in front of a camera, and has spent most of the years since *Hogan's Heroes* on the stage— acting, singing, conducting, and narrating.

His music career has taken him across the country, performing and con- ducting with many of the major and regional symphony orchestras in the United States and Canada. In 1979 he made his debut at the Metropolitan Opera House in a speaking role in Mozart's *Abduction from the Seraglio.* Though he has performed singing roles in several operettas, Klemperer has been more active in the operatic community as a narrator. Explaining his interest in narration, he says, "For me it's a wonderful way to express myself as an actor and gets me close to my love, which is music. To be able to work as a liaison between audience and orchestra and use the spoken voice to cre- ate an atmosphere—that's an interesting acting challenge, and more impor- tantly, it keeps me in front of an audience performing 'live' rather than on film or tape, and that to me is the essence of my work." He narrated *Babar the Elephant* at a special performance at the White House for children of ambas- sadors to the U.S., and has performed as narrator with the Boston Symphony, Chicago Symphony, Columbus Symphony, Los Angeles Philharmonic, the Metropolitan Opera, and the New York Philharmonic, to name a few.

Theater roles have taken Klemperer from the LaJolla Playhouse in California to the Kennedy Center to New York's Broadway and off-Broadway houses. In 1987, he played Herr Schultz, the Jewish green grocer in the Broadway revival of *Cabaret* starring Joel Grey. Klemperer earned rave reviews for *Cabaret,* including *Variety*'s appraisal of his performance as "excellent work." Joel Siegel of ABC-TV said that the role of Herr Schultz was "superbly played by Werner Klemperer—what a fine actor." Klemperer was nominated for a Tony Award as Best Featured Actor in a Musical for his work in *Cabaret.*

Klemperer's next theater role was in another revival—*The Sound of Music.* The off-Broadway production at the New York State Theater was rated poorly in comparison to the original Broadway production and the very successful film version. Werner Klemperer, as agent Max Detweiler, "struck just the right note of arch irony" according to *New York Newsday,* and was termed "diffidently witty" by the *New York Times. USA Today* noted that "the only character projecting any sense of inner life is Werner Klemperer."

In 1993, Klemperer reprised his most famous role, in an episode of the animated Fox series *The Simpsons.* In the episode, Homer Simpson is tempted by a beautiful female coworker, voiced by Michelle Pfeiffer. Homer receives advice from his guardian angel, who takes the form of someone Homer reveres—Colonel Klink. But Homer is less interested in hearing Klink's counsel than he is in discussing the exploits of Stalag 13's inmates.

Homer: Did you know Kinch had a radio in the coffee pot?

Klink (incredulous): He *did?*

The episode was so cleverly written that it made Klemperer go back on his decision to keep Klink in mothballs. He says, "I had sworn that I was not going to appear as Klink again. But when they came up with this totally crazy idea, I thought it was kind of cute. So I did it, and I enjoyed it."

He has also popped up frequently as a guest on Bill Maher's late-night show, *Politically Incorrect,* which he enjoys because of its spontaneity. "It's so free and open that anything can happen," he says.

Fans can expect to see much more of Werner Klemperer, though it might be hard to predict where he'll pop up next—in television, films, opera, or on the Broadway stage.

### Werner Klemperer—Selected Credits

**FILM**

*Death of a Scoundrel* (1956) 'Lawyer'
*Flight to Hong Kong* (1956) 'Bendesh'
*The Wrong Man* (1956) 'Doctor Banay'
*Istanbul* (1957) 'Paul Renkow'
*Five Steps to Danger* (aka *The Wrong Man*) (1957) 'Dr. Simmons'
*Kiss Them for Me* (1957) 'Commander Wallace'
*The Goddess* (1958) 'Mr. Woolsy'
*The High Cost of Loving* (1958) 'Joseph Jessup'
*Houseboat* (1958) 'Harold Messner'
*Operation Eichmann* (1961) 'Adolf Eichmann'
*Judgment at Nuremberg* (1961) 'Emil Hahn'
*Escape from East Berlin* (1962) 'Brunner'
*Youngblood Hawke* (1964) 'Mr. Leffer'

*Dark Intruder* (1965) 'Professor Malaki'
*Ship of Fools* (1965) 'Lieutenant Heebner'
*The Wicked Dreams of Paula Schultz* (1968) 'Klaus'
*The Cabinet of Dr. Ramirez* (1991)

**TELEVISION**

*Philco Television Playhouse,* "Holiday Song" (NBC, 9/14/52)
*The Secret Files of Captain Video,* "The Box" (DUM, 9/5/53)
*Studio One,* "Stirmugs" (CBS, 4/5/54)
*The Red Buttons Show* (NBC, 12/31/54)
*Crusader,* "The Bargain" (CBS, 11/11/55) 'Wilhelm Leichner'
*Alfred Hitchcock Presents,* "Safe Conduct" (CBS, 2/19/56)
*M Squad,* "Face of Evil" (NBC, 10/18/57)
*Maverick,* "Comstock Conspiracy" (ABC, 12/29/57)
*Studio One,* "Balance of Terror" (CBS, 1/27/58) 'Dorfmann'
*Gunsmoke,* "Sunday Supplement" (CBS, 2/8/58) 'Clifton Bunker'
*Perry Mason,* "The Case of the Desperate Daughter" (CBS, 3/22/58) 'Stefan Riker'
*Steve Canyon,* "Iron Curtain" (NBC, 3/5/59)
*Alcoa Presents One Step Beyond,* "The Haunted U-Boat" (ABC, 5/12/59) 'Herr Bautman'
*Alfred Hitchcock Presents,* "The Crystal Trench" (CBS, 10/4/59) 'Mr. Ranks'
*Have Gun Will Travel,* "Fragile" (CBS, 10/31/59) 'Etienne Ledoux'
*Troubleshooters,* "Tunnel to Yesterday" (NBC, 12/4/59) 'Stehlmann'
*The Alaskans,* "Gold Fever" (ABC, 1/17/60)
*The Overland Trail,* "Vigilantes of Montana" (NBC, 4/3/60)
*Alcoa Theater,* "The Observer" (NBC, 4/18/60)
*Rawhide,* "Incident of the Music Maker" (CBS, 5/20/60)
*Men Into Space,* "Flare Up" (CBS, 8/17/60) 'Major Kralenko'
*The Untouchables,* "The Purple Gang" (ABC, 12/1/60)
*Thriller,* "Man in the Middle" (ABC, 12/20/60) 'Clark'
*The Islanders,* "The Pearls of Ratu" (ABC, 3/19/61)
*Have Gun Will Travel,* "The Uneasy Grave" (CBS, 6/3/61)
*Checkmate,* "An Assassin Arrives, Andante" (CBS, 2/21/62) 'Franz Leder'
*General Electric True,* "Man in a Suitcase" (CBS, 11/18/62) 'Captain'
*The Lloyd Bridges Show,* "The Wonder of Wanda" (CBS, 1/8/63) 'Gustavsen'
*My Three Sons,* "The Dream Book" (ABC, 1/31/63) 'Professor Engel'
*Perry Mason,* "The Case of the Two-Faced Turnabout" (CBS, 2/14/63) 'Zenas'

*77 Sunset Strip,* "Escape to Freedom" (ABC, 2/22/63) 'Schtiekel'
*The Dakotas,* "Trial at Grand Forks" (ABC, 3/25/63) 'Colonel Von Bleist'
*General Electric True,* "Heydrich" (CBS, 5/5 and 5/12/63) 'Karl Frank'
*My Three Sons,* "Total Recall" (ABC, 5/9/63)
*Insight,* "The Prisoner" (Syndicated, 1964)
*Perry Mason,* "The Case of a Place Called Midnight" (CBS, 11/12/64) 'Hurt'
*The Man from U.N.C.L.E.,* "The Project Strigas Affair" (NBC, 11/24/64)
*Voyage to the Bottom of the Sea,* "The Blizzard Makers" (ABC, 12/7/64)
   'Cregar'
*The Hollywood Palace* (ABC, 12/25/65)
*Lost in Space,* "All That Glitters" (CBS, 4/6/66) 'Bolix'
*Batman* "Come Back, Shame—It's the Way You Play the Game" (ABC,
   12/1/66) 'Colonel Klink'
*Wake Me When the War is Over* (ABC TVM, 10/14/69) 'Major Mueller'
*Night Gallery,* "The Funeral" (NBC, 1/5/72) 'Ludwig'
*The Doris Day Show,* "Gowns by Louie" (CBS, 2/28/72)
*Assignment: Munich* (ABC TVM, 4/30/72) 'Inspector Hoffman'
*Love, American Style,* "Love and the Unbearable Fiancée" (ABC, 12/22/72)
   'Dad'
*McMillan and Wife,* "The Devil, You Say" (NBC, 10/21/73) 'Dr. Ernest
   Bleeker'
*McMillan,* "All Bets Off" (NBC, 12/5/76) 'Van Doren/Cecil Kaufman'
*The Rhinemann Exchange* (NBC Miniseries, 3/10, 17, 24/77) 'Franz
   Altmuller'
*The Love Boat,* "The Grass Is Always Greener" (ABC, 9/22/79)
*Vega$,* "Heist" (ABC, 2/25/81) 'Klaus'
*Return of the Beverly Hillbillies* (CBS TVM, 10/6/81) 'C. D. Medford'
*Matt Houston* (ABC, 1/9/83)
*Mr. Sunshine* (ABC, 5/17/86) 'Dean'
*Live from Lincoln Center,* "A Mostly Mozart Festival Gala" (PBS, 7/11/90)
   narrator
*Law and Order,* "Star Struck" (NBC, 1/7/92) 'Unger'
*The Simpsons,* "The Last Temptation of Homer" (FOX, 12/9/93) 'Colonel
   Klink'

**THEATER**
*Abie's Irish Rose,* New York (1947) 'Abie'
*Heads or Tails,* Cort Theater, NY (1947) 'Eric Petersen'
*Galileo,* Maxine Elliott's Theater, NY (1947) 'Infuriated Monk'

*The Insect Comedy,* City Center, NY (1948) 'Soldier Ant'
*Lucky Sam McCarver,* DeWitt Clinton Community Center, NY (1950) 'Archie Ellis'
*Twentieth Century,* ANTA Playhouse, NY (1950) '1st Beard'
*Dear Charles,* Morosco Theater, NY (1954–55) 'Jan Letzaresco'
*A Shot in the Dark,* Ivanhoe Theater, Chicago, IL (1970)
*Cyrano de Bergerac,* Ahmanson Theater, Los Angeles (1973)
*The Night of the Tribades,* Helen Hayes Theater, NY (1977) 'Viggo Schiwe'
*The Visions of Simone Machard,* La Jolla Playhouse, CA (1983)
*Hang on to Me,* Tyrone Guthrie Theater, Minneapolis, MN (1984)
*Idiot's Delight,* Kennedy Center, Washington, D.C. (1986) 'Achille Weber'
*Master Class,* Roundabout Theater, NY (1986) 'Prokofiev'
*Cabaret,* Imperial Theater, then Minskoff Theater, NY, and tour (1987–88) 'Herr Schultz'
*The Sound of Music,* New York State Theater, NY (1990) 'Max Detweiler'
*Uncle Vanya,* Circle in the Square, NY (1994)

**OPERA**

*Abduction from the Seraglio,* Metropolitan Opera House, NY (1979–80, 1982–83) 'Pasha Selim'
*Die Fledermaus,* Seattle Opera Company (1981) 'Prince Orlofsky'
*Die Entfuhring Aus Dem Serail,* Metropolitan Opera House, NY (1982)
*Lelio,* Long Beach Symphony Orchestra, CA (1983)
Various performances as narrator of the following symphonies: *Egmont, Oedipus Rex, Gurreleider, Babar the Elephant, Impresario, The Plague, L'Histoire du Soldat, Dido*

**RECORDINGS**

*Gurreleider* by Arnold Schoenberg, with Boston Symphony 'narration in German'
*Lelio,* with the Milwaukee Symphony (Koss Classics, 1991)
*Gerald McBoing Boing* by Dr. Seuss (Delos, 1991)
*Fatherland* by Robert Harris (Random House Audiobooks, 1993) narrator

**AWARDS**

Emmy award, Best Supporting Actor in a Comedy Series for *Hogan's Heroes,* 1968
Emmy award, Best Supporting Actor in a Comedy Series for *Hogan's Heroes,* 1969
Five Emmy Award nominations as Best Supporting Actor in a Comedy Series

Honored by the Catholic Big Brothers, for which he served as national
spokesman, 1980

Tony award nomination, Best Featured Actor in a Musical for *Cabaret,* 1988

Legends in Television Award from MGM/Walt Disney Studios, Orlando,
Florida, 1988

Scroll of Commendation, presented by Los Angeles mayor Tom Bradley, citing his involvement with the Young Musician's Foundation, symphony
orchestras, and *Hogan's Heroes*

Gilmor Brown Award from the Pasadena Playhouse Alumni and Associates
for his enduring career in the theatrical arts

## JOHN BANNER

### *as Sergeant Hans Schultz*

John Banner took the role of a sympathetic guard on *Hogan's Heroes* and ran
with it, nearly stealing the show. Viewer response to his character was over-
whelmingly positive, though critics protested his depiction of Sergeant
Schultz as a harmless, simpleminded oaf. Schultz was tagged a "huggable
Nazi"—a being incomprehensible to most people. In a *TV Guide* interview he
explained his views, "I see Schultz as the representative of some kind of good
in any generation." An Austrian Jew himself, Banner vehemently opposed the
notion that Schultz was an instrument of Hitlerism.

In a *Los Angeles Times* interview printed a few weeks after the series'
premiere, John Banner defended his series against the rash of criticism it was
receiving. He said, "Some people ask me how we can be funny about a
prison camp in the war, and I say to them how was it possible to write about
two little old ladies who killed twelve men and buried them in the basement
and make it funny? Well, somebody did and it was called *Arsenic and Old
Lace*." A year and a half later, the protests had dissipated and Banner told an
interviewer, "They accept us now for what we are—broadly portrayed, funny
people." Certainly Schultz was one of the funniest and most broadly portrayed characters in television history.

Nearly every one of the heroes' plots involved tricking, misleading, or
otherwise gaining the cooperation of Sergeant Schultz. Not one to take sides, the
bulky sergeant was aware of much more of the prisoners' shenanigans than he
let on. Whenever questioned, he would bark, "I know nothing, I see *nothing!*"
That line became his trademark. Of his character's penchant for looking the other
way, Banner once said, "You think Schultz is stupid? Notice that he survives."

While on guard duty, Schultz usually didn't even keep his rifle loaded—it was obvious he would never hurt anyone, enemy or ally.

Lovable, huggable Schultz soon became a notorious scene stealer. Costar Richard Dawson remarked in a 1968 interview that Banner "is so good, he steals scenes even from the dogs on our show." Banner liked to joke that it was a "physical impossibility" to upstage him—referring to his large girth. Always joking, always riotously funny on the set, Banner had a habit of withholding the humorous punches from his performance until the

**John Banner as Sergeant Hans Schultz.**
© Bing Crosby Productions, Inc. Reprinted with permission.

actual filming. Writer Richard M. Powell explains: "The first reading is when you all sit around the table and read the script. It was funny, John Banner had a way of underplaying. He would read the script and he'd be very mild, not terribly funny, but you knew he was holding back for when he got on stage. Then he was tremendously funny."

Banner is the one most often attributed with the hilarity on the set that would sometimes delay scenes being shot. Werner Klemperer says, "He was a lot of fun on the set. He had a great sense of humor." Frequent guest star Henry Corden remembers having difficulty keeping a straight face often during filming. He says, "Sometimes there was a particular scene that tickled us and we couldn't stop laughing! Especially with John Banner. John was a wonderful laugher."

Banner was born on January 28, 1910, in Vienna, Austria. He studied law for two semesters at the University of Vienna, but left school over his parents' objections and entered the Deutsches Volkstheater in Vienna.

"Courtroom dramatics were not for me," he explained. "I wanted the real thing." He was one of twenty students accepted out of over four hundred applicants at the Volkstheater. He made his stage debut there in *Caramba*.

Audiences who only remember Banner for his role as Schultz may find it hard to believe, but as a young man in Vienna, the slim, handsome actor worked steadily as a romantic lead on stage and screen. In 1938, the twenty-seven-year-old actor was performing at Schauspielhaus in Zurich, Switzerland when Hitler's forces invaded Austria. Unable to return to his homeland, he came to the United States as a refugee. Almost immediately he landed a role in a Broadway revue, *From Vienna,* but as he didn't speak English he had to memorize all his lines phonetically. Another Broadway role followed, and soon he was being cast in motion pictures. He appeared in eight films in his first two years in Hollywood.

Banner took a break from moviemaking from 1943 to 1945 to serve in the United States Army Air Corps. Banner, like his TV counterpart, achieved the rank of sergeant. He also served the Army in another way—he posed for a string of Army recruiting posters. After his release from the service, he worked steadily in films and episodic television, usually playing explosive Europeans.

In 1964, Banner's career was in a slump. He was fifty-five years old and was considering giving up show business. Then *Hogan's Heroes* came along. Banner counted his blessings in a *Los Angeles Times* interview: "I still shake my head in wonderment because I know there are an awful lot of good actors out there who are forced to pump gas to make a living. I'm lucky, and I appreciate it."

Banner found inspiration for his role in a novel called *Good Soldier Schweik* by Czechoslavakian author Jaroslav Hasek. Set in World War I, the plot centers around a hapless Austrian private who is drawn into trouble in spite of himself.

On June 19, 1965, three months before the premiere of the series which would make him famous, Banner married Christine Gremenne. She was French, and a gourmet chef. The two shared a love for fine foods and fine wine. Both were excellent cooks. Character actor Leonid Kinskey, best known as Sascha in *Casablanca,* worked on the pilot for *Hogan's Heroes* and was a good friend of the Banners. He remembers, "His wife served the finest French dinners with imported french bread. Usually after dinner John would ask her with his heavy German-Austrian accent, 'Darlink, what are we having for dinner *tomorrrrow?*' " In a 1968 interview, Banner said, "I'm married to the most wonderful cook—and woman—in the world. In that order."

After the cancellation of *Hogan's Heroes,* Banner wasted no time in getting another series. The very next season saw him costarring in a new CBS comedy, *The Chicago Teddy Bears.* The series focused on a gang of bungling mobsters, "teddy bears" who couldn't do anything right. Banner played Uncle Latzi, a lovable guy who was always getting in the way. The show was created by two former *Hogan's Heroes* writers, Harvey Bullock and Ray S. Allen, and several other creative talents from *Hogan's* were involved. Unfortunately *The Chicago Teddy Bears* did not achieve the same success and was yanked from the CBS lineup after only thirteen episodes.

In early 1973, John and Christine Banner were in Vienna, awaiting a shipment of furniture they had ordered for their new home there. On the eve of his sixty-third birthday, the actor suffered an abdominal hemorrhage and was taken to Sofien Hospital. He died the next day. His former *Hogan's Heroes* colleagues dedicated a full-page ad in *Variety* to Banner's memory.

### John Banner—Selected Credits

**FILM**

*Once Upon a Honeymoon* (1942) 'Kleinoch'
*Seven Miles From Alcatraz* (1942) 'Fritz Weinermann'
*The Moon Is Down* (1943) 'Lieutenant Prackle'
*The Fallen Sparrow* (1943) 'Anton'
*The Immortal Sergeant* (1943) 'Officer'
*They Came to Blow Up America* (1943) 'Gestapo Agent'
*This Land Is Mine* (1943) 'German Sergeant'
*Tonight We Raid Calais* (1943) 'Kurz'
*Nocturne* (1946) 'Shawn'
*Rendezvous 24* (1946)
*Tangier* (1946) 'Ferris Wheel Operator'
*The Argyle Secrets* (1948) 'Mr. Winter'
*My Girl Tisa* (1948) 'Otto'
*To the Victor* (1948) 'Lestrac'
*Guilty of Treason* (1949) 'Sandor Deste'
*King Solomon's Mines* (1950) 'Austin'
*Callaway Went Thataway* (1951) 'Headwaiter'
*The Juggler* (1953) 'Emile Halevy'
*Executive Suite* (1954) 'Enrique'
*The Rains of Ranchipur* (1955) 'Ranchid'
*Never Say Goodbye* (1956) 'Oskar'

*The Beast of Budapest* (1958) 'Doctor Kovach'
*The Young Lions* (1958) 'Burgermeister'
*The Blue Angel* (1959) 'Mr. Harter'
*The Wonderful Country* (1959) 'Ben Turner'
*The Story of Ruth* (1960) 'King of Moab'
*Operation Eichmann* (1961) 'Rudolf Hoess'
*20,000 Eyes* (1961) 'Kurt Novak'
*Hitler* (1962) 'Gregor Strasser'
*The Interns* (1962) 'Doctor Duane'
*The Prize* (1963) 'German Correspondent'
*The Yellow Canary* (1963) 'Sam Skolman'
*Kisses for My President* (1964) 'Russian Ambassador'
*36 Hours* (1965) 'Ernst'
*The Wicked Dreams of Paula Schultz* (1986) 'Weber'
*Togetherness* (1970) 'Hippy'

**TELEVISION**

*The Lone Ranger,* "Damsels in Distress" (ABC, 6/8/50)
*Sky King,* "Operation Urgent" (ABC, 4/5/52)
*The Alfred Hitchcock Hour,* "Safe Conduct" (CBS, 2/19/56)
*Private Secretary,* "Cat on a Hot Tin File" (CBS, 3/18/56)
*Sheena,* "The Renegade" (Syndicated, 9/23/56)
*Superman,* "The Man Who Made Dreams Come True" (Syndicated, 10/15/56) 'Bronsky'
*Father Knows Best,* "Brief Holiday" (NBC, 1/9/57)
*Man Without a Gun,* "Headline" (Syndicated, 6/9/58)
*Cimarron City,* "I, the People" (NBC, 10/11/58)
*The Adventures of Rin Tin Tin,* "Grandpappy's Love Affair" (ABC, 11/14/58)
*The Roaring Twenties,* "The Velvet Frame" (ABC, 10/29/60)
*Perry Mason,* "The Case of the Nine Dolls" (CBS, 11/9/60)
*My Sister Eileen,* "Ruth Becomes a Waitress" (CBS, 1960)
*The Many Loves of Dobie Gillis,* "Mystic Powers of Maynard G. Krebs" (CBS, 10/27/60)
*Thriller,* "Portrait Without a Face" (NBC, 12/25/61)
*The Virginian,* "The Small Parade" (NBC, 2/20/63)
*The Wide Country,* "The Quest for Jacob Blaufus" (NBC, 3/7/63)
*The Donna Reed Show,* "Moon-Shot" (ABC, 12/19/63)
*The Rogues,* "The Personal Touch" (NBC, 9/13/64)
*The Man from U.N.C.L.E.,* "The Venetian Affair" (NBC, 12/8/64)

*The Hollywood Palace* (ABC, 12/25/65)
*The Lucy Show,* "Lucy and Bob Crane" (CBS, 2/21/66) 'Schultz'
*The Chicago Teddy Bears* (CBS, 9/17/71–12/17/71) 'Uncle Latzi'
*The Doris Day Show,* "The Crapshooter Who Would Be King" (CBS, 2/7/72)
*Alias Smith and Jones,* "Don't Get Mad, Get Even" (ABC, 2/17/72)
*The Partridge Family,* "Who Is Max Ledbetter and Why Is He Saying All
    Those Terrible Things?" (ABC, 3/17/72) 'Max Ledbetter'

### THEATER
*From Vienna,* Music Box Theater, NY (1939)
*Pastoral,* Henry Miller's Theater, NY (1939) 'Genko'
*The Big Two,* Booth Theater, NY (1947) 'Wirth'
*At the Grand,* Philharmonic Auditorium, LA (1958) 'Direttore Inglehardt'

# ROBERT CLARY

### as Corporal Louis LeBeau

Corporal Louis LeBeau, the Frenchman, didn't venture out of the barracks
too often during the series' first season. His heroic duties consisted mainly of
serving up delectable dishes for the gang. Actor Robert Clary wasn't too
pleased with his limited exposure on camera. "Because I think I was the best
known of all of them when I first signed with *Hogan's Heroes,*" he explains.
"And then I felt like a fifth wheel. And many times, all I had to do was, 'How
are we going to do that, Colonel?' or 'Kraut's coming' or 'How, colonel?' And
that was very frustrating." He recalls an incident which occured one day
when a scene was being filmed in which LeBeau had no lines, and nothing to
do with the plot, but stood in the background with his back to the camera.
Clary became fed up and asked director Howard Morris to remove him from
the scene. "I wasn't doing anything in the scene. And he was very nice, he did
cut me out of it. I don't like what I did," he says today, "I realize now that it
was very unprofessional."

    After that episode, Clary made peace with himself and his role. "I said to
myself there's two things you can do. If you're very unhappy, get out, go to Ed
Feldman and say, 'I'm sick and tired of it' or if you're going to stick with it, shut
up and enjoy what you're doing. And that's what I did for the next five years."

    During the following seasons, the audience got to see more of the 5' 3" actor.
But with a cast as large as *Hogan's Heroes*' it was difficult to display each actor's
talents equally, so the size of his role varied from week to week. He says, "There

were some writers who would write more for me than others. If there was a script by Larry Marks or Artie Julian, I knew I would have a good share of the half hour. It didn't make me too happy to see a script by Richard Powell, because we knew that we were not going to do a lot that week, it's going to be all the guest stars." He concedes that Powell's scripts were brilliant. "They were very funny, but not for the heroes."

In "Cuisine à la Stalag 13," an episode which Clary recalls as one of his favorites, the central action revolved around his character, as the heroes tried to persuade LeBeau not to

**Robert Clary as Corporal Louis LeBeau.**
© Bing Crosby Productions, Inc. Reprinted with permission.

leave Stalag 13. Conversely, in "A Tiger Hunt," the two-parter that has Hogan and LeBeau stowing away with Klink and Schultz on a trip to Paris, LeBeau's presence was gratuitous. "I went because I was French, but I had very little to say." He no longer begrudged his lack of star status, however, and insists that there were never any prima donnas on the set.

Part of Clary's initial reluctance to be relegated to the background revolved around the fact that prior to the show, Clary, unlike most of his costars, had already established a name for himself in show business. At age nineteen, he was a singing star in France. He recorded a hit single consisting of two English-language songs, "Put Your Shoes On, Lucy" and "Johnny, Get Your Girl," which sold a quarter of a million copies. Based on that success, American producers brought him to the United States. He sang "Johnny, Get Your Girl" on a 1950 telecast of *The Ed Wynn Show*. Since he was still learning English at the time, the show's writers created a comedy skit for Clary and Wynn in which Clary got to primarily speak in French.

Clary never had to wait tables, or take any other line of work, like most actors do when they first hit New York. He found work right away in nightclubs, such as the Cafe Gala (now Spago's), where he worked as a singer for over a year. Roles on Broadway soon followed, most notably *New Faces of 1952*.

*New Faces of 1952* was called "an excellent light review" by the *New York Times*' Brooks Atkinson, who called Robert Clary's number, "I'm in Love with Miss Logan," "fascinating." Clary also appeared in the 1954 film version titled *New Faces*.

Clary had been working steadily in variety shows and nightclubs when the call came for *Hogan's Heroes*. He didn't even have to audition for the role. One meeting with the actor convinced producer Ed Feldman that he had found LeBeau.

Close friend Jimmy Komack (television producer/director/writer) had long been urging Clary to move to the West Coast and try to get work there. But it wasn't until Clary heard that the pilot for *Hogan's Heroes* had been sold that he finally made the move. "I decided two things," he says of the day he learned of the pilot's success, "I decided to move to California permanently, and to marry my wife." Clary had met Eddie Cantor's daughter Natalie in 1950, and married her on May 18, 1965, just months before *Hogan's Heroes*' premiere. They are still married today.

Widely recognized then and now as the lovable LeBeau—nicknamed "cockroach" by Schultz and Klink—Clary remembers his work on the series fondly, but does not think it was his best work. "I was capable of doing better than that," he says. "But it was a good living, and a good association. I cannot complain." As happens in the entertainment industry, Clary has lost touch with most of his *Hogan's* costars, with the exception of Werner Klemperer. Though the two live on opposite coasts (Klemperer is a diehard New Yorker), they see each other often.

It surprises many people to learn that this actor, whose fame came from a series that poked fun at World War II, is himself a survivor of the Holocaust. Born Robert Max Wideman on March 1, 1926, in Paris, he was sixteen when he was seized by Hitler's troops, on September 23, 1942. He spent three years in concentration camps. Upon his liberation he learned that of the thirteen members of his family sent to the camps, he alone survived. During his years on *Hogan's Heroes,* Clary rarely discussed his ordeal, preferring to forget all about it. In a 1966 *TV Guide* interview, writer Dick Hobson got him to relate some of his experiences. Clary told Hobson, "When we got to Buchenwald, the SS shoved us into a shower room to spend the night. I had heard the rumors about the dummy shower heads that were gas jets. I thought, *this is it*. But no, it was just a place to sleep. The first eight days there, the Germans kept us without even a crumb to eat. We were hanging on by pure guts, sleeping on top of each other, every morning waking up to find a new corpse next to you."

In 1980, the actor became involved with the Simon Wiesenthal Center, because he realized that "the world just doesn't learn from history," and that as a survivor he needed to speak about his experiences, to ensure that history won't repeat itself. He made a documentary film in 1984 in which he went back to Buchenwald. Making the film was important to him because it will exist "long after the last of us, the survivors, is dead—a permanent refutation to anyone who ever dares say the Holocaust never happened." He also spent years touring the nation's high schools, junior high schools, universities, synagogues, and other organizations lecturing about the horrors of the Holocaust. The Wiesenthal Center has honored Clary for his work, as has the California State Senate. Clary also worked with Steven Spielberg's Shoah Foundation, interviewing Holocaust survivors for archival recordings.

Invariably, at his lectures, someone would ask Clary how he could work on *Hogan's Heroes* after what he went through during World War II. He is weary of repeating himself. "That is the first question I am asked. Always. And I have to tell them that *Hogan's Heroes* was very different. It dealt with prisoner-of-war camps. I'm an actor. I played Louis LeBeau. He was not Jewish, I was never a corporal, I was never a soldier in the Army. And so I played him, and I enjoyed it. Really with the students it's the first question, 'How could you have done *Hogan's Heroes,* which dealt with Nazism?' And I say, not all Germans were Nazis, and not all Nazis were Germans, and we did not deal, really with Nazism, we left that apart. As a comedy you cannot do that."

Some critics of *Hogan's Heroes* confused prisoner-of-war camps with concentration camps and Clary is the first to set the record straight. "I'm not denying or diminishing what the soldiers in prisoner-of-war camps went through in Germany. They were incarcerated, they were prisoners, but there was a big difference. They received Red Cross packages, they had the Geneva Convention, they could write letters and receive letters even though they were censored, they were not forced to go to work, they were not killed, they were not sent to gas chambers."

In 1982, producer Doris Quinlan was putting together a television movie about the gathering of Jewish survivors of the Holocaust in Israel, which happened the previous year. She asked Clary to speak with herself and the scriptwriter (Harold Jack Bloom) about his experiences at the gathering in

**Robert Clary.** Photo courtesy Robert Clary.

Israel. His input resulted in him landing a role in the production. "My agent called and said, 'I just read this script called *Remembrance of Love* and there's a character—Robert Clary.' I guess the writer was impressed with what I was saying and he put my name in it. So I played myself! Again I did not have to audition."

*Remembrance of Love* starred Kirk Douglas as a Holocaust survivor who returns to Israel with his daughter (played by Pam Dawber) and is unexpectedly reunited with his former love, from whom he was separated during World War II. As Clary was playing himself in the film, he changed a lot of the lines he was uncomfortable with. "I went to the producer and the director and I said 'If I'm going to play me, this is the way I talk, this is the way I would say it. And they agreed with it, but they never told Kirk Douglas, and I remember his face when we did the first reading all together. He looked at me like 'What is he doing? He's not following the script!' "

Directly after the cancellation of *Hogan's Heroes,* Clary found it difficult to find acting work; according to his agent he had been 'overexposed.' Not one to sit idle, he took up a hobby—pencil painting. As time passed, and friends praised his talents, he began to take his art more seriously. He has had several gallery showings over the years, and some of his pieces hang in the homes of George C. Scott, Burt Reynolds, Merv Griffin, Jed Allan, and many other famous admirers of his work. His painting style is photo-realism. The works vary in theme from the Atlantic City boardwalks to political slogans on a French subway, but all are vividly moving. "I do things that really have to stir me, otherwise I won't paint it."

After two years without working in show business, Clary was offered a role on the daytime soap opera *Days of Our Lives.* Again, without auditioning, he was cast as Robert LeClare, a role he returned to three times after his initial two-year stint. His character co-owned a nightclub with the soap's central character Doug Williams (played by Bill Hayes). Clary felt that his character, who had married a woman who was pregnant by another man, was a bit of a sad sack in the romance department. He said in a 1977 interview, "My character will sacrifice himself for the lady he loves. I always seem to have someone who likes me but doesn't love me in these parts. I wouldn't be surprised if there *are* people who marry someone who doesn't love them—it's in Dear Abby all the time—but I couldn't.'"

After Clary's initial term on *Days of Our Lives,* he took on another soap opera role. He played Pierre Rolland, a nightclub singer on *The Young and the Restless* from the serial's premiere until 1974, when his character was killed off. The decision to kill off Rolland was one that producer Bill Bell later regretted. He told Clary, "I'm sorry I killed you, I should have killed your wife, but not you!" Bell compensated for his error in 1990 by casting Clary in his new soap opera, *The Bold and the Beautiful*. Clary played Pierre Jourdan, a French saloon singer and confidante to heroine Brooke Logan. The role was remarkably similar to Clary's *The Young and the Restless* character.

In the early 1990s, Clary hosted his own talk show, *A Conversation with Robert Clary,* on Los Angeles' Jewish TV Network. His guests included Ed Asner, Mel Brooks, Carl Reiner, Dick Van Dyke, Martin Landau, and Richard Benjamin. Recently, Clary has returned to his first love, performing live music. He performs in Los Angeles–area nighteries and has released two CDs, *Robert Clary Sings at the Jazz Bakery* and *Robert Clary Sings Rodgers, Hart, and Mercer*. Both recordings have garnered rave reviews, including *Billboard*'s assessment of the *Jazz Bakery* release as "a nostalgic winner." The reviewer concluded, "[Clary] is as fresh as a juvenile lead on the brink of stardom with the added plus, of course, of being a veteran performer... a joyous revelation.'"

### Robert Clary—Selected Credits

**FILM**
*Ten Tall Men* (1951) 'Mossul'
*Thief of Damascus* (1952) 'Aladdin'
*New Faces* (1954)
*A New Kind of Love* (1963) 'Albert Sardou'
*The Hindenburg* (1975) 'Joe Spah'
*Robert Clary A5714: A Memoir of Liberation* (1984) himself

**TELEVISION**

*The Ed Wynn Show* (CBS, 2/11/50)

*The Colgate Comedy Hour* (NBC, 1/20/52)

*Pantomime Quiz* (ABC-CBS, 1954–57)

*Heidi* (NBC Special, 10/1/55) 'Eric'

*The Hollywood Palace* (ABC, 12/25/65)

*The High Chaparral,* "The Last Hundred Miles" (NBC, 12/4/69) 'Charot'

*Love, American Style,* "Love and the Letter" (ABC, 10/6/69) 'Maurice Ravise'

*Days of Our Lives* (NBC, 1972–73, 1975–80, 1981–83, 1985–87) 'Robert LeClare'

*The Young and the Restless* (CBS, 1973–74) 'Pierre Rolland'

*The Legendary Curse of the Hope Diamond* (CBS TVM, 3/27/75) 'Louis XVI'

*Fantasy Island,* "Escape" (ABC, 12/8/78) 'Ipsy Dauphin'

*Remembrance of Love* (NBC TVM, 12/6/82) 'Robert Clary'

*The Bold and the Beautiful* (CBS, 1990–92) 'Pierre Jourdan'

*A Conversation with Robert Clary* (1990s; Los Angeles) host

**THEATER**

*New Faces of 1952,* Royale Theater, New York, and tour (1952)

*Seventh Heaven,* ANTA Theater, New York (1955) 'Fleegle'

*La Plume de ma Tante* (1960)

*Around the World in 80 Days,* Marine Theater, Long Island, NY (1963–64) 'Passepartout' (also 1987 tour)

**RECORDINGS**

*Put Your Shoes On, Lucy/Johnny, Get Your Girl,* 1948

*Meet Robert Clary,* Epic Records

*Hogan's Heroes Sing the Best of World War II,* Liberty Records, 1967

*Robert Clary Sings at the Jazz Bakery,* Original Cast Records, 1997

*Robert Clary Sings Rodgers and Hart, and Mercer,* Original Cast Records, 1997

**AWARDS AND HONORS**

Founders Star Award from the Simon Wiesenthal Center, 1982

Proclamations from Los Angeles Mayor Tom Bradley, Governor Jerry Brown, and Assemblyman Mel Levine, all in honor of Clary's work with the Wiesenthal Center, 1982

Honored by the California State Senate, 1989, for his work with the Wiesenthal Center

# RICHARD DAWSON

## *as Corporal Peter Newkirk*

Before becoming known as the kissing bandit of the game show circuit, Richard Dawson played Corporal Newkirk, the British prisoner with a talent for mimicry and a penchant for pickpocketing. Prior to that, he was a popular standup comedian in London, known as Dickie Dawson.

Born in Gosport, Hampshire, England on November 20, 1934, to poor but hard-working parents, Dawson left home in his early teens to join the merchant marines. After three years, he was back on land working as a waiter, with little or no clue what to do with his future. On a lark, he for a repertory company, hoping to meet girls. He was hired, and spent two years touring with the company.

His career as a comic began with a disastrous performance at a music hall in Plymouth, and flourished steadily with dates at the London Palladium and several London night-clubs. During an engagement at the Stork Room, Dawson met Diana Dors, a statuesque blonde starlet who was looking for a comedian to join her on tour. She hired Dawson for the tour, which took them to the United States. In January 1959, following an appearance on *The Steve Allen Show,* Richard Dawson and Diana Dors were married.

The couple settled in Beverly Hills and had two sons, Mark and Gary. While Dors pursued film roles, she found that she was not in as great demand in America as she had been in England. For that reason, she frequently

**Richard Dawson as Peter Newkirk, lifting Schultz's gun.** © Bing Crosby Productions, Inc. Reprinted with permission.

travelled back to England to work. Dawson found steady work in television, co-hosting a local Los Angeles talk show. His fame was on a much lesser scale than his that of his wife, who had starred in dozens of films in "bombshell" parts. Rumors circulated that Dawson's ego was hurting and that the marriage was in trouble.

Whether Dawson's ego or Dors' frequent absence—or both—were the cause, the couple's marriage crumbled. Dors filed for a divorce in January of 1964, charging mental cruelty. She soon realized that this method of handling the problem was hurtful and dropped the divorce action. Though they were separated from this point onward, the couple did not officially divorce until 1967, and then it was ostensibly to save their house from being taken by Dors' debtors. The Inland Revenue Service (England's equivalent to the IRS) had charged Dors with 40,000 pounds in back taxes, and to protect the house and its assets from being taken by the government, she signed them over to Dawson in their divorce settlement.

Bernard Fox, who played Colonel Crittendon on *Hogan's Heroes,* recalls chiding his compatriot about his tax troubles. "I remember one time, I had a fairly long speech, and Dickie was watching. And I blew it. And Dickie said, 'You'll have to do better than that Bernie, or we'll send you back to England.' And I said, 'I don't care, *I've* paid *my* taxes.' And all the crew went, 'Whooa!' and had quite a laugh."

In the divorce settlement, Dawson was awarded the house and its contents, and more importantly to him, custody of his sons. Dawson told *People* magazine, "People looked down their noses at Diana for leaving me with two young boys, but it was an act of sheer kindness. I don't know what would have happened to me without them."

In 1962, Carl Reiner saw Dawson perform in a nightclub and wrote an episode of his series, *The Dick Van Dyke Show,* especially for him. The episode, "Racy Tracy Rattigan," aired in April, 1963, and featured Dawson as a skirt-chasing British comic. It was Dawson's first experience in situation comedy.

Primarily known as a comedian, it was the 1965 drama *King Rat* that gained Dawson the interest of producer Ed Feldman. Feldman later said of Dawson's *King Rat* role, "He had this one marvelous scene in particular where he was very heroic walking into a Japanese POW camp all alone." Consequently, Feldman tested Dawson for the role of Hogan, but decided against him, in part due to the actor's strong British accent. Feldman was still impressed by Dawson's comic ability and cast him as Newkirk.

During *Hogan's Heroes,* Dawson gained a reputation as a joker. With co-conspirator Larry Hovis, he pulled pranks on other members of the cast and did his best to keep the company in good humor. In a 1981 interview, Ed Feldman insisted that despite his devil-may-care attitude, Dawson was always very professional about being on time and knowing his lines. Today, Hovis says, "Richard Dawson is one of the funniest and most brilliant people I have ever known. We had a lot of fun."

After *Hogan's Heroes,* Dawson and Hovis brought their antics to another series, ABC's *Laugh-In.* Dawson was a regular in the comedy-variety show until its cancellation in 1973. Another sitcom role followed, in *The New Dick Van Dyke Show,* which lasted only one season.

Dawson's career in game shows had begun while he was still on *Hogan's Heroes.* He hosted *Lucky Pair* on a local Los Angeles TV station, and was a panelist and joke-teller on *Can You Top This?,* a syndicated show, in between heroic duties on *Hogan's.* His first national game show venture came in 1973 when he became a regular on the newly resurrected *Match Game.* He resided in one of the six celebrity panelist spots for six years in the daytime version, and held the same position on the syndicated nighttime version, *Match Game P.M.*

Using his popularity on *Match Game* as a springboard, Dawson tried to move into hosting. In 1974 he hosted the syndicated game show *Masquerade Party* (a revival of the 1952–60 version), in which panelists guess the identity of famous people buried under mounds of latex makeup. Nipsey Russell, Jo Ann Worley, and Bill Bixby were the regular panelists.

In 1976, the Goodson-Todman Company, producers of *Match Game,* were planning a new show called *Family Feud.* Dawson's manager pushed for his client for the emcee assignment. Though Dawson did not fit the typical emcee mold, he was given an audition, and ultimately, the job. *Variety* said of *Family Feud*'s nighttime premiere, "Dawson's demeanor sets a proper and welcome pace. Dawson does seem to work hard at being a down-home friendly type, and his sharp humor seemed to be missing as a result."

*Family Feud* soon became one of the most popular game shows in television history, and Richard Dawson's unique style caught on quickly with viewers. His charm with female contestants led to his trademark of greeting each one with a kiss. When this practice drew criticism, he asked viewers to vote. The mail was 14,600 to 704 in favor of the kiss. The contestants themselves apparently didn't mind. Each had to fill out a questionnaire prior to the taping, and one of the questions was "Do you mind if Richard greets you with a kiss?" The producers said they never had a single woman decline. During his tenure on *Family Feud,* Dawson raked in over $250,000 yearly.

As *Family Feud* gained popularity, Dawson lost favor in the Hollywood community. Staff and crew on his show reported that he threw tantrums and that his excessive joking and storytelling during tapings resulted in massive editing to trim each episode down to the proper length. In a *TV Guide* article about game show hosts, colleague Monty Hall said of Dawson, "He has an ego that's gone wild." A former *Family Feud* director said, "The more successful the show gets, the more difficult he is to deal with." Dawson himself refused to be interviewed for the piece unless his photo was guaranteed to be on the cover—alone.

*Family Feud* was canceled in 1985, then revived in 1988, with a new host, Ray Combs. Rather than duplicate Dawson's raucous manner, Combs developed his own style and garnered a large following of his own. But when the show's ratings began to falter, the producers dropped Combs and persuaded Dawson to return. Beset by personal problems, Combs committed suicide in June 1996. Meanwhile, the new version with Dawson also suffered from low ratings and was canceled.

Dawson is known as being somewhat of a recluse, and since his years on *Family Feud* have made him very wealthy, he has worked only sporadically in recent years. His most notable performance was in the 1987 Arnold Schwarzenegger film *The Running Man*. As game show emcee Damon Killian, Dawson received raves from reviewers. Vincent Canby of the *New York Times* called Dawson "wonderfully comic" as the "viciously cheery, lady-kissing, ratings-obsessed emcee." He further noted that Dawson "steals the movie" from superstar Schwarzenegger.

Dawson remarried in 1991, to Gretchen Johnson, whom he met when she appeared as a contestant on *Family Feud*. The couple has an eight-year-old daughter.

Dawson has not remained close to his *Hogan's Heroes* costars. Robert Clary lives just blocks away from Dawson but hasn't seen him in years. "I'm a close neighbor of his, but I never see him. I don't know where he is, what he's doing these days. It's like he disappeared." Clary may not be able to comment on the Dawson of today, but he is very kind in speaking of the Dawson he worked with on *Hogan's*. "It was fun being with him. He was *on* constantly with the jokes and the stories . . . He was so inventive and so marvelous, really."

### Richard Dawson—Selected Credits

**FILM**
*King Rat* (1965) 'Weaver'
*Munster, Go Home* (1966) 'Joey'
*The Devil's Brigade* (1968) 'Hugh MacDonald'
*The Running Man* (1987) 'Damon Killian'

**TELEVISION**

*The Dick Van Dyke Show,* "Racy Tracy Rattigan" (CBS, 4/3/63) 'Tracy Rattigan'

*The Outer Limits,* "The Invisibles" (ABC, 2/3/64) 'Oliver Fair'

*The Alfred Hitchcock Hour,* "Anyone for Murder?" (CBS, 3/13/64) 'Robert Johnson'

*The Hollywood Palace* (ABC, 12/25/65)

*Mr. Terrific,* "The Formula Is Stolen" (CBS, 2/2/67) 'Max'

*Can You Top This?* (Syndicated, 1970) 'Joke Teller'

*McCloud,* "The Stage Is All the World" (NBC, 10/7/70) 'Ted Callender'

*Rowan and Martin's Laugh-In* (NBC, 1971–73) regular cast

*Love, American Style,* "Love and the Groupie" (ABC, 5/21/71) 'Rick'

*Love, American Style,* "Love and the Hiccups" (ABC, 12/10/71) 'Danny'

*Love, American Style,* "The Private Eye" (ABC, 1/28/72) 'Danger'

*Keeping an Eye on Denise* (CBS pilot, 6/19/73) 'British flier'

*Match Game* (CBS, 1973–78) panelist

*The New Dick Van Dyke Show* (CBS, 9/10/73–9/2/74) 'Richard Richardson'

*Masquerade Party* (Syndicated, 1974–75) host

*The Odd Couple,* "Laugh, Clown, Laugh" (ABC, 2/28/75) 'Richard Dawson'

*Match Game P.M.* (Syndicated, 1975–78) panelist

*Hong Kong Phooey* (ABC animated series, 9/6/75–9/4/76) voices

*McMillan and Wife,* "Aftershock" (NBC,11/9/75) 'Roger Stambler/Ken Ryan'

*I've Got a Secret* (CBS, 6/15/76–7/6/76) panelist

*Family Feud* (ABC, 1976–85; CBS, 1994–95) host

*Fantasy Island,* "Call Me Lucky" (ABC, 5/20/78)

*How to Pick Up Girls!* (ABC TVM, 11/3/78) 'Chandler Corey'

*The Love Boat,* "The Song Is Ended" (ABC, 11/4/78)

*Bizarre* (ABC pilot, 3/20/79) host

*Angie,* "Family Feud" (ABC, 11/19/79) 'Richard Dawson'

*Treasure Island* (NBC animated special, 4/29/80) 'Long John Silver'

**RECORDINGS**

*Hogan's Heroes Sing the Best of World War II,* Liberty Records, 1967

**AWARDS**

Emmy Award, Outstanding Game Show Host, for *Family Feud,* 1978

Saturn Award (Academy of Science Fiction, Horror and Fantasy Films), Best Supporting Actor, for *Running Man,* 1988

# IVAN DIXON

## as Sergeant James Kinchloe

Ivan Dixon's reasons for filming the *Hogan's Heroes* pilot, as he revealed in a 1967 interview, were purely financial. "I needed the money," he said. Never thinking the series had a chance, he was surprised when the pilot was picked up and he was offered a supporting role. "Suddenly, I found myself with a guaranteed income for a change," Dixon told the *New York Post*. With three children to support (a fourth was born in October 1965, just after the series' premiere), Dixon was not able to limit his roles to meaningful social dramas as he might have liked.

Not one to bite the hand that fed him, Dixon was thankful for his role as Kinchloe because it gave him exposure and made his name known in the industry. Once he began appearing weekly on television, Dixon's profile helped him to gain other parts. He merely had to express an interest in a production titled "The Final War of Olly Winter" to land the starring role. Broadcast as an episode of CBS's *NET Playhouse*, the critically acclaimed Vietnam war drama earned several Emmy Award nominations, including one for Ivan Dixon as Best Actor.

Ivan Dixon III was born on April 6, 1931, in Harlem, where his father owned a grocery store. The mean streets of Harlem took their toll on young Ivan, who recalls, "I was such a terrible mean little kid, getting into trouble all the time, and it was firmly suggested to my parents that they get me out of the state lest I wind up in reform school." When he was thirteen, his parents sent him to Lincoln Academy, a boarding school in King's Mountain, North Carolina. Dixon credits the southern school system with teaching him more about black history than he ever would have learned in Harlem. At the segregated boarding school, Dixon gained a sense of identity, as he was treated as a person and not "just another black face."

From boarding school, Dixon went to North Carolina College, where he was a pre-law student. He explained, "I had thought that to be someone you had to be a lawyer, doctor, preacher, or teacher, and since the other three didn't appeal to me, I was going to choose law." He eventually abandoned his legal ambitions and graduated with a B.A. in political science and history. A teacher at North Carolina College had recognized Ivan's acting talent when he took part in some school productions, and encouraged him to further his education in the theater.

After graduation, Dixon returned to New York City with his wife Berlie, whom he had met at North Carolina College. He worked as a social case investigator with the New York City Department of Welfare until he earned a Rockefeller Foundation scholarship to study drama at the Western Reserve University in Cleveland. He left Western Reserve before earning his master's degree, opting instead to pursue an acting career in New York City.

In New York, Dixon studied at the American Theater Wing and pounded the pavement for theater roles. He first commanded attention from theatergoers in the 1957 Broadway play *The Cave Dwellers*. A film called *Edge of the City* provided Dixon with his first break in motion pictures. He was hired to act as a stand-in for the film's star, Sidney Poitier. It was the beginning of a fortuitous relationship, as Dixon gained steady

**Ivan Dixon as Sergeant James Kinchloe.**
© Bing Crosby Productions, Inc. Reprinted with permission.

employment doing stunt work and bit parts in Poitier films. In 1958, he moved his family to California, where film and television work was more plentiful.

Acting roles being harder to find for black actors than white, the decision to remain an actor was a tough one. He told the *New York Times* that "most of the people in my college group became teachers and social workers. They would have loved to stay in acting and many were much better than I. But what was the use when there were only two roles a year and both of them played by Sidney Poitier?" In an effort to improve the situation, Dixon helped organize Negro Actors for Action. Now disbanded, the group put pressure on the film and television industries to provide greater opportunities for black actors.

Through his persistence, Dixon gained regular work in films and episodic television. His starring role in the 1964 film *Nothing but a Man* brought him critical acclaim and recognition by his peers. The First International Festival of Negro Arts in Senegal, Africa, named him Best Actor for his performance.

While working with Negro Actors for Action, Dixon met writer Richard M. Powell. Powell recalls, "I was chairing a black writer's workshop and we had quite a few meetings with the actor's groups." When Powell rewrote the *Hogan's Heroes* pilot, he added a black character to the cast and suggested Ivan Dixon for the role. Sergeant Kinchloe was one of few continuing roles for a black actor on television in the mid-sixties.

At the time, Dixon said of his part, "mine is a supporting role. I'm the radio operator. It's the only straight role. The others are really the comedians and I find it enjoyable working with them." Enjoyable, but not fulfilling. Cast mate Robert Clary confides, "Ivan felt very unused. He was not well employed. He's a very, very good actor, and he really had very little to do every week. Of all of us I think he had the least. Once in a while, he would have a big part, but that's maybe once a year. That's not enough. He used to think it was so silly. He used to laugh at everything and say 'What am I doing here?'"

Powell says, "*Hogan's Heroes* gave him exposure, gave him a name, but I guess after five years he felt he really wanted to try other things." Dixon dropped out of the cast at the end of the fifth season. Kenneth Washington was hired as a replacement for Dixon and the series continued for another year. Clary confesses that although the cast liked Washington, they missed Dixon. "But Ivan just didn't want to do it anymore," he says. "He chose the right path and became a very good director."

Bill Cosby gave Dixon his first directorial assignment, an episode of *The Bill Cosby Show*. He directed additional *Bill Cosby Show* episodes as well as the entertainer's 1971 television special. Said Dixon of Cosby, "You couldn't work for or with a better person. It was a gas each time. We worked hard and had fun. Everything came off beautifully." Dixon went on to direct episodes of numerous other television series, including *Julia, Get Christie Love, The Waltons, Starsky and Hutch, The Rockford Files, Little House on the Prairie, Quantum Leap*, and *Magnum, P.I.*

Dixon made his film directing debut in 1972, with *Trouble Man*. The following year he produced and directed *The Spook Who Sat by the Door*, another blaxploitation feature. He returned to acting infrequently in the years after *Hogan's Heroes*, most notably in the controversial 1987 miniseries *Amerika*. He found directing work was more readily available, and in some ways, more fulfilling. He remarked, "Every time I direct a story, it's a little like giving life to something; there's a good feeling when it comes off right—when you know you've applied just the right chemical and creative forces."

Today Dixon lives in Hawaii, where he owns a radio station.

### Ivan Dixon—Selected Credits

**FILM**

*Edge of the City* (1957) extra
*Something of Value* (1957) 'Lathela'
*The Defiant Ones* (1958) stunt double for Sidney Poitier
*Porgy and Bess* (1959) 'Jim'
*Battle at Bloody Beach* (1961) 'Tiger Blair'
*A Raisin in the Sun* (1961) 'Joseph Asagai'
*Nothing but a Man* (1964) 'Duff Anderson'
*A Patch of Blue* (1965) 'Mark Ralfe'
*To Trap a Spy* (1966) 'Soumarin'
*Where's Jack?* [aka *Run, Rebel, Run*] (1969) 'Naval Officer'
*Suppose They Gave a War and Nobody Came?* (1970) 'Sgt. Jones'
*Clay Pigeon* (1971) 'Simon'
*Car Wash* (1976) 'Lonnie'

**AS DIRECTOR**

*Trouble Man* (1972)
*The Spook Who Sat by the Door* (1973) [also producer]

**TELEVISION**

*Studio One,* "Career" (CBS, 12/17/56)
*Studio One,* "Walk Down the Hill" (CBS, 3/18/57)
*DuPont Show of the Month,* "Arrowsmith" (CBS, 1/17/60)
*The Twilight Zone,* "The Big Tall Wish" (CBS, 4/8/60) 'Bolie Jackson'
*Have Gun Will Travel,* "Long Way Home" (CBS, 2/4/61)
*Cain's Hundred,* "Markdown on a Man" (NBC, 10/10/61)
*Follow the Sun,* "The Hunters" (ABC, 11/12/61)
*The New Breed,* "Policemen Die Alone" (ABC, 1/30/62 and 2/6/62) 'Ray Wick'
*Cain's Hundred,* "Blues for a Junkman" (NBC, 2/20/62) 'Joe Sherman'
*Target: The Corruptors,* "Journey Into Mourning" (ABC, 4/13/62) 'Bliss'
*Dr. Kildare,* "Something of Importance" (NBC, 5/3/62) 'Dr. Staples'
*Perry Mason,* "The Case of the Promoter's Pillbox" (CBS, 5/19/62)
*Laramie,* "Among the Missing" (NBC, 9/25/62) 'Jamie Davis'
*The Defenders,* "Man Against Himself" (CBS, 1/12/63) 'Danny Ross'

*Going My Way*, "Run, Robin, Run" (ABC, 3/25/63) 'Robin Green'
*Stoney Burke*, "The Test" (ABC, 5/13/63) 'Dr. Manning'
*Perry Mason*, "The Case of the Nebulous Nephew" (CBS, 9/26/63) 'Caleb'
*The Outer Limits*, "The Human Factor" (ABC, 11/11/63) 'Major Giles'
*Channing*, "Memory of a Firing Squad" (ABC, 11/64)
*Great Adventure*, "The Special Courage of Captain Pratt" (CBS, 2/14/64)
*The Twilight Zone*, "I Am the Night—Color Me Black" (CBS, 3/27/64)
    'Reverend Anderson'
*Dr. Kildare*, "Night of the Beast" (NBC, 4/23/64) 'Detective'
*The Defenders*, "The Non-Violent" (CBS, 6/6/64)
*The Nurses*, "The Warrior" (CBS, 6/18/64)
*The Man from U.N.C.L.E.*, "The Vulcan Affair" (NBC, 9/22/64) 'Soumarin'
*Bob Hope's Chrysler Theater*, "Murder in the First" (NBC, 10/9/64)
*The Fugitive*, "Escape Into Black" (ABC, 11/17/64)
*The Outer Limits*, "The Inheritors" (ABC, 11/21/64 and 11/28/64)
    'Sergeant James Conover'
*I Spy*, "So Long, Patrick Henry" (NBC, 9/15/65) 'Elroy Brown'
*The Hollywood Palace* (ABC, 12/25/65)
*NET Playhouse*, "The Final War of Olly Winter" (CBS, 1/29/67) 'Olly Winter'
*The Fugitive*, "Dossier on a Diplomat" (ABC, 3/28/67)
*Felony Squad*, "The Deadly Junkman" (ABC, 10/16/67)
*Ironside*, "Backfire" (NBC, 11/2/67)
*The Jonathan Winters Show* (CBS, 12/27/67)
*It Takes a Thief*, "Get Me to the Revolution on Time" (ABC, 10/22/68)
*The Name of the Game*, "The Black Answer" (NBC, 12/13/68)
*The Name of the Game*, "The Incomparable Connie Walker" (NBC, 1/24/69)
    'Mayor Conway Walker'
*The Mod Squad*, "Return to Darkness, Return to Light" (ABC, 3/17/70)
*The F.B.I.*, "The Deadly Pact" (ABC, 11/8/70) 'Terry Maynard'
*Love, American Style*, "Love and the Baby" (ABC, 11/12/71) 'Stan'
*Fer-De-Lance* (CBS TVM, 10/18/74) 'Joe Voit'
*Perry Mason: The Case of the Shooting Star* (NBC TVM, 11/9/86) 'Judge'
*Amerika* (ABC Miniseries, 2/15/87–2/22/87) 'Alan Drummond'
*Father Dowling Mysteries*, "The Joyful Noise Mystery" (ABC, 5/2/91)
    'Reverend Johnson'

**AS DIRECTOR:**

Episodes of *The Bill Cosby Show, Julia, Get Christie Love, The Waltons, Delvecchio, Kahn!, Starsky and Hutch, McCloud, Tenspeed and Brownshoe, Baa Baa Black Sheep, Little House on the Prairie, Palmerstown,*

*U.S.A., The Rockford Files, Airwolf, The Greatest American Hero, The A-Team, Magnum, P.I., Quantum Leap, Hawaiian Heat*

**THEATER**

*The Cave Dwellers,* Bijou Theater, NY (1957) 'Jamie'
*Wedding in Japan,* Greystone Theater, NY (1957) 'Sergeant Mallet'
*A Raisin in the Sun,* Ethel Barrymore Theater, NY (1959) 'Joseph Asagai'

**RECORDINGS**

*Hogan's Heroes Sing the Best of World War II,* Liberty Records, 1967

**AWARDS**

First International Festival of Negro Art, Best Actor Award for *Nothing but a Man*
Emmy nomination for *NET Playhouse,* "The Final War of Olly Winter," 1967
Black Filmmakers Hall of Fame inductee, Oscar Micheaux Award, 1980

## LARRY HOVIS

### as Sergeant Andrew J. Carter

In the pilot episode of *Hogan's Heroes,* POWs Newkirk, LeBeau, Kinch, and Minsk aid a lieutenant who is escaping from Germany. After the pilot was sold, actor Leonid Kinskey, who played Minsk, opted not to sign up for the series. Stewart Moss, another actor who was originally intended to be a regular cast member, also decided not to commit to a series. Larry Hovis played the escaping lieutenant in the pilot, planned to be a one-shot role. When Kinskey and Moss withdrew, Hovis was hired as a regular, the fourth hero—Sergeant Andrew Carter. Hovis's dichotomous character was on one hand an explosives expert and Hitler impressionist and on the other a naïve, at times dim-witted, American. The target of countless dumb jokes, Carter was nonetheless a hero, continually risking his life for the Allies.

Hovis was born on February 20, 1936 in Wapito, Washington. He was raised in Houston, Texas, where his family moved when he was a toddler. At the age of seven, he formed a singing act with his older sister Joan. Later he joined a vocal quartet, the Mascots. The highlight of his five years with the group was performing on television in *Arthur Godfrey's Talent Scouts.*

While studying history and philosophy at the University of Houston, Hovis continued to pursue a singing career. He recorded an album for Capitol Records. Capitol promoted the young man as "a new teenage sensation." He performed in nightclubs in and around Houston, wrote for local television shows, and briefly hosted a daytime game show, *Surprise Party*, on Houston's KTRK-TV.

With ambitions of starring in musical theater, Hovis moved to New York City. His sister Joan had already amassed some stage credits of her own, as well as a Theater World Award for the 1957–58 Broadway season. Larry landed roles on Broadway in *From A to Z* and *The Billy Barnes Revue*. In 1963, he and his wife, Ann, relocated to California. He performed stand-up routines in nightclubs and began working in television. He portrayed a marine in ten episodes of *Gomer Pyle, U.S.M.C.*, but

**Carter (Larry Hovis) impersonating a German officer.** © Bing Crosby Productions, Inc. Reprinted with permission.

found the work less than satisfying. "It was very nice that I got some work. And Jim Nabors was nice. But my character was basically a wall, you know, just somebody in the background." Though his role was minor, Hovis was remembered by one of the producers, Ed Feldman, when he was casting the pilot episode of *Hogan's Heroes*.

During the run of *Hogan's Heroes*, Hovis did not remain idle. He continued his scriptwriting efforts and wrote a few television specials. He was a performer and writer on NBC's *Rowan and Martin's Laugh-In* from its premiere in September 1967 until the following season. Some reports state that Hovis's double duty stopped short when CBS realized he was moonlighting for a rival network. He denies that was the case. "I just reached the point where I couldn't do everything," he recalls. "Ann Elder and I were writing

Mitzi Gaynor specials and her nightclub act, and I was writing for other people. And trying to do two shows was just crazy. Plus I had four kids to raise!"

Hovis even tried writing a *Hogan's* script with costar Richard Dawson. He says, "We roughed out an outline of an episode we thought we'd like to write. And Eddie Feldman, who was just the most princely guy in the world, very kindly said, 'Let me think about it.' And then I suddenly realized, he doesn't want to alienate these wonderful writers that we had. They were really good to us, and we should just act and leave the writing to them."

In a cast of seven regulars, Larry Hovis's Carter often got lost in the crowd. A 1970 *TV Guide* interview quoted him as saying, "I wasn't pictured in the *Hogan's* comic book. I wasn't on the bubble-gum trading cards. I was even missing from the *Hogan's* lunch box. I'm the Invisible Man—one of those people whose every vestige of existence is destined to be erased." Either the *TV Guide* reporter mistook tongue-in-cheek statements for serious laments or Hovis's feelings have softened over the years. With no hint of sour grapes, he calls being part of the large *Hogan's* cast "one of the luckiest things in the world." He says, "My goodness, when you really analyze my character, any competent actor could have done what I did. And the fact that Eddie Feldman said 'you're the guy that's going to get to do it for six years'—I mean, who could have a complaint?"

After *Hogan's Heroes* was canceled, Hovis returned to the cast of *Laugh-In*, bringing fellow hero and cohort Richard Dawson along. He also did some episodic television work, including a few appearances on *The Doris Day Show*. Hovis must have felt right at home on Doris's show, as it employed several *Hogan's Heroes* alumni. In his first *Doris Day Show* appearance, he acted alongside frequent *Hogan's* guest stars Arlene Martel, Henry Corden, and Ben Wright, in a script penned by Richard M. Powell. He returned several months later in an episode written by Arthur Julian and directed by Marc Daniels, both former *Hogan's* staffers.

In the years after *Hogan's*, Hovis gradually did less acting and moved more into writing and producing. He had realized that as an actor, television was not the right medium for him. "My whole background is stage. And I realized that I was kind of this nebbish guy-next-door type. I was probably never going to get to do the kind of things dramatically that I really wanted to do. So I returned to theater from time to time, and I wrote and produced."

Like Dawson, Hovis found a niche for a while in television game shows. His most notable venture was *Liar's Club*, a syndicated game show in which panelists made up stories about unusual objects and contestants guessed which one was telling the truth. One of the regular panelists from 1976 to 1978, Hovis was also executive producer for the series. Subsequent game show endeavors were *Anything for Money* and a game show based on the dice game *Yahtzee*.

In 1989, Larry Hovis made headlines when he was fired by Fox Broadcasting as co-producer of *Totally Hidden Video*. The series was intended to be a *Candid Camera*-type series with everyday people being surprised by hidden cameras. Hovis allegedly hired actors to portray "real people" for three segments and was dismissed. About that time, he decided to move back to Texas, where his siblings and his mother still reside.

**Larry Hovis.** Photo courtesy Larry Hovis.

For the past nine years, Hovis has been teaching drama at Southwest Texas State University in San Marcos, Texas. He has performed in several productions at the university, but says, "I think that my performance days as such are behind me. But more and more I love teaching, and I kind of like directing." Still recognized as Carter, Hovis says he is astounded by the series' continued popularity, especially its hit status in Germany. "I'm amazed after all this time that anyone still cares about our show," he says. "I'm so grateful to have been a part of it. It was a wonderful part of my life."

### Larry Hovis—Selected Credits

**FILM**

*Black Jack* [aka *Wild in the Sky*] (1973) 'Captain Breen'
*Shadow Force* (1993) 'Frank Bergmann'

**AS WRITER**

*Out of Sight* (1966)

**TELEVISION**

*Gomer Pyle, U.S.M.C.* (CBS, 9/25/64–6/65) 'Larry'

*The Andy Griffith Show,* "Goober Takes a Car Apart" (CBS, 1/11/65) 'Gilly Walker'

*The Andy Griffith Show,* "The Case of the Punch in the Nose" (CBS, 3/15/65) 'Gilly Walker'

*Ben Casey,* "The Day They Stole the County General" (ABC, 4/26/65)

*The Hollywood Palace* (ABC, 12/25/65)

*ABC Stage 67,* "Where It's At" (ABC, 9/28/66)

*Rowan and Martin's Laugh-In* (NBC, 1967–68, 1971–72)

*The Ghost and Mrs. Muir,* "Dog Gone" (NBC, 1/11/69) 'Norbert Frank'

*The Carol Burnett Show* (CBS, 3/24/69)

*The Doris Day Show,* "The Sorrow of Sangapur" (CBS, 1/10/72)

*The Doris Day Show,* "Peeping Tom" (CBS, 10/9/72)

*Adam-12,* "Venice Division" (NBC, 10/10/73)

*Chico and the Man,* "Borrowed Trouble" (NBC, 10/11/74) 'First Customer'

*The New Daughters of Joshua Cabe* (ABC TVM, 5/29/76) 'Clel Tonkins'

*Holmes and Yoyo* (ABC, 9/25/76–12/11/76) 'Doctor Babcock'

*Liar's Club* (Syndicated, 1976–78) executive producer and panelist

*Sex and the Married Woman* (NBC, 9/13/77) 'Arnie Fish'

*Alice,* "The Indian Taker" (CBS, 10/9/77) 'Fred'

*Alice,* "Close Encounters of the Worst Kind" (CBS, 1/22/78) 'Bill Dovey'

*Another Pair of Aces: Three of a Kind* (CBS TVM, 4/9/91) 'Tillman'

**AS WRITER**

*ABC Stage 67,* "Where It's At" (ABC, 9/28/66)

*Rowan and Martin's Laugh-In* (NBC, 1967–68, 1971–72)

*Mitzi* (NBC, 10/14/68)

*Mitzi's Second Special* (NBC, 10/20/69)

**AS PRODUCER**

*Liar's Club* (Syndicated, 1976–78)

*Anything for Money* (Syndicated, 1984–85)

*Yahtzee* (Syndicated, 1988)

*Totally Hidden Video* (Fox, 1989)

**THEATER**

*From A to Z,* Plymouth Theater, New York (1960) 'Michael Fesco'

*The Billy Barnes Revue,* New York (1959)

*Mr. Roberts,* Alley Theater, 'Ensign Pulver'

*Best Little Whorehouse in Texas,* Wilshire Theater (1981) 'Melvin B. Thorpe'
*Carnival, Southwest Texas University, Glade Theater, 'Schlegel'*
*The Dead President's Club, Southwest Texas University* Theater (1995) 'Truman'

**RECORDINGS**
*My Heart Belongs to Only You,* Capitol Records
*Sweet Swingin' Swing* with the Bill Gannon Trio, Carlton Records
*Hogan's Heroes Sing the Best of World War II,* Liberty Records, 1967

## KENNETH WASHINGTON

### *as Sergeant Richard Baker*

In the sixth—and final—season of *Hogan's Heroes,* a newcomer joined *Hogan's* ranks. Ivan Dixon had departed at the end of the fifth season to pursue other avenues of show business, leaving Hogan minus one hero. Auditions for a replacement character were held in both New York City and Los Angeles, and actor Kenneth Washington attended one of the open calls. Regarding his success in landing the part, he says, "I was one of the many who auditioned and I guess God chose to smile on me."

Rather than recasting Dixon's role of Kinchloe, the producers chose to create a new character, Sergeant Richard Baker. Baker, like his predecessor, ran the underground communications center. As the two characters were radio experts and both were portrayed by black actors, it seemed as though the producers were trying to slip the change by viewers without notice. In fact, nothing was ever mentioned on screen about Kinch's departure or Baker's arrival—it was just business as usual at Stalag 13.

While Baker's arrival was not much heralded on screen, Kenneth Washington was very warmly received offscreen. Werner Klemperer says "We really missed Ivan, but Kenny Washington was very nice. We all enjoyed working with him." Washington is emphatic when he speaks of the cast's friendly treatment of him. "Everybody was very nice, very receptive."

Like his costars, loyal viewers probably missed Ivan Dixon too, but they reacted favorably to the addition of Kenneth Washington to the cast. "I got a lot of fan mail," reflects Washington. "Lots of mail, saying 'best of luck.' And folks who would come on the set were very supportive, wishing me all good fortune. I didn't receive one discouraging letter or remark."

Washington is diplomatic when speaking about the modest size of his role. With a cast of seven regulars and a handful of semiregulars, it was impossible to feature prominently each of the performers every week. The role of

**Kenneth Washington (center) joined the cast in the sixth season. With Richard Dawson, Robert Clary, Bob Crane, and Larry Hovis.** © Bing Crosby Productions, Inc. Reprinted with permission.

Baker was often reduced to a few lines per episode, along the lines of "What next, Colonel?" Rather than feeling resentful, Washington was grateful for the chance to work on the series. "It was only a thirty-minute show, and every actor wants more. But they had to give the lion's share to the three who got the show off the ground—John Banner, Werner Klemperer, and Bob Crane."

Washington's time on *Hogan's Heroes,* though enjoyable, was brief. The series was canceled at the end of the sixth season, only nine months after Washington joined the cast.

In the years since *Hogan's,* Washington has acted in a few feature films and television movies. His principal work, however, has been in the theater. He has performed in numerous plays, from *Hamlet* to *One Flew Over the Cuckoo's Nest,* with lead roles in *Purlie Victorius* and *Lost in the Stars,* among others. He returned to school and earned a degree from Loyola Marymount in Los Angeles, with plans to venture into the teaching field.

### Kenneth Washington—Selected Credits

**FILM**
*Changes* (1969)
*Hook, Line and Sinker* (1969)
*Marooned* (1969)

*Tarzan's Deadly Silence* (1970) 'Akaba'
*Westworld* (1973) 'Technician'
*Ebony, Ivory and Jade* (1977)

**TELEVISION**

*Tarzan,* "The Deadly Silence" (NBC, 10/28/66 and 11/4/66) 'Akaba' [later released as a feature film, *Tarzan's Deadly Silence*]
*I Dream of Jeannie,* "The Girl Who Never Had a Birthday" (NBC, 11/14/66 and 11/21/66)
*My Three Sons,* "Dear Enemy" (CBS, 2/10/68) 'Corporal'
*Adam 12,* "Log 141" (NBC, 9/28/68) 'Miller'
*My Friend Tony,* "Death Comes in Small Packages" (NBC, 1/12/69) 'Coley'
*Star Trek,* "That Which Survives" (NBC, 1/24/69) 'John B. Watkins'
*Petticoat Junction,* "By the Book" (CBS, 3/29/69) 'William Blake'
*Climb an Angry Mountain* (NBC TVM, 12/23/72) 'Huggins'
*Cry Rape!* (CBS, 11/27/73) 'Marshall'
*The Rockford Files,* "2 Into 5.56 Won't Go" (NBC, 11/21/75) 'Guard'
*Steeltown* (CBS pilot, 5/19/79) 'Doc Brinjac'
*Our Family Business* (ABC TVM, 9/20/81) 'Harry'
*Money on the Side* (ABC TVM, 9/29/82) 'Detective White'

**THEATER**

*Happy Ending,* Ebony Theater, Los Angeles
*A Raisin in the Sun,* Inner City Theater, Los Angeles
*Dark, Don't Catch Me Here,* Actor's Theater, Los Angeles
*One Flew Over the Cuckoo's Nest,* Player's Ring, Los Angeles
*Lost in the Stars,* Ebony Theater, Los Angeles
*Purlie Victorious,* Lafayette Players, Los Angeles
*The Hasty Heart,* San Francisco
*The Blacks,* Mark Taper Forum, Los Angeles
*The Training,* Actor's Workspace, Los Angeles
*Hamlet,* Inner City Theater, Los Angeles

# LEON ASKIN

### *as General Albert Burkhalter*

How did Leon Askin approach his role of Klink's cantankerous superior officer? He revealed his secret in a 1966 CBS press release: "In portraying Burkhalter I try always to depict the sort of irritability of a man who realizes he has just swal-

**Leon Askin as General Burkhalter.** © Bing Crosby Productions, Inc. Reprinted with permission.

lowed a rotten olive." The method proved effective, for when Burkhalter bellowed, Klink quivered.

Joining the cast of *Hogan's Heroes* was like old home week for Askin. He had worked on stage with John Banner in his native Vienna, before either emigrated to the United States. And Werner Klemperer was a colleague from the New York stage. Of his long-standing friendship with Klemperer, Askin says "I've never worked with someone in more variety of situations than Werner." Klemperer agrees. "That's true. We were in a Broadway show together, with Jose Ferrer and Gloria Swanson, *Twentieth Century*. We had two small, but very effective, parts in it. And he directed me in a play. I made a commercial in Minneapolis and Leon was also in it. Our lives have just criss-crossed for a long time."

Askin, whose name was Leon Aschkenazy before he shortened it, was born in Vienna, Austria on September 18, 1907. His mother being German, Askin speaks the language fluently—a fact which must have come in handy in the multitude of European roles he played in films and television.

From the time he was a young boy, Askin possessed a driving ambition to be an actor. He spent his free time in his childhood attending as many productions as he could, and he made his first professsional appearance on stage in 1926 in *Schrei aus der Strasse* (*Cry from the Streets*) with the Youth Theater in Vienna. Soon afterwards, he began studying at Max Reinhardt's New School for Dramatic Arts in Vienna. He left the school when he was offered a contract with the Düsseldorf Municipal Theater. He worked his way up in the dramatic world in Germany, and was under contract at the famed

Louise Dumont Playhouse in 1933 when Adolf Hitler was named Chancellor of the Reich. As a Jew, Askin was dismissed from the theater.

In April of that year, he was arrested and beaten by the Gestapo. The Austrian Consul arranged for his release and he fled to Paris. He spent the next several years working in the theater in Austria and Paris. In September 1938, he was interred in a French prison camp because his Austrian citizenship made him an enemy of the French government. Conditions in the camp were primitive, but Askin says that the most of the inmates—Austrian, German, and Italian refugees—did not attempt escape. "We were welcome to 'escape' any time we wished, provided that we left France, but none of us bothered to do it since we had no yen to return to our own countries and it appeared impossible for us to gain admittance anywhere else." After six months in the camp, Askin was released when a U.S. visa he had previously applied for came through. He arrived in the United States on March 1, 1940.

Shortly after his arrival in the U.S., Askin became the artistic director of the Washington Civic Theater in Washington, D.C. He directed several successful productions and founded a drama school at the theater. He left the theater when he was drafted into the U.S. Army Air Corps. During his four-year stint in the military, Askin achieved the rank of technical sergeant. Though he was in the air force, Askin never went into the wild blue yonder. He edited the Orientation Digest and delivered hundreds of lectures to American troops and officers on the military and political history of Germany that led to Hitler's rule.

After the war, Askin returned to New York. For the next seven years, he worked as an actor and director on and off Broadway. In 1952, he went to Hollywood, hoping to find more lucrative work—in the film industry. Askin's first film role was in the Columbia Pictures production *Assignment—Paris*. He was cast as European characters in dozens of movies and television productions. He worked with Richard Burton in *The Robe,* Danny Kaye in *Knock on Wood,* James Cagney in *One, Two, Three,* and Doris Day in *Do Not Disturb*. He recalls, "I was typecast as the funny villain and played Russians, Germans, Swedes, French people, no matter how exact my English could be...There is a slight intonation, and that is enough for Hollywood producers never to cast me as an American or Englishman."

The role of General Burkhalter on *Hogan's Heroes* came naturally to Askin, who had played similar roles throughout his career. What surprised him was the controversy which surrounded the series. He was subjected to questions as to how a Jewish actor could portray a German Nazi in a comedy. "From the beginning," he says, "*Hogan's Heroes* was misunderstood. It was about a POW camp. A stalag. In stalags there are soldiers under the Geneva convention. It was not a concentration camp. If you want to make fun of your enemy, be it French, American, German, whatever—humor is the greatest weapon. The controversy is idiotic." In his opinion, the secret of the series' success was the familial atmosphere. "It was family. Brotherly love. It was a wonderful experience."

In a 1996 interview for *Austria Kultur,* the publication of the Austria Cultural Institute, Askin described his approach to his character, "I played him straight, an Army officer...I had a discussion with a colleague of mine, who played an SS officer. He always said that he couldn't make him straight, but had to portray him as a caricature. But if you do so, you hurt the cause. Because that's not what he was. An SS officer was never a caricature, but a life-threatening person...whether it is Richard III or the SS or General Burkhalter—you have to play the part, the person that he is. You cannot play a caricature of Richard III either. He wasn't exactly a nice guy. That is a great misinterpretation of what acting is supposed to do."

In addition to an extensive list of performing and directing credits, Askin has also been very active in the administrative end of the business. He founded the Actors' Equity Community Theater in 1948, was chairman of several Equity Library Theater committees between 1947 and 1952 and is an honorary lifetime director of ELT. He has served on the boards of the Screen Actors Guild and the American National Theater and Academy (ANTA) West. In 1983 he was appointed president emeritus of ANTA West.

In 1991, Askin added a new role to his repertoire, that of author. His book, *Quietude and Quest,* combines an autobiography with his reflections on the theater and interpretations of some of his historic characters. The book only touches lightly upon his years on *Hogan's Heroes,* instead concentrating on his fascinating experiences in pre- and post-war Europe and his emigration to the United States.

In 1994, Askin returned to his native Vienna. Though wheelchair-bound due to a leg injury, he remains active in theater and film.

### Leon Askin—Selected Credits

**FILM**
*Assignment—Paris* (1952) 'Franz'
*Road to Bali* (1952) 'Ramayana'
*China Venture* (1953) 'Wu King'
*Desert Legion* (1953) 'Major Vasil'

*The Robe* (1953) 'Abidor'
*South Sea Woman* (1953) 'Marchand'
*The Veils of Bagdad* (1953) 'Pascha Hamman'
*Knock on Wood* (1954) 'Gromeck'
*Secret of the Incas* (1954) 'Anton Marcu'
*Valley of the Kings* (1954) 'Valentine Arko'
*Carolina Cannonball* (1955) 'Otto'
*Son of Sinbad* (1955) 'Khalif'
*Spy Chasers* (1956) 'Colonel Alex Baxis'
*My Gun Is Quick* (1957) 'Teller'
*The Last Blitzkrieg* (1958) 'Sergeant Steiner'
*One, Two, Three* (1961) 'Peripetchikoff'
*Lulu* (1962–Austria) 'Son'
*Sherlock Holmes and the Deadly Necklace* (1962–Germany) 'Charles'
*John Goldfarb, Please Come Home* (1964) 'Samir'
*Do Not Disturb* (1965) 'Langsdorf'
*The Terror of Dr. Mabuse* (1965) 'Floke'
*What Did You Do in the War, Daddy?* (1966) 'Kastorp'
*The Caper of the Golden Bulls* [aka *Carnival of Thieves*] (1967) 'Morchek'
*Double Trouble* (1967) 'Inspector De Groote'
*The Perils of Pauline* (1967) 'Commissar'
*Guns for San Sebastian* (1968) 'Vicar General'
*The Wicked Dreams of Paula Schultz* (1968) 'Oscar'
*Lukrezia Borgia* (1968–Rome)
*A Fine Pair* (1969) 'Chief Wellman'
*The Maltese Bippy* (1969) 'Axel Kronstadt'
*The Black Count* (1971–Hungary)
*Hammersmith Is Out* (1972) 'Doctor Krodt'
*Doctor Death: Seeker of Souls* (1973) 'Thor'
*The World's Greatest Athlete* (1973) 'Doctor Gottlieb'
*Perahim* (1973–Germany)
*Young Frankenstein* (1974) 'Herr Waldman'
*Karl May* (1974–Austria)
*Affaire Hofrichter* (1974–Austria)
*Death Knocks Twice* (1975)
*Going Ape!* (1981) 'Zabrowski'
*Airplane II: The Sequel* (1982) 'Moscow Anchorman'
*Frightmare* (1983) 'Wolfgang'
*Savage Island* (1985) 'Luker'

*Odd Jobs* (1986) 'Don Carlutci'
*Deshima* (1987–Japan) 'Frank Nievergelt'
*Hohenangst* (1994–Austria)
*Adolf Lanz–Mein Krampf* (1995–Germany)

## TELEVISION

*Lux Video Theater,* "Return to Alsace" (CBS, 9/24/53) 'Gustave'
*Superman,* "Superman in Exile" (Syndicated, 10/26/53) 'Ferdinand'
*Superman,* "King for a Day" (Syndicated, 12/6/54) 'Valance'
*The Charlie Farrell Show* (CBS, 7/2/56–9/24/56) 'Pierre'
*Lux Video Theater,* "You Can't Escape Forever" (CBS, 11/1/56) 'Mike Czerny'
*Lux Video Theater,* "Christmas in Connecticut" (CBS, 12/13/56) 'Felix'
*The Restless Gun,* "The Shooting of Jett King" (NBC, 10/28/57)
*Walt Disney Presents,* "The Peter Tchaicovsky Story" (ABC, 1/30/59) 'Anton Rubinstein'
*Saints and Sinners,* "The Year Joan Crawford Won the Oscar" (NBC, 1/21/63) 'Baron'
*The Outer Limits,* "The Inheritors" (ABC, 11/21/64 and 11/28/64)
*The Rogues,* "Plavonia, Hail and Farewell" (NBC, 11/29/64)
*My Favorite Martian,* "Martin of the Movies" (CBS, 9/26/65) 'Von Reinbein'
*Honey West,* "The Abominable Snowman" (ABC, 10/1/65) 'Count'
*Russian Roulette* (NBC Special, 11/17/65) 'Chunky Russian'
*The Man from U.N.C.L.E.,* "The Project Deephole Affair" (NBC, 3/18/66) 'Marvin Elom'
*My Favorite Martian,* "Pay the Man the $24" (CBS, 5/1/66) 'Peter Minuit'
*I Spy,* "Will the Real Good Guys Please Stand Up?" (NBC, 11/2/66) 'Boris'
*The Man from U.N.C.L.E.,* "The Off-Broadway Affair" (NBC, 11/18/66) 'Machina'
*It's About Time,* "The Stone Age Diplomats" (CBS, 3/12/67)
*Alfred of the Amazon* (CBS pilot, 7/31/67) 'Herr Futterman'
*Felony Squad,* "The Pat Hand of Death" (ABC, 10/30/67)
*The Monkees,* "The Card-Carrying Red Shoes" (NBC, 11/6/67)
*Daniel Boone,* "Benvenuto . . . Who?" (NBC, 10/9/69) 'Roquelin'
*Mission: Impossible,* "Death Squad" (CBS, 3/15/70) 'Riva'
*The F.B.I.,* "The Buyer" (ABC, 1/2/72) 'Arnold Bebenek'
*McMillan and Wife,* "No Hearts, No Flowers" (NBC, 1/14/73) 'Ingo'
*Genesis II* (CBS pilot, 3/23/73) 'Overseer'
*Switch!,* "The Lady from Liechtenstein" (CBS, 11/23/76 and 11/30/76)

*Visions,* "The Great Cherub Knitwear Strike" (PBS, 11/25/76) 'Mr. Genselheimer'

*The Hardy Boys/Nancy Drew Mysteries,* "The Hardy Boys and Nancy Drew Meet Dracula" (ABC, 9/11/77 and 9/18/77)

*Meeting of Minds* (PBS, 1/24/77 and 1/31/77) 'Doctor Karl Marx'

*Meeting of Minds* (PBS, 3/6/78 and 3/13/78) 'Martin Luther'

*Happy Days,* "Fearless Malph" (ABC, 1978) 'Himmel'

*Three's Company,* "The Bake-Off" (ABC, 2/27/79) 'Mr. Hoffmeir'

### THEATER

*Faust,* Barbizon-Plaza Theater, NY (1947) 'Faust'

*A Temporary Island,* Maxine Elliott's Theater, NY (1948) 'Mr. Prince'

*Twentieth Century,* ANTA Playhouse, NY (1950) '2nd Beard'

*I Remember Mama,* Shubert, New Haven, CT (1951) 'Uncle Chris'

*The Play's the Thing,* Lenox Hill Playhouse, New York (1952) 'Turai'

*Othello,* Hamburg Kammerspiele Theater, Germany (1957) 'Othello'

*Idiot's Delight,* Ahmanson Theater, Los Angeles (1970)

Also producer/director/star of numerous productions, including *Hamlet, Julius Caesar, St. Joan, The Apple Cart,* and *Mrs. Warren's Profession.*

### AWARDS

Medal of Honor, City of Vienna, 1983

Austrian Cross of Honor, 1988

### PUBLICATIONS

*Quietude and Quest: Protagonists and Antagonists in the Theater, On and Off Stage, as Seen Through the Eyes of Leon Askin* (Riverside, Calif: Ariadne Press, 1991)

# HOWARD CAINE

### *as Major Wolfgang Hochstetter*

Most people are surprised to learn that Howard Caine, the ruthless Major Hochstetter, was a Southern born Jew. Born Howard Cohen on January 2, 1928 in Nashville, Tennessee, Caine began his show business career at the tender age of two, when Hal and Jack Roach filmed the original "Our Gang" silent films in Nashville. His older brothers and sister heard about the auditions and dressed Howard up in one of his doll's clothes and brought him to the theater. Howard was cast as Wheezer and performed in a few of the films. The Roach brothers wanted Howard's parents to move the family to California

**Howard Caine as Major Hochstetter.** © Bing Crosby Productions, Inc. Reprinted with permission.

so that Howard could perform in more "Our Gang" shorts. Howard's parents refused to uproot the family, and the toddler's career in show business was put on hold. Bobby Hutchins took the part of Wheezer in rest of the "Our Gang" films.

After a hiatus of more than twenty years, Howard Caine resumed his career as an actor with an appearance on *Goodyear TV Playhouse.* The versatile performer played a wide range of roles, from American to Europeans, in films, television, and theater. In his first feature film, *From the Terrace,* he played Paul Newman's brother-in-law and nemesis. He portrayed Judy Garland's husband in *Judgment at Nuremberg,* which also starred future *Hogan's Heroes* cast mate Werner Klemperer.

While working on the short-lived series *Fair Exchange,* Caine met producer Edward Feldman. Feldman had a reputation of being loyal to actors whose work he liked, and he called Caine to work on his next series, *Hogan's Heroes.*

Caine's initial appearance on *Hogan's Heroes* was in Episode #17, "Happy Birthday, Adolf." The following season, he was called back for "The Battle of Stalag 13," Episode #37. Feldman loved Caine's characterization of ruthless, nasty Gestapo officers in these two episodes, and decided to bring Caine back as a recurring character. Eager to work with Feldman, Caine accepted the offer, and beginning with Episode #54, "Heil Klink," he portrayed Major Hochstetter on a semiregular basis.

Caine had no misgivings about his role. He recalled, "I've had, over these years, many fellow Jews say to me 'how could you play a comic Gestapo like that?' Because I played him as a madman. If I hadn't been there, they would've all been

**Howard Caine.** Photo courtesy Howard Caine.

your sweet, loving, neighborhood Nazis, turned the local shoe salesman or butcher. Sure, I was doing it for laughs, but there was that aspect to it. I wanted to play the madman. My standpoint is that my willingness to do it was to remain true to the concept that they wanted, of the vicious, killer potential Nazi."

In true Gestapo fashion, when Major Hochstetter came onto the scene, his ranting and raving made Klink shake in his boots. What usually sent Hochstetter's pulse racing was Hogan's presence in every situation. Hogan, whom Hochstetter called "the most dangerous man in all of Germany," was invariably on hand when trouble brewed for the Germans, causing Hochstetter to scream "What is this man doing here?" in nearly every episode. Caine explains how his trademark line evolved.

"In the first script as Hochstetter, I had a little exchange where while I'm talking to Klink, Hogan comes in and he says 'pardon me, Colonel Klink, and so on' and Klink says 'not now, Hogan,' and then I say, 'Who is this man?' And the thing goes on again and I say 'Who *is* this man?' and they go on again. And at the reading I had gone, '*Who is this man??!!*' screaming, and everybody went wild around the table. Then when we sat down in a circle on Monday and did it and I read 'Who is this man?' in a normal tone of voice. And Dickie (Dawson) turned to me and said 'Aren't you going to do it the way you did it?' And I said, 'No, that's so hokum.' Eddie was in on the meeting, and he said 'No, no, do it!' I thought it was too extreme, it was hokum, but Eddie said 'No, it's great, he's like a madman!' Which is what I wanted to play. Then when we came back for the next season, it came in again, and I said

'I can't keep saying this, I've got to know *who* Hogan is.' That's when we changed it to 'What is this man doing here?' "

Another running gag Caine enjoyed was between his character and Klemperer's. "Klink, I have a dossier on you that would send you straight to the Russian front," Hochstetter repeatedly threatened.

In a 1989 interview for the hardcover publication of this book, Caine said he was amazed at how frequently he was recognized as Major Hochstetter. "Even with the beard, even with the gray," he laughed. He recalled his years on *Hogan's Heroes* very fondly. "It was a set full of love," he said. "The most wonderful thing in the world to have a place that wonderful to go to work every day, with those people. And the comedy was brilliant. Nobody would ever dream of stepping on anybody. Nor would anybody dream of challenging anybody's timing. It was absolute heaven, it really was."

His long list of credits prior to *Hogan's Heroes* protected Caine from the typecasting that often hurts actors closely identified with a character. "Before *Hogan's Heroes* I had played German roles, I played Latinos, I played Chinese, I played Japanese, Italians. So I never really had that type of problem after the series ended." He played Charles Manson's attorney in the television movie *Helter Skelter*, Billy Wilder in *Marilyn: The Untold Story*, and appeared in the epic miniseries *War and Remembrance*. He also performed in local theater productions, did voice-over work, and was very active in the acting community. He served on numerous union committees and was the founding president of Housing for Entertainment Professionals, involved with building low-cost housing for actors and other show business personnel. A Summa Cum Laude graduate of Columbia University, Caine also taught drama at U.S. International University in San Diego.

A lifelong fan of bluegrass and folk music, Caine mastered the Appalachian five-string banjo, which he had picked up as a hobby in the 1960s. During the filming of *Hogan's Heroes,* he would spend his time in between shots picking on the banjo. From 1970 onward, he began entering banjo and folk-singing contests around Southern California, winning twenty-nine trophies in various categories.

Caine passed away on December 28, 1993, after suffering a heart attack. At his memorial service at Eden Memorial Park in Mission Hills, California, his friends and colleagues remembered him as a headstrong man who fought passionately for actors' rights and other causes he believed in. His son Lyle sang a song he wrote for his father called "Wounded Warrior." He was survived by his second wife, Valerie, whom he married in 1991.

## Howard Caine—Selected Credits

**FILM**

*Our Gang* silent shorts (1929) 'Wheezer'
*From the Terrace* (1960) 'Duffy'
*Pay or Die* (1960) 'Enrico Caruso'
*Judgement at Nuremberg* (1961) 'Wallner'
*Brushfire* (1962) 'Vlad'
*Pressure Point* (1962) 'Tavern Owner'
*The Man from the Diners' Club* (1963) 'Bassanio'
*Alvarez Kelly* (1966) 'McIntyre'
*Watermelon Man* (1970) 'Mr. Townsend'
*1776* (1972) 'Lewis Morris'
*Forced Vengeance* (1982) 'Milt Diamond'

**TELEVISION**

*Goodyear TV Playhouse,* "Marty" (NBC, 5/24/53) 'Lou'
*A Time to Live* (NBC, 7/5/54–12/31/54) 'Quinn'
*The Californians* (NBC, 9/24/57–1958) 'Schaab'
*The Lawman,* "Warpath" (ABC, 2/8/59) 'Newt Whitaker'
*Gunsmoke,* "Big Tom" (CBS, 1960) 'Brady'
*Hallmark Hall of Fame,* "Captain Brassbound's Conversion" (NBC, 5/2/60) 'Cadi of Knatfi'
*Alfred Hitchcock Presents,* "Mrs. Bixby and the Colonel's Coat" (NBC, 9/27/60)
*Michael Shayne,* "Dolls Are Deadly" (NBC, 9/30/60)
*Michael Shayne,* "Death Selects the Winner" (NBC, 12/23/60)
*Two Faces West,* "The Vials" (Syndicated, 5/29/61)
*The Detectives,* "A Piece of Tomorrow" (NBC, 11/10/61) 'Ben Martin'
*My Three Sons,* "Chip Leaves Home" (ABC, 1/4/62)
*Armstrong Circle Theater,* "Securities for Suckers" (CBS, 1/17/62) 'Loomis'
*Straightaway,* "Full Circle" (ABC, 3/14/62) 'Artie Burke'
*Fair Exchange,* "To Each His Own" (CBS, 10/19/62) 'Charley'
*Leave It to Beaver,* "Eddie, the Businessman" (ABC, 11/1/62) 'Foreman'
*Fair Exchange,* "Neville's Problem" (CBS, 12/14/62) 'Frank'
*Fair Exchange,* "'Twas the Fortnight Before Christmas" (CBS, 12/21/62) 'Frank'
*The Twilight Zone,* "He's Alive" (CBS, 12/4/63) 'Nick'
*The Travels of Jaimie McPheeters,* "The Day of the Pawnees" (ABC, 12/29/63) 'Afraid-of-His-Horse'

*The Lucy Show,* "Lucy Goes to an Art Class" (CBS, 1/13/64) 'Harold'
*The Outer Limits,* "The Chameleon" (ABC, 4/27/64) 'Leon Chambers'
*Rawhide,* "Corporal Dasovik" (CBS, 12/4/64)
*The Alfred Hitchcock Hour,* "Thou Still Unravished Bride" (NBC, 3/22/65) 'Mr. Setlin'
*Slattery's People,* "A Sitting Duck Named Slattery" (CBS, 9/17/65)
*My Favorite Martian,* "Bottled Martin" (CBS, 10/31/65)
*Get Smart,* "The Day Smart Turned Chicken" (NBC, 11/6/65) 'Dr. Fish'
*The F.B.I.,* "The Hijackers" (ABC, 12/26/65) 'Arnold McTague'
*Felony Squad,* "The Terror Trap" (ABC, 11/28/66)
*The Doomsday Flight* (NBC TVM, 12/13/66) 'L.A. Dispatcher'
*Rango,* "Gunfight at the K.O. Saloon" (ABC, 2/3/67)
*Get Smart,* "A Man Called Smart" (NBC, 4/8/67, 4/15/67, 4/22/67) 'Dr. Bediyoskin/Dr. Smith'
*The Outcasts,* "Gideon" (ABC, 2/24/69) 'Sam Barnes'
*The High Chaparral,* "Friends and Partners" (NBC, 1/16/70)
*Adam's Rib,* "Illegal Aid" (ABC, 9/14/73)
*Police Story,* "The Other Side of the Fence" (NBC, 1/23/76) 'Higby'
*Helter Skelter* (CBS TVM, 4/1/76–4/2/76) 'Everett Scoville'
*Marilyn: The Untold Story* (ABC TVM, 9/28/80) 'Billy Wilder'
*Bret Maverick,* "The Ballad of Bret Maverick" (NBC, 2/16/82) 'Tertius'
*War and Remembrance* (ABC Miniseries, 11/88 and 5/89) 'Lord Maxwell Beaverbrook'

**THEATER**
*The School for Scandal,* Theater De Lys, NY (1953) 'Sir Oliver Surface'
*Inherit the Wind,* National Theater, NY (1955) 'Hot Dog Man'
*Tiger at the Gates,* Plymouth Theater, NY (1955) 'Abneos'
*Annie Get Your Gun,* DeWitt Clinton Adult Center, NY (1957) 'Sitting Bull'
*Wonderful Town,* Shubert Theater, NY
*Lunatics and Lovers,* Broadhurst Theater, NY
*Damn Yankees,* Adelphi Theater, NY

# CYNTHIA LYNN

### as Helga

Pretty Cynthia Lynn, who escaped from Nazi-occupied Latvia as a child, had only a few professional acting credits (an episode of *Dr. Kildare* and a small role in the 1964 film *Bedtime Story*) before she was signed to *Hogan's Heroes*. Her

**Cynthia Lynn as Helga, with Bob Crane.**
© Bing Crosby Productions, Inc. Reprinted with permission.

role as the kommandant's secretary was minuscule, but costar Werner Klemperer calls her "just exactly right for that part. She was a lovely girl." In an October 1997 interview, Lynn told *Entertainment Tonight* that during her year on the show, she and Bob Crane—both married at the time—had an affair. When her estranged husband begged for a reconciliation, Lynn decided to try to make her marriage work. Her husband insisted that she leave the series, and she complied.

At the time of her departure, series director Gene Reynolds reported to *Variety,* "Cynthia is leaving the show of her own volition due to difficulties not related to the show."

She told *Entertainment Tonight* that leaving the series was her biggest mistake in life. "Hollywood was great to me. But I goofed it up at the height of my career." Lynn's marriage ended in divorce three months later, after she had been replaced on the series by Sigrid Valdis. Lynn returned for two additional episodes during the show's run and appeared in other series, including CBS's *Mr. Terrific,* but she was unable to revive her acting career. Depression over her failed career, combined with nightmares about Bob Crane's murder, led her to attempt suicide in October 1997.

Lynn, who came forward in a February 1998 *Star* tabloid interview with claims that her daughter Lisa is Marlon Brando's child, is working on her autobiography, tentatively titled *Escape to Freedom.*

# SIGRID VALDIS

### as Hilda

When Sigrid Valdis joined the hit series at the start of the second season, CBS touted their new find as a sex goddess. The network's press accounts attributed the casting change to the series' new opposition on NBC—*The Man from U.N.C.L.E.* To compete with *U.N.C.L.E.*, Bing Crosby Productions decided to add some sex appeal to Stalag 13. While Cynthia Lynn's Helga exuded a wholesome form of sex appeal, Valdis was pure vamp. Valdis, whose real name is Patricia Olsen, had worked as a model and a car salesman before turning to acting. Film roles in *Marriage on the Rocks* (1965) and *Our Man Flint* (1966) and guest spots on *The Steve Allen Show* and *Wild, Wild West* were the highlights of her career before *Hogan's Heroes.*

**Sigrid Valdis as Hilda, with Bob Crane.** © Bing Crosby Productions, Inc. Reprinted with permission.

While working on the series, Valdis became involved with Bob Crane. Crane was married when the affair began, but in June 1970, he divorced his wife of twenty years. In October of that year, Crane and Valdis were married. The couple had a son, Robert Scott, the following year. She had a fourteen-year-old daughter, Melissa, and he was the father of three children from his first marriage. The couple was headed for divorce when Crane was murdered in 1978. After *Hogan's Heroes,* Valdis abandoned her acting career.

# BERNARD FOX

## as Colonel Rodney Crittendon

Character actor Bernard Fox has guest starred on numerous series in his career, and is probably most recognized for his roles as Doctor Bombay on *Bewitched* and Colonel Crittendon on *Hogan's Heroes*. Of these two comic creations he says, "Colonel Crittendon was a marvelous schmuck, and I think I probably enjoyed Colonel Crittendon more than Dr. Bombay. It was a wild character and I totally reveled in messing up every attempt to escape." Though he made more appearances on *Bewitched,* he preferred working on *Hogan's*. "The people were equally nice on either show," he says, "but I really liked the outrageous behavior of Colonel Crittendon. And I may have got a little bit more comedy of my own in on *Hogan's Heroes* than I did on *Bewitched*."

**Bernard Fox as British bungler Colonel Crittendon, with Bob Crane.** © Bing Crosby Productions, Inc. Reprinted with permission.

Fox is a fifth-generation actor. Born in South Wales on May 11, 1927, it didn't take him long to follow in the footsteps of his theatrical forebears. "I was carried onstage by my mother at about thirteen months. And on and off, with a short stint out for the Royal Navy during the war, I've been acting all my life."

In the late 1950s, Fox was one of the three stars in a BBC television series called *Three Live Wires*. He became friends with one the show's writers, Ray S. Allen. Allen, an American, told Fox that if he ever came to the States, he'd guarantee him a couple of guest shots on television. When an actors' strike in Britain left him without work, Fox came to America and took his friend up on his offer. Allen had become one of the writers on *The Danny Thomas Show* with his partner Harvey Bullock. They penned an episode for Fox in which he played a mild-mannered waiter, Alfie, patterned on a character Fox had played on *Three Live Wires*. Next, they wrote him into *The Andy Griffith Show* as Malcolm Merriweather, a character he played in three episodes. Pretty soon, he was in high demand, and he went from series to series, creating memorable roles in *The Dick Van Dyke Show, F Troop, I Spy, The Man from U.N.C.L.E., The Girl from U.N.C.L.E.,* and many others.

As Crittendon, Fox appeared in a total of eight episodes over the run of *Hogan's Heroes* and contributed the story idea for his two-part showcase, "Lady Chitterly's Lover." Producer Feldman also had another series in mind for Fox, which would have teamed him with a Frenchman and an American as three news correspondents stationed in Paris. "All three of them fairly inept," he says. "I thought it was a wonderful idea, and it never got off the ground. I was very disappointed about that."

In the 1970s, Fox toured with Bob Crane in *Beginner's Luck* but he was not with the production when it reached Scottsdale, where Crane was murdered. He says, "I liked old Bob. He kind of appreciated the comedy additions that I put in. He used to laugh up a storm. Anything that you could do to make the show funnier. He was very generous that way."

Most recently, Fox appeared in the 1998 blockbuster film *Titanic* as Colonel Archibald Gracie. Ironically, one of his earliest films was also about the doomed ocean liner. He says, "In 1957, I did *A Night to Remember,* which was about the Titanic. I was the fellow that saw the iceberg. And it has taken me forty years to work my way up from the crew to being a first-class passenger!"

Fox is married to actress Jacqueline Holt, whom he met in a production of *The Amorous Prawn* in Rome in 1959.

## KATHLEEN FREEMAN

### *as Gertrude Linkmeyer*

Kathleen Freeman has enjoyed a busy career in film, television, and theater. Since her film debut in *The Naked City* in 1948, she has played a wide variety of comedic and dramatic roles in over 150 films, including ten slapstick comedies with Jerry Lewis. Most recently, she appeared in *Blues Brothers*

*2000.* Her television credits are just as extensive, and range from such classics as *The Lucy Show, The Dick Van Dyke Show,* and *The Man from U.N.C.L.E.* to contemporary series *Murphy Brown, Duckman,* and *Party of Five.*

Freeman is also a respected drama coach, and founder of the Players Ring and Gallery Theaters.

# NITA TALBOT

### as Marya

Few women were able to take the spotlight away from the large cast of male stars on *Hogan's Heroes.* In each of her appearances as Marya, the Russian spy intent on involving herself with *Hogan's* missions—and with Hogan himself—Nita Talbot always created quite a splash. Her performance in Episode #77, "The Hostage," earned her an Emmy nomination as Best Supporting Actress in a Comedy Series. She was the only guest-starring performer in *Hogan's Heroes'* history to be nominated for an Emmy.

**Bob Crane with two of Hogan's paramours, Marya (Nita Talbot) and Tiger (Arlene Martel).** © Bing Crosby Productions, Inc. Reprinted with permission.

Talbot began modeling at age thirteen. At eighteen, she was signed as a contract player at Warner Bros. Her striking looks were often compared to Lauren Bacall's. The busy actress was a guest on over 100 television series, and was a regular on *Joe and Mabel* (1955–56), *The Thin Man* (1958–59), and *Starting from Scratch* (1988–89).

# EPISODE GUIDE

## Regular and Supporting Cast

*Colonel Robert Hogan:* Bob Crane

*Colonel Wilhelm Klink:* Werner Klemperer

*Sergeant Hans Schultz:* John Banner

*Corporal Louis LeBeau:* Robert Clary

*Corporal Peter Newkirk:* Richard Dawson

*Sergeant James Kinchloe:* Ivan Dixon (seasons 1–5)

*Sergeant Andrew Carter:* Larry Hovis

*Sergeant Richard Baker:* Kenneth Washington (season 6)

*General Albert Burkhalter:* Leon Askin

*Major Wolfgang Hochstetter:* Howard Caine

*Helga:* Cynthia Lynn (season 1)

*Hilda:* Sigrid Valdis (seasons 2–6)

**Schultz, Hogan, and Klink.**
© Bing Crosby Productions, Inc. Reprinted with permission.

# FIRST SEASON (1965–66)

Aired Fridays, 8:30–9:00 P.M.,
opposite *The Addams Family* on ABC
and *Convoy* on NBC.

### First Season Technical Credits

Producer: Edward H. Feldman
Associate Producer: Bernard Fein
Score: Fred Steiner
Theme Music: Jerry Fielding
Production Supervisor: William A. Calihan
Editorial Supervisor: Jerry London
Director of Photography: Gordon Avil
Art Directors: Rolland M. Brooks, Howard Hollander
Film Editors: Jerry London, Michael Kahn
Assistant Directors: Major Roup, Donald Gold, Floyd Joyer
Set Decorators: Robert Priestly, Edward M. Parker
Sound Engineers: S. G. Haughton, Leon Leon
Post-Production Supervisor: Houseley Stevenson
Music Supervisor: Richard Berres
Supervising Sound Editor: William Andrews
Costumes: Reeder Boss, Marjorie Wahl
Casting: Lynn Stalmaster, Milt Hamerman
Filmed at Desilu Studios for Bing Crosby Productions

## EPISODE 1. "THE INFORMER"

Original airdate: September 17, 1965
Teleplay by: Richard M. Powell, Bernard Fein, and Albert S. Ruddy
Story by: Bernard Fein and Albert S. Ruddy
Directed by: Robert Butler
Guest cast: Leonid Kinskey (Vladimir Minsk), Noam Pitlik (Wagner), Leon Askin (Colonel Burkhalter), Larry Hovis (Lieutenant Carter), Stewart Moss (Olsen), Richard Sinatra (Sergeant Riley), Walter Janowitz (Oscar Schnitzer)

Germany, 1942. Camp 13 welcomes two new arrivals—Carter, an American lieutenant who escapes *into* camp for processing, and Wagner, a new inmate who is actually a German spy. Wagner tries to expose Hogan's operation to his commander, Colonel Burkhalter, but the men cleverly discredit the spy. As punishment for his preposterous claims, Wagner is sent to the Russian front, and the secrets of Hogan's "heroes" remain safe beneath the confines of Camp 13.

**Notes:** The pilot episode introduced each of the characters and their individual talents and set the tone for the rest of the series. In most respects, the series remained true to the format set up in the pilot. But there were a handful of differences worth noting. For example, hard-to-believe luxuries such as the underground steam room were toned down in the series to lend some credibility to the operation. Werner Klemperer's Klink was a much harsher character in the pilot than in the remainder of the series. His sharp accent softened in subsequent episodes, with the result that Klink was perceived as more of a fool than a villain.

The character of Vladimir Minsk, a Russian POW, was intended as a regular role, but actor Leonid Kinskey opted not to continue with the series. Stewart Moss, who portrayed Olsen, also declined the offer to be a regular, but did make a handful of return appearances. Larry Hovis's character, meanwhile, was intended as a guest-starring role in the pilot only, but producer Ed Feldman was impressed by his performance. When Kinskey and Moss backed out of the series, Hovis was offered a regular role. A lieutenant in the pilot, Carter was a sergeant in the series. Hovis recalls, "When CBS picked up the series, Eddie Feldman decided to make me a regular. And he said, 'We'll just make you a sergeant instead of a lieutenant, because sergeants are more sympathetic.'" Hovis pointed out to Feldman that his character had escaped at the end of the pilot, to which the producer responded, "No one will care."

In another change of rank, Leon Askin played Colonel Burkhalter in the pilot, but was promoted to general by the time the series aired, probably to make his character more threatening to Colonel Klink.

The pilot is the only episode of the series that was filmed in black-and-white. Color was in an experimental stage in 1965, and many series, including *The Addams Family*, *Bewitched*, and *The Dick Van Dyke Show*, were still being filmed in black-and-white. Though color processing was more expensive, the foresighted Feldman insisted on shooting the remainder of the series in color, to increase its value in syndication.

The closing credits in the pilot were run over outtakes from the episode. From the second episode forward, the credits aired over a picture of Hogan's cap sitting atop Klink's World War I spiked helmet.

In the pilot, the prisoner-of-war camp is referred to as Camp 13, but in the rest of the series, it was known as Stalag 13. The term "stalag" originated in World War II. It was derived from the German *stammlager* (*stamm*: stem, trunk, something stable or constant; and *lager*: camp). The term became familiar to the American public through *Stalag 17*, a 1951 Broadway play that was adapted into a film starring William Holden in 1953.

## EPISODE 2. "HOLD THAT TIGER"

Original airdate: September 24, 1965
Writer: Richard M. Powell
Director: Robert Butler
Guest cast: Arlene Martel (Tiger), Henry Rico Cattani (General Hofstader), Jon Cedar (Corporal Langenscheidt)

In order to get blueprints of the Germans' new Tiger tank, the heroes pull off an audacious plan—they steal one, drive it into camp, and hide it in the recreation hall. After the gang dismantles the tank and draws up blueprints, Newkirk—disguised as a Gestapo officer—drives the tank right out of camp through the front gate. After all, who can stop the unstoppable Tiger tank? Meanwhile, underground agent Tiger smuggles the plans out of camp.

**Highlight:** The heroes rig the rec hall so that one wall opens on hinges. Newkirk drives the tank into the hall, and the men quickly replace the wall.

**Notes:** The German Tiger tank was introduced in August 1942. It had a reputation as one of the war's most formidable fighting machines: Its 88 mm gun could pierce 100 mm armor at a range of 1000 meters and its own frontal armor was virtually impenetrable. The tank used in this episode bears little likeness to the actual Tiger tank.

Beginning with this episode, the end credits ran over a photo of Hogan's cap perched on top of Klink's spiked helmet, representing the Allies' domination over the Germans in the series. Jerry London, then an editor on the series, came up with this idea for the end title logo. He says, "It kind of tells the whole story, doesn't it?"

This episode marks the first appearance of the beautiful French underground agent, Tiger, played by Arlene Martel. Tiger assisted Hogan and his men on four espionage missions, and Martel took different roles in two additional episodes.

***Viva la différence:*** LeBeau is seen wearing a blue uniform in this episode instead of his trademark red.

## EPISODE 3. "KOMMANDANT OF THE YEAR"

Original airdate: October 1, 1965
Writer: Laurence Marks
Director: Robert Butler
Guest cast: Woodrow Parfrey (Doctor Schneider), William Allyn (Major Hauser), James Beggs (Commando #1), Victor French (Commando #2), Kurt Lewin (Courier)

Knowing the Allies won't bomb a POW camp, the Germans stash an experimental rocket-bomb at Stalag 13. London sends an Allied scientist, Dr. Schneider, to photograph and sabotage the bomb. Hogan's plan to get Schneider near the bomb involves exploiting Klink's vanity by naming him Kommandant of the Year. Schneider and his commandos enter camp in German uniforms to present Klink with the phony award. During Klink's long-winded acceptance speech, Schneider slips away and changes the rocket's course. When the rocket launches it strikes a German—not Allied—target.

**Familiar faces:** Victor French is best remembered for his roles on *Little House on the Prairie* (1974–83) and *Highway to Heaven* (1984–89).

## EPISODE 4. "THE LATE INSPECTOR GENERAL"

Original airdate: October 8, 1965
Writer: Richard M. Powell
Director: Robert Butler
Guest cast: John Dehner (General von Platzen), Stewart Moss (Olsen), Jon Cedar (Corporal Langenscheidt), Walter Janowitz (Oscar Schnitzer)

The heroes delay their plan to blow up a munitions train when Inspector General von Platzen makes an unexpected visit to Stalag 13. Hogan fears that if Klink receives a poor rating he'll be replaced with a more rigid kommandant. The men convince the general that Klink is a cold disciplinarian. The plan works, but too well: Klink is promoted to a post in Berlin! The heroes reverse von Platzen's opinion of Klink's efficiency, but again they go too far: Klink is arrested. The heroes solve both their problems at once when they destroy the munitions train with von Platzen aboard.

**Familiar faces:** John Dehner played Doris's boss, editor Cy Bennett, on *The Doris Day Show* (1971–73).

## EPISODE 5. "THE FLIGHT OF THE VALKYRIE"

Original airdate: October 15, 1965
Writer: Richard M. Powell
Director: Gene Reynolds
Guest cast: Bernard Fox (Colonel Crittendon), Louise Troy (Lili), Jon Cedar (Corporal Langenscheidt), Walter Janowitz (Oscar Schnitzer), Frank G. Tallman (Pilot)

Hogan must help Lili, a German baroness who has been working as a spy for the Allies, escape to England. An American plane is shot down outside of camp and Hogan decides to use the plane to fly Lili to England. The plot almost fails when Colonel Klink transfers a British prisoner to Stalag 13. The new prisoner, Colonel Crittendon, believes that a POW's primary responsibility is to escape, and his repeated attempts nearly ruin Hogan's plan to get Lili out of Germany. To protect his no-escape record, Klink transfers the British bungler to another camp.

**Notes:** Bernard Fox's characterization of the inept Colonel Crittendon, originally a one-shot role, was so popular that he was brought back for seven more episodes. Often causing Hogan more trouble than the Germans did, it was hard to believe they were on the same side!

Werner Klemperer and actress Louise Troy first met when she guest-starred in this episode. They were married in 1969 and divorced five years later.

Frank Tallman was one of the movie industry's leading stunt pilots, with several big pictures to his name, including *It's a Mad Mad Mad Mad World, Catch 22, The Great Waldo Pepper,* and *Capricorn One.* Gene Reynolds recalls, "We had a real airplane actually making a run on the 40 Acres back lot, and this marvelous pilot, Frank Tallman. And he revved that thing up, then of course they had to slam on the brakes because they had just towed it in there; it wasn't flying, but just appeared to be flying."

## EPISODE 6. "THE PRISONER'S PRISONER"

Original airdate: October 22, 1965
Writers: Ray S. Allen and Harvey Bullock
Director: Gene Reynolds
Guest cast: Roger C. Carmel (General Schmidt), John Orchard (Sergeant Walters), Inge Jaklin (Fraulein)

While completing a sabotage mission, Carter and Hogan are surprised by a German general. They overpower the general and smuggle him into camp along with a group of new prisoners. Hogan learns that General Schmidt's troops are preparing for an attack, and London wants to know where they are stationed. Schmidt refuses to talk. Through a series of deceptions, the heroes convince Schmidt that he is suffering from a rare disease. Believing he is dying, Schmidt tells Hogan where his aide can be contacted. The information is relayed to London, resulting in total destruction of Schmidt's troops.

**Highlight:** The "Mighty Hogan Art Players" pull out all the stops in convincing Schmidt that he is suffering from shaklitis, but LeBeau's theatrics take top honors for comedic value.

## EPISODE 7. "GERMAN BRIDGE IS FALLING DOWN"

Original airdate: October 29, 1965
Writer: Laurence Marks
Director: Gene Reynolds
Guest cast: Forrest Compton (Pilot), Hal Lynch (Co-pilot), Jon Cedar (Corporal Langenscheidt)

After several botched attempts to demolish a German bridge, Hogan plots to blow up the bridge using the Germans' own ammunition. Hogan gets his men assigned to paint the storage building. While they are painting they sneak inside and steal the explosives. They plant the explosives on a courier whose route takes him over the bridge. The plot is almost foiled when Schultz bribes the courier into straying from his scheduled route. Hogan convinces Klink to keep the courier on course and the bridge blows as planned.

**Familiar faces:** Forrest Compton returned for four more missions on *Hogan's Heroes* (see Episodes #12, #44, #113, and #139). From 1971 to 1984, he played district attorney Mike Karr, one of the central characters on the daytime drama *The Edge of Night*.

## EPISODE 8. "MOVIES ARE YOUR BEST ESCAPE"

Original airdate: November 5, 1965
Writer: Laurence Marks
Director: Howard Morris

Guest cast: Henry Corden (General von Kaplow), John Crawford (Lieutenant Ritchie), William Christopher (Lieutenant Donner), Jon Cedar (Corporal Langenscheidt)

A visiting general has secret documents in a briefcase handcuffed to his wrist. At a dinner party, the heroes keep the general distracted (by the lovely Helga) and detained (by Klink's awful violin solo) long enough for Newkirk to pick the lock and retrieve the documents. Hogan's plan to get the documents out of camp involves convincing Klink that Germany is losing the war so he'll allow two German officers to film the friendly atmosphere of Stalag 13. The filmmakers, really escaping RAF officers in disguise, leave camp with the documents hidden inside their phony movie camera.

**Highlight:** To convince Schultz that the Russians are coming to liberate Stalag 13, Hogan teaches the POWs the rudiments of the Russian language. Ever eager to be friends with the winning side, Schultz joins the class.

**Notes:** Henry Corden, whose extensive list of credits includes the voice of Fred Flintstone on *The Flintstones,* reveals that the most difficult aspect of working on *Hogan's Heroes* was trying to keep a straight face. "Sometimes there was a particular scene that tickled us, and we couldn't stop laughing. Especially John Banner—he was a wonderful laugher! This would happen very often. But somehow we got it all done, and everything was fine." Corden adds that the friendly atmostphere aided the creative process. "There was never any animosity going around. So if you goofed in any way, it was no big thing. And if you feel free to goof, then you're also free to create."

## EPISODE 9. "GO LIGHT ON THE HEAVY WATER"

Original airdate: November 12, 1965
Writer: Arthur Julian
Director: Howard Morris
Guest cast: John Stephenson (Captain Mueller), Lawrence Montaigne (Sergeant Steinfeld), Eddie Firestone (POW Scotty)

A German captain brings a heavily guarded truck to Stalag 13 for safekeeping. Hogan is determined to find out what is inside the truck, but the Germans insist that it is only a barrel of water. Further investigation reveals that it is heavy water, to be used in nuclear research. Ordered by London to get rid of the special water, Hogan tries to trick Colonel Klink into drinking it by claiming it stimulates hair growth. When that fails, the heroes stage a fire, and on the pretense of protecting the valuable cargo, they replace the heavy water with tap water.

**Familiar faces:** If his face isn't familiar, his voice should be. A popular voice actor, John Stephenson provided the voice of Mr. Slate, Fred Flintstone's boss on *The Flintstones,* and Dr. Benton Quest on *Johnny Quest,* among others. Stephenson appeared in eight episodes of *Hogan's Heroes.*

**Notes:** One of the benefits of having a large cast was that when one of the supporting actors needed time off for other projects, their dialogue could be rewritten for another actor. In this episode, Eddie Firestone plays a prisoner who participates in the mission. He fills in for Robert Clary, who does not appear in the episode. Bob Crane and Werner Klemperer are the only regular cast members who appear in every one of the 168 episodes.

This entry stands out as one of Werner Klemperer's personal favorites.

## EPISODE 10. "TOP HAT, WHITE TIE AND BOMB SIGHT"

Original airdate: November 19, 1965
Writer: Laurence Marks
Director: Gene Reynolds
Guest cast: Leon Askin (General Burkhalter), Edward Knight (Major Klopfer), Monroe Arnold (Willie), Sigrid Valdis (Gretchen), Thordis Brandt (Elsa)

When Hogan discovers that Klink has bugged his office, he uses the hidden microphone to convince Klink that he is switching over to the Germans' side. Hinting that he worked on the Norden bombsight, Hogan strikes a deal with his captors: In exchange for a night in town, he'll reveal all he knows about the Norden. Hogan uses his trip into town to pass information to an underground contact. Back at camp, he willingly sketches the Norden for Klink and Burkhalter, who are outraged when they realize that Hogan is not drawing the Norden bombsight, but the Norden vacuum cleaner!

**Notes:** Sigrid Valdis's guest appearance as Klink's date led to her being cast as Hilda the following season.

## EPISODE 11. "HAPPINESS IS A WARM SERGEANT"

Original airdate: November 26, 1965
Writer: Laurence Marks
Director: Gene Reynolds

Guest cast: Bruce Yarnell (Captain Jeb Winslow), Norman Alden (Sergeant Krebs), Jon Cedar (Guard), Norbert Schiller (Max)

Schultz gets drunk while escorting prisoner Newkirk to the dentist in town, and Klink replaces him with a tougher guard, Sergeant Krebs. To get Schultz reinstated, the prisoners stage an escape attempt and arrange for Schultz to capture them while Newkirk's card tricks distract Krebs. The phony escape also diverts attention from the actual escape of an American POW who had been hiding in the tunnel.

**Highlight:** Newkirk wheels Schultz back to camp in a wheelbarrow and the drunken sergeant calls Klink "Kommandant Big Shot" to his face. This seemingly preposterous scene has its roots in reality. In a 1967 interview for *TV Scout*, Leon Askin related an incident that occurred when he was interred in a French POW camp during World War II. "One day another prisoner and I and a guard were sent on an errand to a nearby village. The guard deserted us, got drunk in a saloon, passed out, and we brought him back to camp in a wheelbarrow."

**Familiar faces:** The escaping Texan, whose appetite for barbecued foods causes LeBeau to bristle, is played by Bruce Yarnell. Yarnell previously starred as deputy marshal Chalk Breeson in the western series *The Outlaws* (1961–62).

**Notes:** "This was a show that worked out particularly well for me as a director," Gene Reynolds says. "I thought we had some very good stuff in it, and I loved John Banner in this episode."

## EPISODE 12. "THE SCIENTIST"

Original airdate: December 3, 1965
Writer: Laurence Marks
Director: Howard Morris
Guest cast: Parley Baer (Professor Altman), Maurice Marsac (Henry DuBois*), Forrest Compton (First Officer), Buck Young (Second Officer), Jayne Massey (Marie DuBois), Bard Stevens (Captain Krug), Robert Champion (German Sergeant)
*listed as Emil DuBois in the credits

A captured French scientist is brought to Stalag 13 to conduct experiments for the Germans. LeBeau, assigned to assist his fellow countryman, learns that DuBois is not working for the enemy willingly—they are holding his daughter captive. The heroes help the scientist and his daughter flee

Germany, but they risk being caught when a German professor arrives at camp for a demonstration of DuBois' findings. Hoping to stall long enough for DuBois and his daughter to get out of Germany safely, LeBeau takes the scientist's place and bluffs his way through the experiment.

**Highlight:** Posing as a vicious German general, Hogan destroys the lobby of the hotel where Marie DuBois is being held. He threatens to send everyone to the Russian front—including the hotel itself.

LeBeau has no knowledge of chemistry but must convince the visiting Germans that he is the scientist, DuBois. With only Carter's pharmacy handbook to guide him, LeBeau concocts a synthetic fuel "emulsion," which he claims also relieves nasal congestion. When the ruse succeeds, LeBeau laughs, "What a crazy war!"

***Was ist los?*** Carter says he cannot teach LeBeau anything about chemistry because he's not a chemist—he ran a drugstore in Muncie, Indiana and hopes to take the pharmacy exam when he returns home. But Carter somehow acquires the expertise to become the unit's resident chemist and explosives expert in subsequent episodes.

**Familiar faces:** Character actor and old-time radio star Parley Baer played Mayor Stoner on *The Andy Griffith Show,* and appeared in hundreds of guest-starring roles on television series ranging from *Father Knows Best* to *Star Trek: Voyager.*

## EPISODE 13. "HOGAN'S HOFBRAU"

Original airdate: December 10, 1965
Writer: Laurence Marks
Director: Gene Reynolds
Guest cast: Frank Marth (Captain Milheiser), Paula Stewart (Hilda), Willard Sage (Lieutenant Durnitz*), Roger Heldfond (Soldier)
*Called Durnitz in the episode, but listed as "Lt. Schmidt" in the closing credits.

An elite panzer division moves into the area and Hogan wants details of their strength and mission. In the guise of a German officer, Major Hoople, Hogan goes to the hofbrau and tries to pry information from two members of the panzer division, Captain Milheiser and Lieutenant Durnitz. Coincidentally, Milheiser and Durnitz have been extorting money from Klink. Klink nearly blows Hogan's cover, but Hogan/Hoople hands 5,000 marks to the officers, saving Klink's life.

**Familiar faces:** Frank Marth, who played German officers in several episodes, called the *Hogan's Heroes* set "one of the most pleasant and relaxed I've ever worked on." He adds, "The regular cast made you feel as though you were members of the permanent company—they were all very helpful and pleasant."

## EPISODE 14. "OIL FOR THE LAMPS OF HOGAN"

Original airdate: December 17, 1965
Writer: Laurence Marks
Director: Howard Morris
Guest cast: Leon Askin (General Burkhalter), William Mims (Fritz Bowman), Jon Cedar (Corporal Langenscheidt)

Burkhalter plans to build a synthetic fuel plant at Stalag 13, where it will be safe from Allied bombing. The prisoners are to be transferred to other camps, bringing Hogan's operation to an end. To prevent this, Hogan convinces Klink that there is a vast supply of crude oil under Stalag 13. With visions of postwar riches, Klink tries to retain control of the camp. When this fails, Hogan stages a phony bombing raid on the camp. Leaflets are dropped warning that if the fuel plant is built there, it will be bombed. The plans are abandoned.

## EPISODE 15. "RESERVATIONS ARE REQUIRED"

Original airdate: December 24, 1965
Writer: Laurence Marks
Director: Gene Reynolds
Guest cast: Robert Hogan (Braden), Dennis Robertson (Mills), Mike Murphy (Corporal Walter Comminsky)

Twenty escapees from Stalag 9 arrive at Stalag 13 seeking Hogan's assistance. Outfitting twenty men is time consuming, and two of the prisoners get restless and try to break out on their own. Their blunder causes Klink to tighten security around the camp. In order to get the men out of camp, Hogan gives up the location of their escape tunnel. While Klink is looking for the tunnel entrance, the twenty men leave through the other end.

**Highlight:** Newkirk, pretending to be sleepwalking, calls Schultz "fraulein" and caresses his face. Both men's expressions when Newkirk's fingers reach Schultz's mustache are priceless.

## IS THAT WHY IT'S CALLED THE UNDERGROUND?

Perhaps the most unbelievable aspect of Hogan's operation was the extensive tunnel system that existed under Stalag 13. During World War II, tunneling was a primary activity of prisoners-of-war, and those tunnels were nothing short of astounding. Ed Feldman and his staff researched prison camps and learned that at one such camp the prisoners had built so many tunnels that they caved in on one another. The tunnels built by *Hogan's Heroes* were based in reality, but were exaggerated in TV tradition.

Paul Brickhill's *The Great Escape* and Arthur A. Durand's *Stalag Luft III* (both books are recommended as studies of real life in a prisoner-of-war camp) recount the story of a mass escape made from Stalag Luft III in which eighty prisoners escaped through a tunnel originating under a stove in a barracks. The tunnel was one of several constructed by the POWs at Stalag Luft III, which were ingeniously designed and engineered. They tapped into the camp's electricity for lighting and built air pumps to provide a steady flow of oxygen. The tunnels were lined with boards taken from the prisoners' beds, and equipped with small trolleys, which ran on tracks to carry the prisoners or supplies from one end of the tunnel to the other. (Unfortunately the "Great Escape" did not have a sitcom ending. All but three of the escapees were recaptured, and fifty of those men were shot.)

The heroes' primary tunnel entrances:

A lower bunk in Hogan's barracks
Under the dog house in the kennel
Tree stump in the woods outside of camp
Under the stove in Klink's quarters
In the cooler ★

**Notes:** Robert Hogan, who played Mills in this episode, was a friend of co-creator Bernie Fein's. He recalls, "One night I was talking to Bernie on the phone and he said they had changed the name of the show (to *Hogan's Heroes*). Good name. He said, half jokingly, that it might do me some good. Since that time I cannot tell you how many people, on hearing my name say 'Oh, one of *Hogan's Heroes,* huh?' You can't tell everyone and they really don't care so I smile weakly and nod." Through his friendship with Fein, Hogan landed a guest-starring role in this episode. Hogan also played Scott Banning on *Days of Our Lives* (1970–71) and commanded the Sea Tiger as Lieutenant Commander Haller during the second season of *Operation Petticoat* (1978–79).

**A rare sight:** Klink is seen smoking in this episode. More accurately, he is seen holding a cigarette, but he never actually takes a puff. This out-of-character bit of business was inserted to set up one of Hogan's insubordinate deeds. He removes the spike from Klink's World War I helmet and offers it to the kommandant to catch the ashes from his cigarette.

## EPISODE 16. "ANCHORS AWEIGH, MEN OF STALAG 13"

Original airdate: December 31, 1965
Writers: David Chandler and Jack H. Robinson
Director: Howard Morris
Guest cast: Leon Askin (General Burkhalter), Fredd Wayne (Kristman), Michael St. Clair (Captain Michaels), Jon Cedar (Corporal Langenscheidt)

With the submarine out of commission, Hogan has to find a way to get an escaped British POW and a new German gunsight to London, across eighty miles of open sea. To solve this dilemma, the heroes build Klink an officer's club in the shape of a ship. Then they convince the kommandant that Burkhalter will disapprove of the lavish "yacht club," so Klink sends the vessel to sea, with the Englishman and the gunsight stowed away on board.

**Highlight:** LeBeau, placed in charge of constructing the club due to his "French sense of style and decor," gets to order Klink's guards around.

**Notes:** Burkhalter is incorrectly listed in the credits as a colonel, which was his rank in the pilot episode only.

## EPISODE 17. "HAPPY BIRTHDAY, ADOLF"

Original airdate: January 7, 1966
Writer: Laurence Marks
Director: Robert Butler
Guest cast: Howard Caine (Major Keitel)

Hogan and the men must disable a gun emplacement before an Allied attack scheduled for Hitler's birthday. Hogan poses as a German major and presents phony orders to the commanding officer, Major Keitel, that he replace Keitel during the birthday celebration. On the night of the party, Keitel refuses to abandon his post, until he sees Helga and her pretty friend arrive. With Keitel thus distracted, the heroes sabotage the guns. When the Allied raid begins, Keitel's men commence firing. But instead of ammo, flags reading "Happy Birthday Adolph" pop out of the guns. The Allied raid is successful.

**Notes:** This was the first of two guest-starring appearances for Howard Caine before the character of Major Hochstetter was created. Caine recalls chiding Teddy, the prop man, for using the American spelling of Adolph on the flags. Hitler spelled it with an 'f.'

*Was ist los?* LeBeau mentions in this episode that he is married—he "volunteered" the same way Hogan volunteers him for a dangerous mission. His marriage is never brought up in subsequent episodes.

## EPISODE 18. "THE GOLD RUSH"

Original airdate: January 14, 1966
Writer: Laurence Marks
Director: Howard Morris
Guest cast: Tom Hatten (Lieutenant Edward H. Martin), Rick Traeger (Major Krieger), Pitt Herbert (German)

A shipment of gold stolen by the Germans from the Bank of France is being stored at a local bank. Hogan persuades Klink to have the gold bars moved to Stalag 13 for safekeeping. The men tamper with the stairs leading to Klink's office. When the steps collapse, Hogan offers to rebuild them using brick. The POWs steal the gold bars from the delivery truck. They dip the bars into red paint, and the bricks into gold paint. The gold-painted bricks are placed on the truck and the phony "bricks" are used to build Klink's new steps, which Hogan proclaims are "good as gold."

**Notes:** Tom Hatten had been a friend of Bob Crane's prior to Hogan's Heroes and was an occasional guest on Crane's radio show, promoting theater productions or his local cartoon show, *Popeye and Friends* (1956–64) on KTLA. His four guest appearances on *Hogan's Heroes* were partially the result of his friendship with Crane. The two actors also costarred in stage productions of *Send Me No Flowers* and *Who Was That Lady I Saw You With?* Hatten says, "Bob was wonderful to work with on stage—he was so spontaneous."

*Was ist los?* For the rest of the series, the steps leading to Klink's office are once again made of wood.

## EPISODE 19. "HELLO, ZOLLE"

Original airdate: January 21, 1966
Writers: David Chandler and Jack H. Robinson
Director: Gene Reynolds

Guest cast: Gavin MacLeod (Major Zolle), Albert Green (General Hans Stofle), Britt Nilsson (Ingeborg), Ramon Bieri (Steiner), Horst Ebersberg (Gunther)

General Stofle, an old chum of Klink's, comes for a furtive visit to Stalag 13. London orders Hogan to detain the general for twenty-four hours—long enough for the Allies to mount an attack on Stofle's forces. When Stofle demands to leave camp, Hogan contrives to have the general arrested by the Gestapo. Afraid of being charged with complicity, Klink won't back up his old friend's claim of innocence.

**Familiar faces:** This was the first of four guest-starring appearances by Gavin MacLeod, who is best known for his roles as Murray on *The Mary Tyler Moore Show* (1970–77) and Captain Stubing on *The Love Boat* (1977–86). He says, "the *Hogan's* gang was fun—a very relaxed set." The tables were turned when Bob Crane guest starred on MacLeod's series *The Love Boat* in 1978. MacLeod says of that appearance, "Bob was excellent in a very out-of-type character for him."

## EPISODE 20. "IT TAKES A THIEF... SOMETIMES"

Original airdate: January 28, 1966
Writer: Richard M. Powell
Director: Howard Morris
Guest cast: Michael Constantine (Captain Heinrich), Claudine Longet (Michelle), Chris Anders (Wolfgang), Edgar Winston (Adolph)

Hogan decides to join forces with a new underground unit operating near Stalag 13. When the group leader turns up at camp, Hogan learns that they are actually undercover Gestapo agents out to trap the real saboteurs. Hogan and the men continue to meet with the spies, pretending to be unaware of their identity. While plotting a phony attack on Stalag 13, Hogan leads the spies into a trap while also destroying the real target—a local railroad tunnel.

**Notes:** Chris Anders, a native German, made a career out of playing European roles in feature films and television series. He appeared in several episodes of *Hogan's Heroes*. "Once I worked on it, I was always called back," he recalled. "They enjoyed my work and I enjoyed being on the show." Anders never felt that *Hogan's Heroes* was derisive towards Germans. He recalled, "I did so many other war shows and sometimes I felt they made the Germans look stupid, but I never felt it on this show. Because it wasn't meant to be. It was just humorous, not to be taken seriously. It was a comedy, not a drama of life, like *Combat* and other war shows."

**Familiar faces:** Michael Constantine played principal Seymour Kaufman on *Room 222* (1969–74), winning a Best Supporting Actor Emmy for the role in 1970.

## EPISODE 21. "THE GREAT IMPERSONATION"

Original airdate: February 4, 1966
Writer: Laurence Marks
Director: Gene Reynolds
Guest cast: Bert Freed (Major Bernsdorf), James Frawley (Gestapo Captain)

LeBeau, Newkirk, and Carter are captured by a German patrol. The three prisoners are being held at Stalag 4 for questioning. In order to free them, Colonel Hogan persuades Schultz to masquerade as Klink, and demand that the prisoners be turned over to him. It isn't easy turning the soft-hearted sergeant into a convincingly nasty colonel, and Schultz almost gives up too easily. A Gestapo captain comes looking for the man who took the prisoners, but the only one who fits the physical description is Schultz, and who could believe that Schultz is a fierce officer?

*Was ist los?* Carter laments that he doesn't know why he was drafted, since he doesn't know anything about war. Apparently the writers were just as confused—in Episode #45, Carter says he enlisted early to get in the war before it got too crowded.

**Notes:** James Frawley left acting to become a prominent television director, with credits including *Magnum, P.I., Chicago Hope, Law and Order, The Practice,* and *Ally McBeal.*

## EPISODE 22. "THE PIZZA PARLOR"

Original airdate: February 11, 1966
Writer: Arthur Julian
Director: Gene Reynolds
Guest cast: Hans Conried (Major Bonacelli), Joey Tata (Tony Garlotti), Ernest Sarracino (Mr. Garlotti), Jack Good (Captain Henderson), Harry Lauter (Submarine Captain), Elisa Ingram (British Sergeant), Jon Cedar (Corporal Langenscheidt), Bard Stevens (German Driver)

Major Bonacelli, an Italian POW camp kommandant, is sent to Stalag 13 to train under Colonel Klink, but the war-hating major tries to defect to Switzerland. With the help of a pizza and a few choruses of "Santa Lucia," Hogan persuades Bonacelli to work for the Allies. The plan almost backfires when Bonacelli is accused of being a traitor. Hogan repairs Bonacelli's reputation by arranging the escape of several prisoners so the major can "recapture" them. Bonacelli, believed to be loyal to the German cause, returns to his camp as a spy for the underground.

**Highlights:** Hogan's British contacts incredulously relay Hogan's request for a pizza recipe from Garlotti's Pizzeria in New Jersey over the radio. Garlotti not only comes through with the recipe, he also belts out "Santa Lucia" upon Hogan's request. Later, the heroes serenade Bonacelli with the Italian song while the smell of pizza lures him into the barracks.

**Familiar faces:** Among Hans Conried's most memorable roles are Uncle Tonoose on *The Danny Thomas Show* and Wrongway Feldman on *Gilligan's Island.*

## EPISODE 23. "THE 43RD, A MOVING STORY"

Original airdate: February 25, 1966
Writers: James Allardice and Tom Adair
Director: Howard Morris
Guest cast: Leon Askin (General Burkhalter), Sandy Kenyon (Major Hans Kuehn), Hal Lynch (Lynch)

Hogan's plan to destroy a German mobile antiaircraft battery is interrupted by Major Kuehn, Klink's new second-in-command. The power hungry Kuehn has doubled the guards, making it impossible for the men to sneak out of camp. The antiaircraft unit is defending a chemical plant, which the Allies plan to bomb. If it remains in place it will wipe out the Allied bombers. Hogan feeds Kuehn false information about an attack on Hammelburg. The battery is moved into Hammelburg, to guard against the phony attack. The Allies bomb the chemical plant and the antiaircraft battery isn't there to defend it.

**Notes:** Sandy Kenyon recollects of his five guest-starring appearances, "mostly just fun, good work, and an appreciation of the fact that so many of us playing Germans were strongly antifascist—indeed had fought in a war against that sort of poison." Kenyon played Revered Kathrun on *Knots Landing* (1984–85) and guest-starred on many series, including *The Twilight Zone, Gunsmoke, M\*A\*S\*H, Hart to Hart,* and *Designing Women.*

## EPISODE 24. "HOW TO COOK A GERMAN GOOSE BY RADAR"

Original airdate: March 4, 1966
Writer: Phil Sharp
Director: Gene Reynolds
Guest cast: J. Pat O'Malley (General Tillman Walters)

An elderly American corporal is brought to Stalag 13. The men don't care for Corporal Tillman's attitude and arrange to have him transferred to another stalag. But the corporal reveals that he's actually General Tillman Walters, and he's on a mission: to plant a radar device inside camp that will direct Allied bombers to their target—a rocket fuel depot thirty miles away. The men must stall Tillman's transfer long enough for them to plant the radar unit on top of the guard tower. Distracting the guards is accomplished by persuading Helga to pose outside in a bathing suit.

**Familiar faces:** Character actor J. Pat O'Malley's notable roles included Tim's (Bill Bixby) boss Mr. Burns on *My Favorite Martian* (1963–64) and Bert Beasley on *Maude* (1975–77).

## EPISODE 25. "PSYCHIC KOMMANDANT"

Original airdate: March 11, 1966
Writer: Phil Sharp
Director: Gene Reynolds
Guest cast: Leon Askin (General Burkhalter), Joseph Mell (Kintzler)

To avoid punishment for gambling, the prisoners convince Klink they were conducting ESP experiments, and lead Klink to believe that *he* has extra sensory perception. The Luftwaffe's new silent aircraft is brought to the stalag for testing, and the heroes quickly steal its engine. While Klink tries to use his psychic abilities to locate the missing engine, the men dismantle and photograph it before replacing it in the aircraft. When the noiseless aircraft is demonstrated for a group of Luftwaffe officers, it is no longer silent—thanks to Hogan's modifications.

## EPISODE 26. "THE PRINCE FROM THE PHONE COMPANY"

Original airdate: March 18, 1966
Writer: Richard M. Powell
Director: Gene Reynolds

Guest cast: Ivan Dixon (Sergeant Kinchloe/Prince Makabana), Isabelle Cooley (Princess Yawanda), Lee Bergere (Count Von Sichel), Stewart Moss (Lieutenant)

An African prince parachutes into Stalag 13 when his plane is shot down. Noting the prince's resemblance to Kinch, Hogan concocts a scheme to obtain new German currency for his operation by substituting Kinch for the prince. The prince's wife easily discerns that Kinch is not her husband—but she doesn't mind. The princess helps Kinch pull off his royal charade: setting up a German submarine base in his country in exchange for 60,000 new German marks. By the time the Germans learn they've been double-crossed, Kinch has changed back into his fatigues.

**Notes:** Lee Bergere, who appeared in this episode and in #165 ("Kommandant Gertrude"), remembers his experience on the show as

### IS THAT A DAMSEL IN DISTRESS OR A HERO IN A DRESS?

With the wide range of disguises used by the POWs in their schemes, it was inevitable that before long a script would call for one of the boys to dress as a woman. A comedy device made popular by Jack Lemmon and Tony Curtis in *Some Like It Hot* (1959) and comedians from Milton Berle to Flip Wilson, dressing three of the characters in drag in Episode #28 ("I Look Better in Basic Black") proved to be such a laugh-getter that the ploy was repeated a handful of times. Corporal Newkirk balked at having to don ladies' clothing in "Basic Black," but in subsequent episodes he was called upon most frequently to do so.

"Happy Birthday, Adolf"—LeBeau dresses as an old lady on a reconaissance mission.

"I Look Better in Basic Black"—Hogan, Newkirk, and LeBeau dress as women and take the place of three female prisoners.

"Reverend Kommandant Klink"—Carter is mother of the bride in the POWs' play.

"Drums Along the Dusseldorf"—Newkirk dresses as a little old lady.

"Color the Luftwaffe Red"—Newkirk again.

"The Gasoline War"—Newkirk dresses as a little old lady.

"Gowns by Yvette"—Schultz models a wedding dress.

"That's No Lady, That's My Spy"—Newkirk crashes a tea party for German officers' wives.

"The Sergeant's Analyst"—Newkirk plays a very masculine-looking female psychiatrist called to camp to hypnotize Schultz. ★

"exhilarating and insane." He recalls, "Bob Crane played his drums at each interval and I kept coming to attention—those boots will do it every time!"

## EPISODE 27. "THE SAFECRACKER SUITE"

Original airdate: March 25, 1966
Writer: Laurence Marks
Director: Howard Morris
Guest cast: Walter Burke (Alfie the Artist), Anthony Eustrel (Major Kronman), Booth Colman (Captain Guenther), Eric Lord (Burgermeister)

Klink's reunion with an old war buddy comes to an abrupt end when the man is arrested for conspiring to assassinate the Führer. Before Major Kronman is hauled off to jail, he slips Hogan a key to a hotel safe deposit box. Afraid that the contents of the box might incriminate him, Klink cooperates with Hogan's scheme. Newkirk's pal Alfie, a master safecracker, helps the gang break into the safe and steal the contents—a list of conspirators in the plot against Hitler. Hogan sends the list to London and gives Klink a phony copy with the kommandant's name at the top.

**Notes:** Newkirk, LeBeau, and Carter sing "This Is the Army Mister Jones." The song also appears on the album, *Hogan's Heroes Sing the Best of World War II*, which was released in 1967.

## EPISODE 28. "I LOOK BETTER IN BASIC BLACK"

Original airdate: April 1, 1966
Writer: Arthur Julian
Director: Howard Morris
Guest cast: Jean Hale (Kathy Pruitt), Edward Knight (Captain Heinrich), Jayne Massey (Ginger Wilson*), Jackie Joseph (Charlene Hemsley), Peter Hellman (Guard)
*The closing credits list her as 'Ginger Flintrin' but she says 'Wilson' in the episode.

Hogan's men aren't interested in tunneling into the barracks where three new prisoners are being held—until they learn that the prisoners are women. The women are being held by the Gestapo because they accidentally learned the location of a new German rocket factory. Hogan, Newkirk, and LeBeau don ladies' clothing and switch places with the three special prisoners when Captain Heinrich arrives to escort them to Berlin. Along the way, the heroes

**Bob Crane, Robert Clary, Werner Klemperer, and Richard Dawson, during the filming of "I Look Better in Basic Black."** Photo courtesy Stephen Cox. © Bing Crosby Productions, Inc. Reprinted with permission.

overpower their guards and get away. Meanwhile, the real ladies escape through the emergency tunnel.

***Was ist los?*** Hogan says that the tunnel the men dug to the perimeter wire is half as long as the one they'll have to dig to reach Barracks 3. But Barracks 3 is directly behind Hogan's quarters; it is often visible through the barracks' door.

## EPISODE 29. "THE ASSASSIN"

Original airdate: April 8, 1966
Writer: Richard M. Powell
Director: Edward H. Feldman
Guest cast: Bernard Fox (Colonel Crittendon), Larry D. Mann (Doctor Vanetti), Leon Askin (General Burkhalter)

The men are uneasy with their latest assignment—the assassination of Dr. Vanetti, a German nuclear scientist working on an atomic bomb at Stalag 13. To make matters worse, Colonel Crittendon insists on being the assassin. But before the bungling Britisher can do the deed, Vanetti confides in Hogan that he wants to defect. Hogan agrees to help Vanetti get out of Germany, but Crittendon keeps trying to kill the scientist. Hogan sends Klink and Crittendon out of camp on a wild goose chase. While they are gone, he sneaks Vanetti out of camp and blows up the lab.

**Notes:** Not only were the characters uneasy about the prospect of an assassination, but the actors playing them were as well. Writer Richard M. Powell recalls that at the reading "I could see the cast got quite nervous about that—it was a departure from what they had been doing, and I guess they were all thinking 'could this be funny, in the context of actually trying to kill someone?' Well of course Crittendon's attempt to kill the person failed completely because he was a complete bungler and the comedy came out of that."

## EPISODE 30. "CUPID COMES TO STALAG 13"

Original airdate: April 15, 1966
Writer: Phil Sharp
Director: Howard Morris
Guest cast: Leon Askin (General Burkhalter), Kathleen Freeman (Gertrude Linkmeyer), Inger Stratton (Lottie), George Tyne (Captain Ferguson)
Colonel Klink's failure to win a promotion has him walking the grounds all night, making it impossible for Hogan to sneak a prisoner out of Stalag 13. General Burkhalter suggests that marrying into the right family would do wonders for Klink's career. The general is trying to marry off his widowed sister Gertrude, but Klink believes that he is intended for the general's beautiful niece. Klink is crushed when he learns that Gertrude is the one he is expected to wed. Hogan tells Gertrude that Klink has volunteered for the Russian front. Not wanting to be widowed twice, she flees the situation.

**Familiar faces:** This was the first of four appearances for character actress Kathleen Freeman as General Burkhalter's sister Gertrude. Freeman counts *Hogan's Heroes* among over two hundred other acting credits. Recent television appearances include *Party of Five, ER,* and *Duckman.* She also appeared in the 1998 feature film *Blues Brothers 2000.*

## EPISODE 31. "THE FLAME GROWS HIGHER"

Original airdate: April 22, 1966
Teleplay: David Chandler, Jack H. Robinson, and Laurence Marks
Story by: David Chandler and Jack H. Robinson
Director: Howard Morris

Guest cast: Susanne Cramer (Eva), Hannie Landman (Margit), Charles Radilac (Willy), Irene Tedrow (Jenny), Todd Martin (Gestapo Officer), Jerry Ayres (Captain Warren)

Hogan learns that there is a weak link in the escape route chain. He tells Klink that there is a forest fire outside of camp and gets his men assigned to extinguish it. Hogan, LeBeau, and Newkirk break away from the fire-fighting group and follow the underground escape route themselves. They determine that Eva and Margit, two lovely innkeepers at one of the checkpoints, are Gestapo spies. Hogan and the boys circumvent the trap that Eva and Margit have laid for them, while implicating the girls as double agents.

## EPISODE 32. "REQUEST PERMISSION TO ESCAPE"

Original airdate: April 29, 1966
Writer: Laurence Marks
Director: Edward H. Feldman
Guest cast: Mary Mitchell (Mady), Martin Blaine (Gestapo Officer), John Crawford (Officer #1), Brett Parker (Officer #2), William Christopher (German Private), Horst Ebersberg (Soldier)

Carter receives a Dear John letter from his girlfriend back home and wants to escape so he can go win her back. The men try to plead, cajole, and trick Carter into staying. Hogan eventually grants Carter permission to escape, but gets him to consent to one last mission—passing fake battle plans to the enemy. After his mission is accomplished, Carter surprises everyone by announcing that he is not going home, but back into town to see Mady, the barmaid at the hofbrau who befriended him.

**Highlight:** Luckless Carter can't seem to do anything right. He walks right up to German officers in the hofbrau stating that he is an escaped prisoner carrying valuable military information, but he can't find anyone who'll arrest him.

# SECOND SEASON (1966–67)

Aired Fridays, 8:30–9:00 P.M.,
opposite *Time Tunnel* on ABC and
*The Man from U.N.C.L.E.* on NBC.

Cast changes: Sigrid Valdis joined the cast as Hilda, Colonel Klink's secretary, replacing Cynthia Lynn as Helga. Howard Caine first appeared as Major Hochstetter in Episode #54, and thereafter became a semiregular.

## Second Season Technical Credits

Producer: Edward H. Feldman
Associate Producer: William A. Calihan
Theme Music: Jerry Fielding
Editorial Supervisor: Jerry London
Director of Photography: Gordon Avil
Art Directors: Rolland M. Brooks, Eugene H. Harris
Film Editor: Michael Kahn
Assistant Director: Floyd Joyer
Set Decorator: Edward M. Parker
Post-Production Supervisor: Houseley Stevenson
Sound Engineer: Wallace Bearden
Makeup: Armand Delmar
Costumes: Ray R. Harp, Marjorie Wahl
Music Supervisor: Milton Lustig
Supervising Sound Editor: James J. Klinger
Filmed at Desilu Studios for Bing Crosby Productions

## EPISODE 33. "HOGAN GIVES A BIRTHDAY PARTY"

Original airdate: September 16, 1966
Writer: Richard M. Powell
Director: Gene Reynolds
Guest cast: James Gregory (General Biedenbender), Peter Marko (Lieutenant Karras), L. E. Young (Lieutenant Hardy)

Hogan induces Klink to conduct experiments on the superiority of Luftwaffe versus Allied fighter pilots. Klink's motive: to win a promotion. Hogan's: to gain access to a German fighter plane and use it to bomb a heavily defended oil refinery. The plan is thwarted by the arrival of General Biedenbender, the man responsible for Hogan's capture. The general has studied Hogan's actions for years and correctly concludes that Hogan plans to steal the plane. But he doesn't predict Hogan's next move—kidnapping the general and using his plane to bomb the refinery.

**Highlight:** Schultz, the prisoners' hostage on the bombing mission, must parachute back into camp. The bulky sergeant is terrified of making the jump and insists that he's too heavy. He has a point.

**Familiar faces:** James Gregory is perhaps best known for his role as Inspector Luger on *Barney Miller* (1975–82).

## EPISODE 34. "THE SCHULTZ BRIGADE"

Original airdate: September 23, 1966
Writer: Richard M. Powell
Director: Gene Reynolds
Guest cast: Leon Askin (General Burkhalter), Parley Baer (Colonel Burmeister), Lou Krugman (Colonel Bussie)

Colonels Bussie and Burmeister, kommandants of two other POW camps, try to enlist Klink in their plot to discredit General Burkhalter. Klink is eventually swayed into going along, but before they can implement their plan, Burkhalter arrives at Stalag 13 and places the three conspirators under arrest. If they lose Colonel Klink, the prisoners may get stuck with a competent kommandant. Hogan arranges for Bussie and Burmeister to escape to London, then breaks Klink out of the cooler to save Burkhalter from a staged assassination attempt. Klink is cleared of suspicion, and the heroes' operation is saved.

**Was ist los?** Carter's German accent is so bad, Hogan tells him not to talk during the mission. But in earlier episodes, Carter had demonstrated his proficiency with German voices, including a convincing Hitler impression.

## EPISODE 35. "DIAMONDS IN THE ROUGH"

Original airdate: September 30, 1966
Writer: Laurence Marks
Director: Gene Reynolds
Guest cast: Paul Lambert (Major Hegel), Ulla Stromstedt (Myra), Martin Blaine (Secret Policeman)

The heroes walk into a trap set by Major Hegel, a Gestapo agent. Hegel knows all about Hogan's operation and demands one million dollars' worth of diamonds for his silence. London denies Hogan's request for a million dollars in diamonds, but complies with a second request—for phony diamonds. Hogan enlists Klink's help in getting rid of Hegel. When Hogan turns over the phony gems in a barn outside of town, Klink and his guards surround the barn. Hegel tries to leave, but Klink sees the gun in his hand and orders his guards to fire, killing the diabolical major.

## EPISODE 36. "OPERATION BRIEFCASE"

Original airdate: October 7, 1966
Writer: Laurence Marks
Director: Gene Reynolds

Guest cast: Oscar Beregi (General Stauffen), Willard Sage (Major Gunther), Barry Ford (Hercules), Eddie Firestone (Sergeant Wilson), Peter Hellman (Guard), Chris Anders (Sentry)

Hogan receives a briefcase wired with a delayed-action bomb, which is to be used in an assassination plot against Hitler. Hogan's contact, German General Stauffen, arrives at Stalag 13 carrying a briefcase that is identical in appearance to the booby-trapped case. Hogan switches the two cases and instructs the general on how to use to bomb. Sergeant Schultz endangers the plan when he accidentally activates the timer on the case as the general is leaving camp. Hogan and the men scramble to catch up with the general. They deactivate the briefcase with fifteen seconds to spare.

**Notes:** This episode was based on an actual event in history. On July 20, 1944, Count von Stauffenberg left a briefcase containing a bomb under a table at Hitler's headquarters in an attempt to assassinate the Führer. Hitler escaped injury and exacted savage revenge: Stauffenberg and three others involved in the plan were shot, Rommel was forced to take poison, and seven thousand other suspects were arrested and executed.

**Familiar faces:** Eddie Firestone had worked on Ed Feldman's *Fair Exchange* before the producer hired him for small roles on *Hogan's*. Though he calls himself an "unimportant entity" on *Hogan's Heroes,* he says the experience was always enjoyable and adds, "The writing was just about the best of any show of that period. Larry Marks was a genius."

## EPISODE 37. "THE BATTLE OF STALAG 13"

Original airdate: October 14, 1966
Writer: Richard M. Powell
Director: Robert Sweeney
Guest cast: Jacques Aubuchon (General von Kattenhorn), Janine Gray (Greta), Howard Caine (Colonel Feldkamp), Walter Alzmann (Schneider)

A Wehrmacht general and a Gestapo colonel fight for control of Stalag 13. General Von Kattenhorn intends to convert the stalag into a rest camp for weary German officers, while Colonel Feldkamp wants to use it as his headquarters. In order to save the camp and his operation, Hogan plays the two officers against one another. He steals both their staff cars, blaming the thefts on the other. When Feldkamp and von Kattenhorn are on the verge of a hostile confrontation, Hogan returns the cars. Shortly after leaving camp, both officers are killed when their vehicles explode. Each death is blamed on the other—a double double cross.

**Notes:** Producer Ed Feldman was so pleased with Howard Caine's portrayal of the nasty Gestapo officer in this episode that he asked Caine if he would like to do a recurring role. Caine replied, "Sure, I love working with you, anytime." Feldman promised that the next time Caine played a Gestapo officer who was not killed in the end (as Feldkamp was in this episode) he would turn it into a semiregular role. The producer was true to his word, and Howard Caine returned later in the season to play Major Hochstetter, a role he would fill in thirty-seven episodes of the series. Even though Caine did not play Hochstetter in this episode, he utters the line that would become Hochstetter's trademark: "Who is this man?"

## EPISODE 38. "THE RISE AND FALL OF SERGEANT SCHULTZ"

Original airdate: October 21, 1966
Writer: Laurence Marks
Director: Gene Reynolds
Guest cast: Whit Bissell (General Kammler), Laurie Main (Colonel Franz), Edward Knight (Gestapo Officer)

Sergeant Schultz begins to carry a lot of weight around camp when an old fighting buddy who is now a general shows up at camp. General Kammler insists that Schultz be given special treatment. Klink complies, and before long Schultz's ego is overinflated. To free a captured underground agent, Hogan arranges for Schultz to be decorated for bravery in a ceremony at the hotel where the agent is being held. During the presentation, the men start a fire and free the agent in the confusion. Schultz's days on easy street end abruptly when Kammler is transferred to the Eastern front.

## EPISODE 39. "HOGAN SPRINGS"

Original airdate: October 28, 1966
Writer: Laurence Marks
Director: Gene Reynolds
Guest cast: Leon Askin (General Burkhalter), Sidney Clute (Sparrow), Walter Janowitz (Oscar Schnitzer), David Frank (Driver)

Hogan frees four underground leaders from their German captors and sneaks them into camp. The men must be smuggled to England, but a problem arises when a leaky pipe under the camp causes water to spring up in the middle of the compound. Hogan fears that if Klink investigates the leak by digging, he will soon find the tunnel system. He convinces Klink that the geyser is spouting mineral water and volunteers his men to build a bath house for German officers. While Klink, Burkhalter, and two other officers are bathing, the four underground agents leave camp wearing their uniforms.

**Notes:** The slogan painted over the bath house entrance, "Strength through Water," was a parody of "Strength through Joy," a Nazi program which subsidized leisure-time activities for workers. By making such luxuries as cruises and mountain excursions available to the working class, the Nazi party hoped to instill in them a sense of being an integral part of a national community. Workers were also given the opportunity to purchase an automobile, the Volkswagen, a symbol of wealth still largely reserved at that time to the upper classes. The Volkswagen, or "People's Car," was originally called the "Strength through Joy Wagon."

## EPISODE 40. "A KLINK, A BOMB AND A SHORT FUSE"

Original airdate: November 4, 1966
Writer: Phil Sharp
Director: Edward H. Feldman
Guest cast: Leon Askin (General Burkhalter)

The prisoners manage to photograph Klink's code book, but they can't transmit the code to London because Burkhalter has been snooping around camp with a radio signal finder. Hogan orders Carter to assemble a phony bomb and plant it in the prison yard. When the bomb is discovered, Burkhalter leaves camp, taking his signal finder with him. Hogan puts on a show of nervousness when disarming the bomb, but his nerves are really put to the test when he learns that Carter is trapped in the tunnel with the fake bomb and the one in the camp yard is real.

**Highlight:** The heroes fool Klink into posing for pictures with them while LeBeau holds the code book open behind his back. To butter him up, Hogan tells Klink that the men's nickname for him—Klink the FINK—stands for Firm, Impartial, Nazi Kommandant.

***Was ist los?*** Klink doesn't question the prisoners' possession of a camera and film, but in other episodes, those items are strictly verboten. In "Man's Best Friend Is Not His Dog" (#98), Klink searches the entire camp for a contraband roll of film.

## EPISODE 41. "TANKS FOR THE MEMORY"

Original airdate: November 11, 1966
Writer: Laurence Marks
Director: Gene Reynolds
Guest cast: Leon Askin (General Burkhalter), Vincent Van Lynn (German Major), Robert Gibbons (Civilian Technician), Margareta Sullivan (Girl)

A new radio-controlled tank is brought to Stalag 13 for testing. The prisoners tunnel into the building where the tank is being kept. While dismantling and photographing the tank, they are surprised by the arrival of General Burkhalter, who has come for a demonstration of the weapon. There's no time to replace the control box, so LeBeau climbs inside the tank and maneuvers it during the demonstration. When the tank goes behind the barracks, the prisoners help LeBeau out and place dynamite in his stead. The tank circles back and commences firing on the German brass.

**Was ist los?** How does the tank turn on its own after LeBeau is out and the control box is still gone?

## EPISODE 42. "A TIGER HUNT IN PARIS, PART 1"

Original airdate: November 18, 1966
Writer: Richard M. Powell
Director: Robert Sweeney
Guest cast: John Dehner (Colonel Backscheider), Nita Talbot (Marya), Arlene Martel (Tiger), George Neise (Captain Mueller), David Morick (Corporal Sontag), David Frank (Bouchet)

Underground agent Tiger is arrested by the Gestapo and held in Paris for questioning. Hogan and LeBeau stow away in Klink's staff car as Klink and Schultz head for Paris on leave. In Paris, Hogan assumes the identity of Frank Dirken, an American black marketeer. He makes contact with Colonel Backscheider, the Gestapo agent who is holding Tiger. Backscheider's fortune teller, a Russian spy named Marya, agrees to help Hogan, for a price—the location of German fighter bases. The operation nearly falls to pieces when Klink believes he has spotted Hogan in Paris.

**Familiar faces:** Dave Morick appeared frequently on *Hogan's Heroes*, usually playing German guards. In his own words, "I was always the dumb German guard, or the dumb Gestapo, or the dumb Wermacht Oberlieutenant." He worked on over twenty episodes and recalls *Hogan's Heroes* as "one of the most enjoyable shows to work on." He adds, "Werner Klemperer was kind enough to give me a hand with my German accent." Morick's other credits include episodes of *The Brady Bunch, The Rockford Files, Cannon, Airwolf,* and *The Mary Tyler Moore Show.*

## EPISODE 43. "A TIGER HUNT IN PARIS, PART 2"

Original airdate: November 25, 1966
Writer: Richard M. Powell
Director: Robert Sweeney
Guest cast: Nita Talbot (Marya), Henry Corden (Himmler/Antonovich), John Dehner (Colonel Backscheider), Arlene Martel (Tiger), George Neise (Captain Mueller), David Morick (Corporal Sontag)

To keep Klink out of his hair, Hogan implicates the kommandant as part of the spy ring working with Tiger, and he is arrested by the Gestapo. Marya teams up with Hogan despite their mutual distrust. She recruits an actor to impersonate Heinrich Himmler. Hogan and the phony Himmler storm Gestapo headquarters. "Himmler" frees Tiger and ransacks the office until he finds the map of the fighter-base locations. He also arranges for Klink's release—in twenty-four hours. Their mission accomplished, Hogan and LeBeau stow away in Klink's staff car for the trip home to Stalag 13.

**Notes:** This two-part episode was the first to feature the exotic Russian spy, Marya. Marya was one of Richard M. Powell's favorite characters, and he put her in six of his scripts.

**Historical notes:** Heinrich Himmler (1900–45) was the head of the SS, Hitler's personal bodyguard. In the last years of World War II, he was the second most powerful man in the Third Reich, next to Hitler himself. After the German surrender, Himmler tried to flee Germany but was captured by British troops. While in custody, he swallowed a vial of cyanide, killing himself.

## EPISODE 44. "WILL THE REAL ADOLF PLEASE STAND UP?"

Original airdate: December 2, 1966
Writer: Laurence Marks
Director: Gene Reynolds
Guest cast: Leon Askin (General Burkhalter), Bonnie Jones (Christina), Forrest Compton (Major Krantz), William Christopher (Foster)

The POWs take over a local cafe in order to steal plans of German fortifications from a German major. They photograph the plans without the major's knowledge, but smuggling the film to the Allies proves trickier. Klink has tightened security and the heroes' only chance of getting the film out of camp is to drive it through the front gate. This seemingly impossible task is accomplished by disguising Carter as Adolf Hitler. Carter, as the Führer, convinces Klink that he has stopped by Stalag 13 for a surprise inspection. After nearly overplaying his role, Carter leaves camp to deliver the film.

**Highlight:** Carter is so effective as Hitler that he gets carried away with the act and stays too long. General Burkhalter arrives at camp, and would surely spot the phony Führer, but Carter begins screaming about the laziness and stupidity of his generals, "One day the goose will hang high!" Burkhalter hastily retreats.

**Familiar faces:** Actor William Christopher first met Gene Reynolds while working on this episode and believes his work on *Hogan's Heroes* helped him land the role of Father Mulcahy on *M\*A\*S\*H,* which Reynolds later produced and directed. But Reynolds remembers differently, "We used another actor for the pilot of *M\*A\*S\*H* as Father Mulcahy. We weren't terribly happy with him. [*M\*A\*S\*H* producer] Burt Metcalfe saw Bill Christopher in *Beyond the Fringe* and brought him in for Mulcahy. When I met him again, I didn't really remember that we had worked together on *Hogan's Heroes*."

## EPISODE 45. "DON'T FORGET TO WRITE"

Original airdate: December 9, 1966
Writer: Laurence Marks
Director: Gene Reynolds
Guest cast: Leon Askin (General Burkhalter), Dick Wilson (Captain Fritz Gruber), Sandy Kenyon (Colonel Bessler), George Tyne (Luftwaffe Doctor)

Colonel Klink's boasting gets him assigned to a combat post at the Russian front. Klink accepts the prisoners' advice that he fail his physical so he'll be turned down for combat duty. When the doctor arrives, Klink is in terrible shape, but he passes the one requirement for active duty on the Russian front: He is breathing! Klink's tough-as-nails replacement, Captain Gruber, is making the prisoners' lives miserable. To discredit the new kommandant, three of the prisoners escape. When Gruber is unable to find the escapees, Klink recaptures them, and is reinstated as kommandant.

**Familiar faces:** Character actor Dick Wilson gained fame as "Mr. Whipple" in a series of Charmin commercials.

## EPISODE 46. "KLINK'S ROCKET"

Original airdate: December 16, 1966
Writers: Art Baer and Ben Joelson
Director: Bob Sweeney
Guest cast: Harold Gould (General Von Lintzer), John Orchard (Billett)

Hogan plans to bring down a few Luftwaffe bombers by luring them over a warehouse loaded with antiaircraft guns. He leads Klink to believe that the warehouse is the site of an Allied factory manufacturing deadly rocket guns. Carter is elected to "leak" the location of the warehouse to Klink, but he forgets the name of the town! Hogan bursts into the room on the pretext of saving Carter from torturous interrogation methods. Under faked duress, Hogan himself divulges the location. The Germans lose sixty-two planes in their attack on the fake factory.

**Familiar faces:** On television, Harold Gould has portrayed Stefanie Powers's father on *The Girl from U.N.C.L.E.*, Rhoda's father Martin Morgenstern on *Rhoda,* and Rose's beau Miles Webber on *The Golden Girls,* to name a few. He describes his experience on *Hogan's Heroes* as very enjoyable and remarks, "Those Nazi uniforms make you look awfully good, and straighten up your posture!"

## EPISODE 47. "INFORMATION PLEASE"

Original airdate: December 23, 1966
Writer: Laurence Marks
Director: Edward H. Feldman
Guest cast: Leon Askin (General Burkhalter), John Stephenson (Major Kohler), Sam Melville (Lieutenant James Crandall/Schmidt), Don Knight (RAF Lieutenant)

General Burkhalter feeds false information to the prisoners regarding the location of a war plant. Hogan falls into the trap and orders an attack on the plant, which turns out to be abandoned. Burkhalter knows that the leak is in Stalag 13 and plants a spy among the prisoners. From the start, Hogan suspects that the new prisoner, Crandall, is a spy. The men use Crandall to help implicate Burkhalter's aide, Major Kohler, in the attack on the plant. Once freed of suspicion, the POWs rid themselves of the spy in their barracks by ordering him to escape—at gunpoint.

## EPISODE 48. "ART FOR HOGAN'S SAKE"

Original airdate: December 30, 1966
Writer: Laurence Marks
Director: Gene Reynolds
Guest cast: Leon Askin (General Burkhalter), Ina Victor (Suzette), John Crawford (First Gestapo Man), Norbert Schiller (Verlaine), Jon Cedar (Corporal Langenscheidt)

LeBeau is enraged when he discovers that General Burkhalter has "requisitioned" a famous painting from the Louvre. He steals the painting from Klink's office. Hogan tells the kommandant that LeBeau has destroyed the painting. Desperate to replace the painting before Burkhalter returns, Klink permits Hogan and LeBeau to travel to Paris to have an artist reproduce it. LeBeau's friend Verlaine renders an excellent copy of the painting and keeps the original for safekeeping until after the war. The jig is almost up when the Gestapo visits Verlaine's studio, but Schultz's impersonation of a German general saves the day.

**Highlight:** Emboldened by wine, Schultz scares off the Gestapo with his enactment of a fierce general. He threatens to report the agents to their superiors, all the way up the chain of command until he reports them to himself. And then, oh boy!

## EPISODE 49. "THE GENERAL SWAP"

Original airdate: January 6, 1967
Writers: Ray S. Allen and Harvey Bullock
Director: Gene Reynolds
Guest cast: Leon Askin (General Burkhalter), John Myhers (Field Marshal von Heinke), Frank Gerstle (General Aloysius Barton)

A captured American general is brought to Stalag 13. When General Barton learns that Hogan has been at Stalag 13 for two years without trying to escape, he calls the colonel a disgrace to the uniform. Hogan is hurt by the insult, but like it or not, his orders are to help the general escape. The men abduct General von Heinke, a German field marshal, and offer a trade for General Barton. An exchange is arranged. Before Barton is shipped out,

Newkirk fills him in on their operation, and the general shows his respect for Hogan with a salute.

**Highlight:** In one of their most unorthodox plots yet, the prisoners convince von Heinke he has been captured by British commandos and flown to England. Von Heinke thinks he's being held in a British POW camp, but he's really in Hogan's quarters. The field marshal remarks with disdain that the Germans would never keep *their* prisoners in such a pig sty.

## EPISODE 50. "THE GREAT BRINKSMEYER ROBBERY"

Original airdate: January 13, 1967
Writer: Phil Sharp
Director: Bob Sweeney
Guest cast: Joyce Jameson (Mady Pfeiffer), Theo Marcuse (Ludwig Strasser), Arthur Hanson (Bank Manager)

The heroes plan to purchase a map of German rocket installations with 100,000 marks provided by the Allies. When the money is destroyed, they must come up with another 100,000 marks. Hogan, Newkirk, and LeBeau get themselves thrown in the cooler so they can escape without being missed at roll call. They go into town to rob a German bank, which adjoins a young woman's apartment. While Hogan entertains the woman, Newkirk and LeBeau chisel away at the brick wall between her bedroom and the bank vault. They steal the money, repair the wall, and return to the cooler before their sentence is up.

## EPISODE 51. "PRAISE THE FÜHRER AND PASS THE AMMUNITION"

Original airdate: January 20, 1967
Writer: Jack Elinson
Director: Robert Sweeney
Guest cast: Frank Marth (Colonel Deutsch), David Frank (SS Guard)

A ruthless SS officer, Colonel Deutsch, plans to stage war games outside of Stalag 13. Colonel Hogan decides to substitute live ammunition for the phony explosives to be used in the games. The evening before the games are to take place, the prisoners keep Colonel Klink and Deutsch entertained by putting on a show in honor of Klink's birthday. While the others are on stage, Hogan slips away and raids Stalag 13's ammunition supply. He plants real explosives among the dummy stuff in the SS stockpile. When the war games commence the following day, Colonel Deutsch is among the casualties.

**Highlight:** This episode gave the actors, especially Robert Clary and Richard Dawson, a chance to display their considerable talent as entertainers. Clary sings "Alouette," and Dawson impersonates Humphrey Bogart, Peter Lorre, and Sydney Greenstreet. It's a special treat to see the usually solemn Ivan Dixon, who joins Clary and Dawson in a trio, get a chance to sing and lighten up in this episode.

*Was ist los?* Klink celebrates his fiftieth birthday in this episode. But in "Get Fit or Go Fight" (#134), which aired three years later in January 1970, Klink says he is forty-nine. Klink's reverse aging allowed the actor playing him to catch up. Werner Klemperer was only forty-six when this episode was filmed, and when Episode #134 aired, Klink and Klemperer were the same age—forty-nine.

**Notes:** As suggested by this episode, the tactics of the SS (*Schutzstaffel* or Elite Guard) were far different than those of the Luftwaffe. Under the leadership of Heinrich Himmler, the barbarous SS was in charge of concentration camps during World War II. At the Nuremberg Trial after the war, the SS was condemned for innumerable atrocities, including persecuting and exterminating Jews, administering slave labor programs, and mistreating and murdering prisoners of war.

## EPISODE 52. "HOGAN AND THE LADY DOCTOR"

Original airdate: January 27, 1967
Writer: Laurence Marks
Director: Gene Reynolds
Guest cast: Ruta Lee (Dr. Suzanne Lechay*), Leon Askin (General Burkhalter), Curt Lowens (Gestapo Captain), Bard Stevens (Lab Duty Officer), Karl Bruck (Dr. Krull)
*The credits say Suzette, but she is called Suzanne in the episode.

Hogan clashes with Dr. Suzanne Lechay, a French underground agent in charge of the demolition of a synthetic fuel plant. Hogan feels the mission is too risky, but the strong-willed doctor pulls rank and orders Hogan to follow her plan. Suzanne allows herself to be captured by the Gestapo. As predicted, the Germans put her to work in the fuel plant. Hogan and the men overpower Lechay's guards and plant explosives at the lab. Lechay is presumed dead in the explosion and escapes to London with the help of Hogan, whose opinion of the lady doctor has softened.

**Notes:** Actress Ruta Lee called her experience on *Hogan's Heroes* "a laugh a minute!" Lee had worked with Werner Klemperer prior to *Hogan's* in the film *Operation Eichmann* (1961).

## EPISODE 53. "THE SWING SHIFT"

Original airdate: February 3, 1967
Writers: Art Baer and Ben Joelson
Director: Edward H. Feldman
Guest cast: Leon Askin (General Burkhalter), Hal Smith (Hans Spear), David Wiley (Major Pintz), David Frank (Inductee Kraus), Otto Waldis (Doctor), Buck Young (Factory Inspector)

Hogan and the men steal German identity cards and go to work in a German cannon factory, in order to halt production of the cannons. They tamper with the equipment so that the cannons are manufactured with a solid barrel! A shocking development occurs when foreman Newkirk, aka Mueller, is drafted into the German army. Hogan convinces the factory owner that Mueller is indispensable at the factory. Just as he's being sent to his new guard post at Stalag 13, Mueller is released from the army. The prisoners wire the factory so that it will blow up after they leave.

## EPISODE 54. "HEIL KLINK"

Original airdate: February 10, 1967
Writer: Richard M. Powell
Director: Edward H. Feldman
Guest cast: John Banner (Wolfgang Brauner/Schultz), Howard Caine (Major Hochstetter), Arlene Martel (Tiger)

Wolfgang Brauner, the "evil genius behind the Nazi money empire," has defected and wants Hogan to smuggle him out of Germany. Hogan decides to hide Brauner at Stalag 13. In order to keep Brauner tucked away, Hogan convinces Klink that Brauner is really Hitler and he has come to Stalag 13 to hide from assassins. When Hochstetter arrives looking for Brauner, Klink places him under arrest. Hogan discovers that after shaving off Brauner's beard, he looks like Schultz. While the real Schultz is kept busy squelching a prisoner riot, the imposter drives out of camp in a staff car.

**Notes:** In Nazi Germany, the greeting "Heil Hitler!" (hail Hitler) took the place of the former standard "Guten Tag" (good day). Adults were required to greet each other with "Heil Hitler" by law. School study periods were opened with the salutation, and every child was expected to use the phrase 50 to 150 times each day.

## EPISODE 55. "EVERYONE HAS A BROTHER-IN-LAW"

Original airdate: February 17, 1967
Writer: Laurence Marks
Director: Edward H. Feldman
Guest cast: Leon Askin (General Burkhalter), Cliff Norton (Captain Kurtz), Mary Mitchell (Eva)

Carter, Newkirk, and LeBeau place dynamite charges along a stretch of railroad track to blow up a munitions train, but when the train is delayed, Carter wires the charges into an emergency telephone near the tracks. The next person to lift the receiver will set off the explosion. General Burkhalter's brother-in-law, Captain Kurtz, is appointed as Klink's adjutant. The ambitious captain beefs up security, making the prisoners' lives miserable. Hogan asks Kurtz to take him to the railroad tracks on the pretext of leading him to an underground unit. Kurtz picks up the phone to turn Hogan in, thereby setting off the dynamite. The munitions train is demolished along with Kurtz's career: His fingerprints are on the receiver.

## EPISODE 56. "KILLER KLINK"

Original airdate: February 24, 1967
Writers: Harvey Bullock and Ray S. Allen
Director: Bob Sweeney
Guest cast: Parley Baer (Doctor Pohlmann), Barbara Morrison (Mrs. Gretchen Schultz), Walter Janowitz (Oscar Schnitzer)

Hogan's underground contact in Heidelberg needs new radio parts, but the POWs can't make the delivery. Hogan conceals the parts in a flower pot and enlists Schultz to make the delivery when he goes home to Heidelberg on a pass. Schultz gets into hot water with his wife and the kommandant and ends up restricted to camp. Hogan tricks Klink into believing that Schultz is sick, by sending a frail, elderly man to take Schultz's physical exam. "Killer" Klink feels responsible for Schultz's ill health and sends him on a furlough. Schultz delivers the flowers to Hogan's contact in Heidelberg.

## EPISODE 57. "REVEREND KOMMANDANT KLINK"

Original airdate: March 3, 1967
Teleplay by: Richard M. Powell, Ben Joelson, Art Baer
Story by: Ben Joelson and Art Baer
Director: Gene Reynolds
Guest cast: Howard Caine (Major Hochstetter), Felice Orlandi (Lieutenant Claude Boucher), Susan Albert (Suzanne Martine)

A captured French flier is brought to Stalag 13 for questioning by the Gestapo. Major Hochstetter tries to deceive Boucher into revealing the location of his unit by claiming that his fiancée has been unfaithful with German

### THE WICKED DREAMS OF PAULA SCHULTZ

When filming closed down after *Hogan's Heroes'* second season, several of the cast members decided to spend the hiatus working together on another project. *Hogan's Heroes* was at the height of its popularity and film producer Edward Small obviously wanted to capitalize on that success. He cast Bob Crane, Werner Klemperer, John Banner, and Leon Askin in his film *The Wicked Dreams of Paula Schultz*. His gambit was not a successful one. The film received dismal reviews and remains an embarrassment to many involved.

The plot of *Wicked Dreams* had Paula Schultz, an East German Olympic athlete (played by Elke Sommer), pole-vaulting over the Berlin Wall to freedom. Bob Crane played a black marketeer who helped her, then double-crossed her to the East Germans, later fell in love with her, and helped her escape again. Werner Klemperer played a lecherous propaganda minister with designs on Paula. Banner and Askin played East Germans working for Klaus.

When *The Wicked Dreams of Paula Schultz* opened in January of 1968, it was met with harsh criticism from reviewers. Renata Adler for the *New York Times* called the film "unrelievedly awful" and claimed that "no one in the film has any comic talent whatever." Adler also called the film pornographic, a tag Bob Crane believed cost them audience members. Pornography it was not, but the film did exploit every possible opportunity to show Elke Sommer losing an article of clothing, tearing her skirt during an escape attempt, or otherwise becoming partially disrobed. "With Elke, of course, you're not going to hide her under a fur coat," Crane quipped in an interview later that year.

officers. The despondent flier is on the verge of talking, until Hogan intervenes. He sends LeBeau to Paris to find Boucher's fiancée Suzanne and bring her back to Stalag 13. The prisoners put on a play, during which Boucher and Suzanne are married by Klink. His spirits revived, Boucher responds to Hochstetter's questions with just his name, rank, and serial number.

**Highlights:** Carter as the homely mother of the bride is a sight to behold. For a war-based comedy, this episode is surprisingly sentimental. Orlandi and Albert are very convincing as the couple in love.

**Familiar faces:** Felice Orlandi returned to aid Hogan and his men in three separate missions as French underground agent Maurice Dubois (see Episodes #70, #73, and #74). Orlandi is married to actress Alice Ghostley,

---

The *New York Times*' criticisms were echoed by reviewers from the *New York Post* ("an overextended floperoo"), the *Los Angeles Times* ("hopelessly silly and pointlessly tasteless"), and the *Hollywood Reporter* ("prospects appear slim"). However, the negative vote was not quite unanimous. The *Film Daily* reviewer was unreserved in his praise, calling it "rousing and frivolous fun...quite original and funny...audiences should enjoy it heartily." *Box Office* magazine recognized that the plot was far-fetched, but still called it "one of the better recent comedies."

Among the film's harshest critics is its costar, Werner Klemperer. Klemperer states, "It was the worst film...I mean, a woman pole-vaulting over the Berlin Wall! Come on!" He maintains that he had fun doing the film, though they all knew it would flop. One good thing to come of the film for Klemperer was his working with Elke Sommer, who became a good friend.

Crane later admitted the film was a mistake, at least from a marketing standpoint. "If we don't go our separate ways during hiatus, we'll be forever identified with those characters. Last year we didn't and it was a mistake. People saw *Wicked Dreams of Paula Schultz* and thought 'that's the old Hogan's gang again.'"

The writers on *Hogan's* even poked fun at the movie in Episode #151, "Kommandant Schultz." In what seems to be an inside joke directed at the film, Hogan insists that two of his men escaped by pole-vaulting over the barbed wire fence. Klink takes hold of the pole and attempts the feat himself, but falls on his face.

Nowadays the film pops up infrequently on late night television, to the amusement of *Hogan's* fans and to the chagrin of Werner Klemperer, who still winces when he hears its name. Leon Askin sums up the experience, "We had great fun in a bad movie." ★

also a guest star on *Hogan's Heroes*. The pair did not appear in any episodes of the series together.

## EPISODE 58. "THE MOST ESCAPE-PROOF CAMP I'VE EVER ESCAPED FROM"

Original airdate: March 10, 1967
Writer: Bill Davenport
Director: Edward H. Feldman
Guest cast: Leon Askin (General Burkhalter), Edward Knight (Colonel Stieffer), Mickey Manners (Sergeant Malcolm Flood), Karl Bruck (OSS Agent Huebler), Bard Stevens (Sergeant Schmidt)

Klink's no-escape record is in jeopardy when British escape artist Malcolm Flood is incarcerated at Stalag 13. Flood has escaped from nine other prison camps and intends to make Stalag 13 his tenth, despite Hogan's pleas that he stay put. Flood quickly escapes, jeopardizing Hogan's scheduled rendezvous with an OSS agent. Under the pretense of helping with the search party, Hogan meets up with his contact. Once the rendezvous is completed, Flood's escape is no longer a concern to Hogan, but the Englishman has a change of heart and returns of his own free will.

**Highlight:** When Carter is appointed to guard Flood, the escape artist easily outwits Carter.

## EPISODE 59. "THE TOWER"

Original airdate: March 17, 1967
Writer: Laurence Marks
Director: Gene Reynolds
Guest cast: Leon Askin (General Burkhalter), Willard Sage (Captain Berger), Elisa Ingram (Lili)

The Germans erect a new radio tower near Stalag 13, which could be deadly to the Allies because it transmits warning signals to German fighter squadrons. Destroying the tower is easy enough for the heroes, but they must find a way to keep Klink—who has been placed in charge of the tower's security—out of hot water. Hogan enlists a beautiful underground agent, Lili, in his scheme. Lili gets Burkhalter into some compromising positions while Kinch snaps incriminating photographs. The heroes, through Lili, use the photos to blackmail Burkhalter into publicly announcing Klink's innocence in connection with the tower.

## EPISODE 60. "COLONEL KLINK'S SECRET WEAPON"

Original airdate: March 24, 1967
Writer: Phil Sharp
Director: Gene Reynolds
Guest cast: Milton Selzer (Sergeant Reinhold Franks), Stewart Moss (Lieutenant Bigelow), Sidney Clute (Max), John Stephenson (Inspector General)

After receiving a poor rating from the Inspector General of prison camps, Colonel Klink brings in a new sergeant to discipline the prisoners. Sergeant Franks has gained a reputation as a "discipline machine" at other stalags and Klink thinks he's just the ticket for Stalag 13. But once Franks takes over the camp, Klink is no more fond of the sergeant than are his weary prisoners, who have been forced to suffer early roll calls, strenuous exercise, and no rest periods. Hogan and the men conspire to discredit Franks, who is subsequently removed from his post.

**Highlight:** The comic high point of this episode is Franks's humiliation in front of the Inspector General. When the inspector arrives, the grounds are covered with clothing and litter and the prisoners are unmanageable. As Franks parades in front of the assembly, his uniform falls apart at the seams, revealing a peace sign boldly decorating his undershirt.

**Familiar faces:** Milton Selzer played Abe Werkfinder, Jon Cryer's boss on *The Famous Teddy Z* (1989–90).

## EPISODE 61. "THE TOP SECRET TOP COAT"

Original airdate: March 31, 1967
Writer: Bill Davenport
Director: Howard Morris
Guest cast: Leon Askin (General Burkhalter), David Wiley (Herr Gruber), Inger Wegge (Maid)

A German traitor will hand over top secret plans to Hogan at a party, which Hogan plans to attend as Colonel Klink. The plot is foiled when General Burkhalter, alerted that a traitor will be at the party, insists that Klink attend. At the party, the information is planted in Klink's top coat. Back at camp, Hogan cannot get Klink to remove his coat. Carter dons a Gestapo uniform and questions Klink. Upon leaving the office, Carter switches his own top coat for Klink's. Hogan clears Klink from suspicion by convincing the Germans that Carter was the traitor.

**Hogan and Klink trade places in "The Reluctant Target."** © Bing Crosby Productions, Inc. Reprinted with permission.

## EPISODE 62. "THE RELUCTANT TARGET"

Original airdate: April 7, 1967
Writer: Phil Sharp
Director: Bob Sweeney
Guest cast: Larry D. Mann (SS General Brenner), Theo Marcuse (Pierre), John Hoyt (Field Marshal von Galter)

Hogan's plan to spring a captured underground agent from camp involves convincing Klink that he's the target of a mystery assassin. The fearful kommandant hides out while Hogan takes his place. While Hogan is masquerading as Klink, three German officers decide to use Klink's office for a maximum security war council. Hogan listens in on their meeting and learns the location of a secret stockpile of munitions to be used in an offensive against the Allies. He arranges for the underground agent to escape with the information. The attempts on Klink's life cease and he regains control of the camp.

**Familiar faces:** This was the first of John Hoyt's seven guest-starring appearances on *Hogan's Heroes*. He played Grandpa Stanley Kanisky on the NBC sitcom *Gimme a Break* (1982–87) starring Nell Carter.

# THIRD SEASON (1967–68)

Aired Saturdays, 9:00–9:30 P.M.,
opposite *The Lawrence Welk Show* on ABC and
*The NBC Saturday Night Movie* on NBC.

### Third Season Technical Credits

Producer: Edward H. Feldman
Associate Producer: William A. Calihan
Theme Music: Jerry Fielding
Editorial Supervisor: Jerry London
Director of Photography: Gordon Avil
Art Directors: Rolland M. Brooks, Eugene H. Harris
Film Editor: Michael Kahn
Assistant Director: Floyd Joyer
Unit Production Manager: W. A. Calihan
Set Decorator: Edward M. Parker
Post-Production Supervisor: Houseley Stevenson
Sound Engineer: Wallace Bearden
Makeup: Armand Delmar
Costumes: Ray R. Harp, Marjorie Wahl
Sound Editors: Bob Henderson, James J. Klinger
Filmed at Desilu Studios (later renamed Paramount Studios) for Bing Crosby
    Productions

## EPISODE 63. "THE CRITTENDON PLAN"

Original airdate: September 9, 1967
Writer: Richard M. Powell
Director: Gene Reynolds
Guest cast: Bernard Fox (Colonel Crittendon), Naomi Stevens (Nadya), Cliff
Osmond (Marko), Laurie Main (Major Shawcross), Angela Dorian (Carla),
Dave Morick (Sergeant)
    London orders Hogan to blow up a rocket fuel convoy and the tunnel it
is going to run through. They insist he spring Colonel Crittendon from
another stalag and implement his plan. Hogan's reluctance proves
well-founded: Crittendon's plan involves planting geraniums along airport
runways. Another Colonel Crittendon in another POW camp authored the

real Crittendon Plan, but it is too late to reach him. Crittendon's presence nearly foils the whole mission, but he redeems himself by attaching a time bomb to the lead truck just before the convoy enters the tunnel. When the convoy is inside the tunnel, the bomb goes off.

## EPISODE 64. "SOME OF THEIR PLANES ARE MISSING"

Original airdate: September 16, 1967
Writer: Laurence Marks
Director: Gene Reynolds
Guest cast: Leon Askin (General Burkhalter), John Doucette (Colonel Richard Leman), Stewart Moss (Olsen), Rick Traeger (Conrad), Walter Janowitz (Oscar Schnitzer)

Hogan uncovers a Luftwaffe plot to destroy British bombers. Using captured RAF planes, the Luftwaffe plans to infiltrate groups of British bombers and shoot them down. To avert such a tragedy, Hogan plans to destroy the captured British planes. Hogan pretends to get drunk at a party in Klink's quarters. He "passes out" in the bedroom. Sergeant Olsen, who has a similar build, trades places with Hogan. Hogan and his men leave camp in Luftwaffe uniforms, force their way on to the airbase and destroy the bombers.

**Familiar faces:** Stewart Moss substituted for Richard Dawson, who does not appear in this episode. Moss's other credits include episodes of *Star Trek, Murder, She Wrote, Hart to Hart, Hawaii Five-O, Rockford Files,* and *Magnum, P.I.*

## EPISODE 65. "D-DAY AT STALAG 13"

Original airdate: September 23, 1967
Writer: Richard M. Powell
Director: Gene Reynolds
Guest cast: Harold Gould (General von Scheider), Gail Kobe (Lilli von Scheider), John Hoyt (General Bruner), Ivan Triesault (General von Katz), J. Pat O'Malley (British General)

As D-Day approaches, Hogan is ordered to immobilize the German generals' staff while the Allies invade France. The generals are meeting at Stalag 13 because it is safe from Allied bombing. In order to delay a German retaliation against the attack, Hogan concocts a plan to confuse the German generals by convincing them that Klink has been named their leader. Once Klink takes over command, he learns of the assault on Normandy. The weak-kneed colonel is indecisive when it comes to issuing orders. As Klink stalls and the generals bicker over what action should be taken, the Allies move in.

**Notes:** On D-Day, June 4, 1944, more than 130,000 Allied troops landed along the coast of Normandy, France. The invasion was the first step on the final road to victory for the Allies in Europe. Prior to the invasion, Allied land, naval, and air forces were marshaled in preparation for the assault. The Allied forces photographed enemy defenses, dropped supplies to the resistance, bombed railways, reconnoitered the beaches, and otherwise trained and prepared for the attack.

**Familiar faces:** After starring on soap operas *Bright Promise* and *Peyton Place,* Gail Kobe switched gears and became a soap producer. After the cancellation of *Texas,* which she helmed, she took over as executive producer on *Guiding Light* in 1983.

## EPISODE 66. "SERGEANT SCHULTZ MEETS MATA HARI"

Original airdate: September 30, 1967
Writer: Laurence Marks
Director: Gene Reynolds
Guest cast: Howard Caine (Major Hochstetter), Joyce Jameson (Eva Mueller), Sidney Clute (Kurt)

Major Hochstetter concludes that Colonel Hogan must have something to do with the sabotage epidemic near Stalag 13. After a search of the camp turns up no evidence to substantiate his charges, Hochstetter decides to attack Stalag 13's weak link: Sergeant Schultz. He assigns Eva Mueller, an attractive Gestapo agent, to charm Schultz and probe him for information. The heroes learn of Eva's motives and implicate her in their latest act of sabotage: the bombing of a shell factory. Hogan sends the dishonored Mata Hari to a British POW camp.

**Highlight:** Sergeant Schultz is practically dancing on air when he returns to the prisoners' barracks after meeting Eva.

**Notes:** The original Mata Hari, Margaretha Zelle (1876–1917), was a Dutch spy during World War I. She had a number of high-ranking Allied officers as lovers, gathered classified information from them, and relayed it to the Germans. Her trial, and subsequent execution, attracted so much public attention that her pseudonym 'Mata Hari' (which means "eye of the dawn") has since become used to describe any femme fatale who acts as a spy or betrays someone.

## EPISODE 67. "FUNNY THING HAPPENED ON THE WAY TO LONDON"

Original airdate: October 7, 1967
Writer: Laurence Marks
Director: Gene Reynolds
Guest cast: Lloyd Bochner (Captain Roberts/Lieutenant Baumann), Howard Caine (Major Hochstetter), Peter Hellman (Gestapo Agent)

Hogan's old friend, RAF Captain Roberts, is brought to Stalag 13 and given the VIP treatment. Roberts appears to be involved in a plot to assassinate Winston Churchill. But the Gestapo has found a German lieutenant, Baumann, who is an exact double for Roberts. While the real Roberts is being held in the cooler, Lieutenant Baumann is to escape to England as Roberts. Once there, he will assassinate the prime minister. Hogan's counter plan involves switching the look-alikes so that the real Roberts is allowed to escape back to England and Baumann is kept in confinement by the Gestapo.

## EPISODE 68. "CASANOVA KLINK"

Original airdate: October 14, 1967
Writer: Bill Davenport
Director: Edward H. Feldman
Guest cast: Leon Askin (General Burkhalter), Kathleen Freeman (Gertrude Linkmeyer), Woodrow Parfrey (Hugo Hindmann), Carl Carlsson (Bartender)

Hogan must gain access to Klink's safe to retrieve documents that outline a trap set for the underground. Burkhalter's sister Gertrude has been filling in as Klink's temporary secretary, and she refuses to leave the office until it is completely organized. Hogan persuades Klink that Gertrude is working for the Gestapo. Klink romances Gertrude so that she will turn in a favorable report. As the couple dines out, the heroes raid Klink's safe and relay details of the trap to the underground, which changes its strategy. Hogan saves Klink from the love-struck Gertrude by telling her that the kommandant also romanced Hilda.

**Notes:** Should Klink have married Frau Linkmeyer? This question was posed to over 200 *Hogan's Heroes* fans in a recent survey. Each and every respondent answered with an emphatic "No!"

## EPISODE 69. "HOW TO WIN FRIENDS AND INFLUENCE NAZIS"

Original airdate: October 21, 1967
Writer: Phil Sharp
Director: Bob Sweeney
Guest cast: Leon Askin (General Burkhalter), Karl Swenson (Dr. Karl Svenson), Doris Singleton (Magda Tischler), Edward Knight (Grosser)

A famous neutralist scientist comes to Stalag 13 to work on a metal alloy that could help the Germans win the war. Hogan and the men must stop Dr. Svenson before he turns his formula over to the Nazis. As part of his plan to sway Svenson over to the Allies, Hogan plays Cupid for Svenson and a beautiful singer, Magda. His romance with Magda causes Svenson to neglect his work on the alloy. The lovebirds are arrested by the Gestapo, but Carter's exploding pen takes care of the arresting officer, and Svenson and Magda escape to England.

**Familiar faces:** Doris Singleton played the recurring role of Caroline Appleby on *I Love Lucy*. *Lucy* fans will recall the extreme lengths the redhead went to to impress or outdo Caroline, including impersonating Harpo Marx. Karl Swenson portrayed Lars Hanson, the mill owner, in *Little House on the Prairie* from 1974 to 1978.

## EPISODE 70. "NIGHTS IN SHINING ARMOR"

Original airdate: October 28, 1967
Writer: Laurence Marks
Director: Gene Reynolds
Guest cast: Leon Askin (General Burkhalter), Felice Orlandi (Maurice Dubois), Chris Anders (Captain Franz)

Hogan receives a special shipment from an Allied airplane: a dozen bulletproof vests. The underground sends an agent, Maurice Dubois, to pick up the vests and bring them to occupied France for use by resistance forces. One man cannot possibly carry the heavy vests out of camp, so Hogan comes up with an alternate plan. Dubois convinces Klink that he made the vests in the camp workshop. Burkhalter orders the vests—and their inventor—sent to Berlin for a demonstration. The heroes stop the car transporting Dubois and abduct the driver, leaving Dubois to drive the vests to France unhindered.

## EPISODE 71. "HOT MONEY"

Original airdate: November 4, 1967
Writer: Laurence Marks
Director: Bob Sweeney
Guest cast: Sandy Kenyon (SS Major Bock), Jon Cedar (Herman Stoffel)

The Germans set up a new counterfeiting plant inside Stalag 13, manufacturing American and British currency. Hogan intends to dismantle the plant before it starts mass production. Hogan's attempt to get Newkirk assigned to work as a forger fails. Plan B involves convincing Herr Stoffel, the expert forger, that he is to be executed as soon as he finishes the counterfeit plates. Stoffel then conspires with the heroes to destroy the counterfeit plates.

## EPISODE 72. "ONE IN EVERY CROWD"

Original airdate: November 11, 1967
Writer: Laurence Marks
Director: Bob Sweeney
Guest cast: Paul Picerni (Jack Williams), John Crawford (Captain Hermann), John Stephenson (Felix), Barbara Babcock (Maria Schmidt)

Hogan's latest enemy comes from within his own ranks. POW Williams offers Klink information on Hogan's sabotage activities in exchange for safe passage to Berlin. The traitor may interfere with Hogan's latest plan: to destroy the German's new S-5 gun being guarded at Stalag 13. Williams unknowingly signs a false confession, which states that an attack will be made on an arms factory in Hammelburg. Klink orders all of his guards to accompany him to the factory, leaving Williams and the S-5 gun unguarded. The heroes demolish the gun and make it appear that Williams was killed in the explosion.

**Highlight:** A brawl breaks out in the barracks, but when Klink enters, the quick-thinking POWs pair up and pretend to be dancing. LeBeau even asks the kommandant to dance.

**Familiar faces:** Barbara Babcock played Dorothy on the CBS western drama *Dr. Quinn, Medicine Woman* (1993–98).

Paul Picerni played agent Lee Hobson on *The Untouchables* (1960–63). Picerni and Bob Crane had been friends and neighbors prior to working together on *Hogan's Heroes*. He recalls, "Bob lived around the corner from me. I had been a guest several times on his radio show before working with him on *Hogan's Heroes*. I tried to get him a guest part on *The Untouchables*, but it didn't work."

## EPISODE 73. "IS GENERAL HAMMERSCHLAG BURNING?"

Original airdate: November 18, 1967
Writer: Richard M. Powell
Director: Edward H. Feldman
Guest cast: Barbara McNair (Kumasa/Carol Dukes), Felice Orlandi (Maurice Dubois), Paul Lambert (General Hammerschlag), David Morick (Aide)

The French Underground comes to Hogan for help in preventing a Nazi plan to level Paris. The plan was created by General Hammerschlag, whose one weakness is a spiritual advisor named Kumasa. Kumasa turns out to be Carol Dukes, an old schoolmate of Kinchloe's. At Kinch's urging, Kumasa conducts a seance in which Hammerschlag communicates with his idol—Prince Otto Bismarck—through Hogan. During the seance, Kinch tosses the plans out the window to a waiting underground agent. The plans are photographed and returned before the seance ends. When Hammerschlag puts the plan into action, the underground will be ready.

**Highlight:** This is one of few episodes to prominently feature Ivan Dixon. He and Bob Crane play off each other well, particularly when Kinch takes the lead on the mission. Improvising, Kinch announces that Hogan is a mute bus boy. Rendered "mute" by Kinch's story, Hogan can only react with with his facial expressions, which denote that Kinch will get an earful when they get back to the barracks.

**Was ist los?** In this episode, Kumasa remembers Kinch as Ivan Kinchloe from Detroit. An earlier episode established Kinch's first name to be James.

**Notes:** Prince Otto von Bismarck was chancellor of Germany from 1871 to 1890. During the reign of William I, Bismarck ruled as a virtual dictator, provoking wars with Denmark, Austria, and France, dissolving parliament, and illegally levying taxes for the army.

## EPISODE 74. "A RUSSIAN IS COMING"

Original airdate: November 25, 1967
Writer: Phil Sharp
Director: Bob Sweeney
Guest cast: Leon Askin (General Burkhalter), Bob Hastings (Igor Piotkin), Felice Orlandi (Maurice Dubois), Bard Stevens (German Officer)

Igor Piotkin, a downed Soviet pilot, has refused the usual escape route to England, demanding to be sent to Russia instead. A series of phone calls from

Hogan and Kinch convince Klink that the Russian has been captured, and that a nonexistent lieutenant has defected. Klink is instructed to ship the defector to the Russian front, should he turn up at Stalag 13. Hogan outfits Piotkin in a German lieutenant's uniform and turns him over to Klink, who sends the man to Russia. Hogan muses, "Wouldn't it be funny if he really wanted to go to the Russian front?!"

## EPISODE 75. "AN EVENING OF GENERALS"

Original airdate: December 2, 1967
Writer: Laurence Marks
Director: Bob Sweeney
Guest cast: Leon Askin (General Burkhalter), Maurice Marsac (Sergeant Jacques Mornay), Ben Wright (General Felix Mercer), John Hoyt (General Bruner)

Klink is placed in charge of security for a banquet for Germany's top generals. The generals are convening for a briefing prior to an offensive. The heroes are ordered to kill the generals. Carter devises bombs disguised as centerpieces. After the bombs are in place, Hogan learns that one of the guests is General Mercer, an Allied spy. Mercer insists that getting the plans for the offensive is more imortant than killing the generals. Mercer exposes the bombs and clears the room. LeBeau enters the room through the dumbwaiter and retrieves the plans, seconds before the bombs go off.

**Was ist los?** The timeline of *Hogan's Heroes* had to progress slowly, as the series ran for six years, nearly twice as long as the prisoners would have been interred at the camp. The pilot is set in 1942 and the camp would have been liberated in April 1945. For that reason, it's understandable when Hogan says he's been at camp for two years in Episode #49, which aired in January 1967, and he's *still* been in camp for two years in Episode #95, in October 1968. But in this episode, time has actually moved backwards. "D-Day at Stalag 13" (Episode #65), which aired a few months earlier, was set in June 1944. According to the poster for the prisoners' upcoming talent show, it's only 1943 in this episode.

## EPISODE 76. "EVERYBODY LOVES A SNOWMAN"

Original airdate: December 9, 1967
Writer: Arthur Julian
Director: Bob Sweeney

Guest cast: Howard Caine (Major Hochstetter), Noam Pitlik (Captain Morgan), Robert Pickering (Lieutenant Rosen)

An American bomber crew led by Captain Morgan is hiding out in the heroes' tunnel while the Gestapo searches for them. To prevent the Gestapo from finding their escape tunnel, Hogan lets them uncover a new tunnel as a decoy. As punishment, the prisoners are moved to a new barracks. Unfortunately, it's the only barracks in camp that they do not have a tunnel under! As recent snowstorms have turned the camp into a winter wonderland, Hogan requests permission for his men to build a snowman. Captain Morgan and his crew escape through a tunnel built underneath the giant snowman.

**Familiar faces:** After a successful acting career, which included regular roles on *The Bob Newhart Show* and *Sanford and Son*, Noam Pitlik became a noted television director. His directorial credits include *Barney Miller, Taxi,* and *Wings*.

## EPISODE 77. "THE HOSTAGE"

Original airdate: December 16, 1967
Writer: Richard M. Powell
Director: Edward H. Feldman
Guest cast: Nita Talbot (Marya), Theo Marcuse (General Freidrich von Heiner)

A rocket fuel depot constructed just outside of camp seems too easy a target for the heroes. General von Heiner has planted the depot there hoping to trap Hogan. The men tunnel under the depot and plant a bomb, set to explode during the prisoners' roll call. The general throws a curve—he holds Hogan hostage at the depot. The others cannot get to the bomb in time to save Hogan's life. But von Heiner's lady friend, the Russian spy Marya, arranges for Hogan's release moments before the bomb explodes, killing von Heiner.

**Notes:** Nita Talbot's performance in this episode earned her an Emmy nomination as Best Actress in a Supporting Role in a Comedy Series. She lost to Marion Lorne of *Bewitched*.

**Familiar faces:** This was the third *Hogan's* episode to feature character actor Theodore Marcuse, who had also guest-starred in *Star Trek, Batman, The Twilight Zone,* and numerous other series, and had joined several *Hogan's* cast members in the feature film *The Wicked Dreams of Paula Schultz*. He was killed in an automobile accident on the Hollywood Freeway two weeks before this episode aired.

**Carter and LeBeau.** © Bing Crosby Productions, Inc. Reprinted with permission.

## EPISODE 78. "CARTER TURNS TRAITOR"

Original airdate: December 23, 1967
Writer: Richard M. Powell
Director: Howard Morris
Guest cast: Antoinette Bower (Leni Richter), John Myhers (General Wittkamper)

The heroes stage a three-way assassination attempt on Carter's life to convince their captors that the POW has turned traitor. Carter fabricates a background in chemical warfare so that he will be put to work in the German's chemical warfare factory. His story is so convincing that one of the chemists, Leni Richter, tries to poison him. Richter, a traitor to Germany, has been working in the factory and sabotaging it every step of the way. Hogan arranges for Richter's escape and the bombing of the factory.

## EPISODE 79. "TWO NAZIS FOR THE PRICE OF ONE"

Original airdate: December 30, 1967
Writer: Phil Sharp
Director: Bruce Bilson

Guest cast: Howard Caine (Major Hochstetter), Alan Oppenheimer (Herman Freitag), Jon Cedar (Mannheim), Barbro Hedstrom (Ilse Praeger)

Gestapo agent Herman Freitag knows all about Hogan's espionage activities, but hasn't blown the whistle yet. He offers Hogan $50,000 and safe passage to Switzerland in exchange for information about the U.S. atom bomb project. Hogan knows nothing about the "Manhattan Project," but doesn't let on. He decides that Freitag knows too much already and must be eliminated. He plans to assassinate Freitag but is beaten to it by Freitag's second-in-command, Mannheim, who despised his commander for not confiding in him.

**Highlight:** When Mannheim opens fire on Hogan, Klink, and Schultz, the three hide behind office furniture. Klink orders Schultz to go after the assailant. "I can't, Herr kommandant, I lost my rifle," Schultz announces as he hides his weapon behind a file cabinet. Once the assassin is captured, Schultz feigns surprise at seeing the rifle behind the cabinet, "Oh, here it is! I found my rifle. I knew it was someplace!"

**Notes:** The Manhattan Project was the code name given to the U.S. project begun in the early 1940s with the aim of developing an atom bomb. The research was carried out with great secrecy and haste, as the United States believed the Germans were already at work on a similar project. The Manhattan Project culminated in the testing of the first atom bomb in July 1945 and its first use in war at Hiroshima on August 6, 1945.

## EPISODE 80. "IS THERE A DOCTOR IN THE HOUSE?"

Original airdate: January 6, 1968
Writer: Arthur Julian
Director: Edward H. Feldman
Guest cast: Leon Askin (General Burkhalter), Howard Caine (Major Hochstetter), Brenda Benet (Janine Robinet), Anthony Eustrel (Doctor Kronk)

A beautiful French model is hiding in the escape tunnel until the heroes can smuggle her out to an underground contact. Their plan calls for Janine to hide in the trunk of Klink's car when the kommandant drives to his staff meeting. Klink's bout with the flu nearly ruins the plan, but LeBeau's home remedy—a Bernaise sauce plaster—has the kommandant feeling much better. Before Klink can leave camp, Hochstetter arrives with tracking dogs to search for Janine. But the dogs pick up the scent of the Bernaise sauce instead, and chase Klink up a tree.

**Notes:** This episode marks a notable occasion, the first time Major Hochstetter and General Burkhalter appear in the same episode. In past episodes, the two characters were virtually interchangeable. In fact, when Leon Askin was working in Europe and was unavailable for filming, all the scripts featuring Burkhalter were changed to Hochstetter.

**Familiar faces:** Brenda Benet took her own life in 1982, a year after the sudden death of her only son, six-year-old Christopher Bixby, from her marriage to actor Bill Bixby. The thirty-six-year-old actress had been playing the villainous Lee DuMonde on *Days of Our Lives* at the time of her death.

## EPISODE 81. "HOGAN, GO HOME"

Original airdate: January 13, 1968
Writer: Bill Davenport
Director: Edward H. Feldman
Guest cast: Bernard Fox (Colonel Rodney Crittendon), David Morick (SS Guard)

A message comes from London ordering Hogan to return to the States for a hero's welcome. Initially overjoyed at the news, Hogan has a change of heart and decides to stay. But it is too late, his replacement is on the way. Worse yet, it's Colonel Crittendon. Crittendon keeps botching his first assignment—preventing Hogan from boarding the Berlin Express, which is scheduled for attack by the Allies. The heroes eventually succeed in rescuing Hogan, who announces he is going home—to Stalag 13.

**Highlights:** A favorite with many fans, this episode contains several classic scenes. Klink relishes in telling Hogan that the new prisoner is Hogan's nemesis Colonel Crittendon and that Crittendon outranks Hogan, making him the new senior POW. "Chop, chop, chop!" chirps the gleeful kommandant, who says that being evil makes him feel good all over. Another gem comes when Crittendon chops down a tree, hoping to block the truck's passage, but the tree falls the wrong way.

## EPISODE 82. "STICKY WICKET NEWKIRK"

Original airdate: January 20, 1968
Writer: Richard M. Powell
Director: John Rich
Guest cast: Howard Caine (Major Hochstetter), Ulla Stromstedt (Gretel), Jay Sheffield (Sergeant), Stewart Moss (Captain Anderson)

Newkirk is captured while romancing a German woman in town, and as punishment for his escape, Klink transfers him to another stalag. Hogan gives Newkirk a gun so he can escape en route to the other camp. Rather than going to London as Hogan ordered, Newkirk returns to Stalag 13 with Gretel, his girl from town. Once she has seen Hogan's operation, Gretel reveals she works for the Gestapo. When Hochstetter arrives, the heroes discredit Gretel's claims and incriminate her as an informant for the Allies. Newkirk talks his way out of trouble with Klink, but has a tougher time getting off the hook with his mates.

**Highlight:** Newkirk's defense of his actions is well played for comic effect. His explanation for why he misjudged Gretel: "lack of practice." His suggested remedy: frequent passes into town!

## EPISODE 83. "WAR TAKES A HOLIDAY"

Original airdate: January 27, 1968
Writers: Art Baer and Ben Joelson
Director: Bruce Bilson
Guest cast: Howard Caine (Major Hochstetter), Frank Marth (Inspector General Busse), William Christopher (Thomas), Peter Marko (Albins), Chris Anders (Hermann)

The Gestapo is holding four underground leaders at Stalag 13 under heavy guard. Newkirk's statement that they won't get out until the war is over sparks Hogan's idea to end the war! Using phony radio broadcasts and newspaper headlines, Hogan convinces Colonel Klink and Major Hochstetter that the war is over. Stalag 13's regular inmates stick around for the celebration, but the freed underground leaders leave camp. Hogan even induces Hochstetter into loaning them his staff car. Moments later, General Busse arrives in camp and puts an end to the charade.

**Notes:** William Christopher plays one of the heroes in this episode. Larry Hovis does not appear.

## EPISODE 84. "DUEL OF HONOR"

Original airdate: February 3, 1968
Writer: Richard M. Powell
Director: Edward H. Feldman
Guest cast: Howard Caine (Major Hochstetter), Antoinette Bower (Erika Weidler)

Underground agent Erika Weidler brings Hogan a list containing the names of people who plan to kill Hitler. Hogan plans to use Klink as a courier to get the list to England. Erika feigns a passionate crush on Klink. Klink is smitten too, until he learns that she is married to a saber-wielding general. As the vicious "Tiger" Weidler, Carter challenges Klink to a duel. Predictably, the cowardly kommandant decides to flee the country instead. A plane is scheduled to pick up Klink—and more importantly, the list. When Hochstetter arrives on the scene, the heroes pose as Abwehr agents and scare off the Gestapo.

**Highlight:** Erika's seduction of Klink provides some of the series' funniest moments. The vain colonel wears his cap on his date, until Erika reveals that she hates hair, prompting Klink to expose his bald pate. Erika's passion for Klink and his "magnificent leonine head" disappears as quickly as it heated up when she announces that she hates him for making her love another man while she's married.

Larry Hovis's masquerade as Tiger Weidler is one of the actor's favorite memories from his work on the series. He says, "I got to whack everything with my saber. I loved doing that."

**Notes:** The Abwehr was the counterintelligence department of the high command of the German armed forces. During World War II, the Abwehr became a focus of opposition to Hitler, who favored the rival SD (*Sicherheitsdienst*), the intelligence branch of the SS. After several Abwehr leaders were implicated in the 1944 plot to overthrow Hitler, the Fuhrer ordered that the Abwehr be merged with the SD.

## EPISODE 85. "AXIS ANNIE"

Original airdate: February 10, 1968
Writer: Laurence Marks
Director: John Rich
Guest cast: Howard Caine (Major Hochstetter), Louise Troy (Anna Gebhart), Chet Stratton (Blue Fox), Karl Bruck (Vandermeer), L. E. Young (Diner in Hotel), Bard Stevens (Gestapo Guard)

Complications prevent Hogan from passing information to an underground contact in Hamelburg. Hogan's crew grants pro-Nazi interviews to broadcaster Axis Annie of the Propaganda Ministry, in exchange for an evening in Hamelburg. Hochstetter, Klink, and Schultz go along as guards when Axis Annie entertains Hogan, Newkirk, and LeBeau in Hamelburg. The prisoners start a fire, and in the ensuing riot Hogan gets the information to the contact, Vandermeer. Back at camp, Carter and Kinch start a fire of their own to destroy the prisoners' traitorous recordings.

**Notes:** The character of Axis Annie was inspired by an actual historical figure, American-born Mildred Gillars, who went to Germany as a music student in the 1920s and became a popular propaganda broadcaster for the Nazis during World War II. Gillars, dubbed Axis Sally by American GIs, greeted American troops with such statements as "Go home and forget the war!" After the war, she was arrested by Allied authorities and sentenced to twelve years in prison.

## EPISODE 86. "WHAT TIME DOES THE BALLOON GO UP?"

Original airdate: February 17, 1968
Writer: Arthur Julian
Director: Marc Daniels
Guest cast: Howard Caine (Major Hochstetter), Peter Brooks (Christopher Downes), Lincoln Deyman (Master Sergeant McMahon)

The heroes think Hogan has lost his marbles when he suggests they take up basket weaving, tent making, and kite flying in order to free a captured British agent. Hogan's outlandish plan calls for the men to construct a hot air balloon to fly Downes out of camp. Hochstetter squashes the prisoners' kite flying activity, but not before they have gathered sufficient meteorological information to plan the flight. That evening, the POWs distract the Germans while the balloon—constructed from old parachutes and a giant basket—lifts off right in the middle of camp.

## EPISODE 87. "LEBEAU AND THE LITTLE OLD LADY"

Original airdate: February 24, 1968
Writer: Arthur Julian
Director: Bruce Bilson
Guest cast: Howard Caine (Major Hochstetter), Celeste Yarnall (Wilhelmina), Sivi Aberg (Juliana)

None of the other prisoners will volunteer to take over LeBeau's weekly visits to an underground contact, whom he describes as a "mean little old lady." In truth, the contact, Wilhelmina, is a beautiful woman whom LeBeau has fallen in love with. When Wilhelmina's life is endangered, LeBeau risks his life to save hers. The heroes arrive at Wilhelmina's apartment only moments ahead of the Gestapo bloodhounds. Ironically, to get Wilhelmina past the Gestapo, the prisoners disguise her as an old lady.

**Familiar faces:** As Chuck Barris's beautiful assistant on *The Gong Show* (1976–80), Sivi Aberg was known for adding a touch of class to the tasteless proceedings.

## EPISODE 88. "HOW TO ESCAPE FROM A PRISON CAMP WITHOUT REALLY TRYING"

Original airdate: March 2, 1968
Writer: Bill Davenport
Director: Edward H. Feldman
Guest cast: Leon Askin (General Burkhalter), Willard Sage (Colonel Krueger), Edward Knight (Colonel Nikolas), Lyn Peters (Audrey St. Laurence), Chet Stratton (Bruno), Tom Hatten (Sergeant), Jay Sheffield (Corporal)

Hogan is ordered to detain the entire 6th SS Division for two days while the Allies organize a surprise attack. But can five unarmed men pin down ten thousand SS soldiers? While Klink is vacationing at a ski resort, Hogan arranges for thirty prisoners to escape and hide in the tunnel. The 6th SS Division is tied up for three days trying to track down the prisoners, thus the heroes' mission is accomplished. Once Klink is back in command and the Allied counterattack is organized, the thirty escaped men suddenly reappear in their barracks.

**Highlight:** Unaware that Burkhalter is standing behind him, Klink instructs the hotel clerk to tell the general he's not in, then proceeds to call Burkhalter a nasty old tub of lard.

## EPISODE 89. "THE COLLECTOR GENERAL"

Original airdate: March 9, 1968
Writer: Laurence Marks
Director: Bruce Bilson
Guest cast: Gavin MacLeod (General Metzger), Heidy Hunt (Lisa), John Stephenson (Karl), David Morick (Guard)

General Metzger arrives from Paris with orders for Colonel Klink to guard a truckload of ammunition. Hogan does not believe the general's story. LeBeau sneaks inside the truck and confirms Hogan's hunch—the truck is filled with valuable pieces of art stolen from France, not ammunition. With the aid of two underground agents, Hogan and crew steal the artwork from the truck and arrange for its return to France. When Metzger threatens retaliation, Hogan calls his bluff. "When you steal from a thief, he'll never call the cops."

**Highlight:** The German soldier (played by David Morick) guarding Metzger's truck delights in learning a new American word, "emergency."

## EPISODE 90. "THE ULTIMATE WEAPON"

Original airdate: March 16, 1968
Writer: Richard M. Powell
Director: Marc Daniels
Guest cast: Leon Askin (General Burkhalter), Marian Moses (Colonel Karla Hoffman)

Hogan must arrange to have German fighter planes moved away from Zuglitz so the Allies can bomb the city. Hogan convinces his captors that Sergeant Schultz is a military genius. He tape-records radio broadcasts and plays them back to Klink after feeding the information to Schultz. When Schultz correctly "predicts" military advances for seven days, Burkhalter calls him "the ultimate weapon." When Schultz guesses that Berlin will be the Allies' next target, all available fighter planes are moved to Berlin. Left undefended, Zuglitz is an easy target for the Allies.

## EPISODE 91. "MONKEY BUSINESS"

Original airdate: March 23, 1968
Writer: Arthur Julian
Director: Bob Sweeney
Guest cast: Leon Askin (General Burkhalter), Laurie Main (Colonel Wembley), Jack Good (Submarine Officer), Elisa Ingram (Radio Operator)

The bombing of the Hammelburg Zoo has the woods around Stalag 13 filled with runaway animals and German guards trying to recapture them. Carter, on a mission to deliver a spare radio part to the underground, is unable to get past the guards. He returns to camp with the radio part and a pal—a chimpanzee he encountered in the woods. The heroes grow attached to the chimp, whom they name Freddy, but they give him up to accomplish their mission. They sew the radio part into his pocket, to be retrieved by a contact waiting at the zoo.

## EPISODE 92. "DRUMS ALONG THE DÜSSELDORF"

Original airdate: March 30, 1968
Writer: Arthur Julian
Director: Bob Sweeney
Guest cast: David Frank (Sergeant)

The heroes' attempt to blow up a truck carrying an experimental new jet fuel fails, but they get a second chance when the truck is rerouted to pass by Stalag 13. The men can't get near the front gate. Carter, whose Sioux heritage is revealed when he gets a letter addressed to "Little Deer Who Goes Swift and Sure through Forest," shoots a flaming arrow in the direction of the truck as it passes by camp. Carter misses, but Newkirk grabs the bow and arrow and hits the target. The truck goes up in flames as Newkirk reveals he's a descendant of Robin Hood.

**Highlight:** Dressed as a little old lady, Newkirk detains the truck driver with talk of her granddaughter the fan dancer.

# FOURTH SEASON (1968–69)

Aired Saturdays, 9:00–9:30 P.M.,
opposite *The Lawrence Welk Show* on ABC and
*The NBC Saturday Night Movie* on NBC.

### Fourth Season Technical Credits

Executive Producer: Edward H. Feldman
Producer: William A. Calihan
Associate Producer: Jerry London
Theme Music: Jerry Fielding
Editorial Supervisor: Jerry London
Directors of Photography: Gordon Avil, Robert Moreno
Art Directors: Rolland M. Brooks, Eugene H. Harris
Film Editors: Michael Kahn, Thomas Neff, Clay Bartels
Assistant Director: Floyd Joyer
Unit Production Manager: William A. Calihan
Set Decorator: Edward M. Parker
Sound Engineer: Wallace Bearden
Makeup: Armand Delmar

Costumes: Ray R. Harp, Marjorie Wahl
Post-Production Supervisor: Houseley Stevenson
Music Supervisor: Milton Lustig
Sound Editors: Bob Henderson, Ross Taylor
Filmed at Paramount Studios for Bing Crosby Productions

## EPISODE 93. "CLEARANCE SALE AT THE BLACK MARKET"

Original airdate: September 28, 1968
Writer: Laurence Marks
Director: Edward H. Feldman
Guest cast: Gavin MacLeod (Major Kiegel), Doris Singleton (Maria), Lou Krugman (Hermann), Bard Stevens (Karl)

While visiting a waitress at the hofbrau, Schultz walks in on the owner and a Gestapo major conducting a shady transaction. To keep his secret safe, Major Kiegel orders Schultz transferred to the Eastern front. Hogan must intervene to save Schultz, and the heroes' operation. He learns that Kiegel has been running a black market operation out of the hofbrau. When the major doesn't give in to Hogan's threats of blackmail, the heroes take photographs of Kiegel and his men loading their loot into a truck and send the film to Berlin. Kiegel is arrested, and Schultz's transfer is revoked.

## EPISODE 94. "KLINK VS. THE GONCULATOR"

Original airdate: October 5, 1968
Writer: Phil Sharp
Director: Bruce Bilson
Guest cast: Leon Askin (General Burkhalter), Noam Pitlik (Major Lutz), Victoria Carroll (Lila), David Morick (Captain Dingel)

Hogan must help a German major who has been working for the underground get out of Germany with a stolen radio homing-device. The men arrange for Major Lutz to be brought to camp by convincing the Germans that Carter's electronic rabbit trap is a "gonculator," a top-secret military device, which they can't finish assembling without the "Lutz" diagram. When Lutz experiments with the gonculator, the device explodes. Obscured by the smoke, Hogan leads Lutz down into the tunnel and the major escapes to London with the homing device. The major is presumed dead in the explosion.

**Highlight:** Neither Klink nor Burkhalter will admit to not knowing what a gonculator is, so they each pretend that they don't recognize the prisoners' version because it differs from the superior German model.

**Familiar faces:** Victoria Carroll appeared in six episodes of *Hogan's Heroes,* but is perhaps most recognized for her recurring role on *Alice* as Mel's (Vic Tayback) girlfriend Marie. She says of her work on *Hogan's:* "I always felt welcomed. Everyone was there to help out, give you a suggestion, make you feel comfortable, make you feel at home. I recall Richard Dawson making me laugh a lot—he'd say something totally outrageous, and just make me laugh. And Larry Hovis was also very funny."

## EPISODE 95. "HOW TO CATCH A PAPA BEAR"

Original airdate: October 12, 1968
Writer: Laurence Marks
Director: Bruce Bilson
Guest cast: Alan Oppenheimer (Wilhelm), Fay Spain (Myra), Jay Sheffield (Gestapo Officer), Horst Ebersberg (SS Sergeant)

The news that Klink is planning a surprise bed-check prevents Hogan from meeting with a new underground unit calling themselves "North Star." Newkirk takes his place and falls into a trap set by the Gestapo. Gestapo agent Myra extracts Hogan's radio frequency from Newkirk and tries to lead Hogan and the others into a trap. Hogan knows she is Gestapo because she did not utilize the secret code Hogan and Newkirk agreed upon before the mission. Hogan avoids the trap and frees Newkirk by sending Myra's contacts on a wild goose chase away from Gestapo headquarters.

## EPISODE 96. "HOGAN'S TRUCKING SERVICE . . . WE DELIVER THE FACTORY TO YOU"

Original airdate: October 19, 1968
Writer: Bill Davenport
Director: Edward H. Feldman
Guest cast: Howard Caine (Major Hochstetter), Bernard Fox (Colonel Crittendon), Bob Garrett (Corporal Kohler), Peter Bourne (Leader Four)

The heroes devise a clever plan to blow up a ball-bearing plant by parking a truck loaded with dynamite nearby. Colonel Crittendon is assigned to watch the plant until midnight and report on the damage. But he gets the time wrong and returns to Stalag 13 three hours early in a truck he found parked near the plant. It's *the* truck, of course, and he parks it just outside the barracks. Quick thinking enables Hogan to arrange for Hochstetter to drive the dynamite truck back to the ball bearing plant just in time for the explosion.

## EPISODE 97. "TO THE GESTAPO WITH LOVE"

Original airdate: October 26, 1968
Writer: Arthur Julian
Director: Bruce Bilson
Guest cast: Howard Caine (Major Hochstetter), Sabrina Scharf (Inge Wagner), Christiane Schmidtmer (Heidi Baum), Inge Jaklin (Anna Mannheim)

Carter loses a uniform button at a sabotage site. The "U.S." imprint on the button causes Hochstetter to suspect Hogan's crew. He arrives at camp with a new interrogation team, made up of three beautiful women. The moonstruck prisoners all fight for the girls' attention. After LeBeau inadvertently spills some secret information, Hogan breaks up the team by turning the girls against each other. But first he uses his time alone with one of the frauleins to finish a sabotage job on a bridge.

## EPISODE 98. "MAN'S BEST FRIEND IS NOT HIS DOG"

Original airdate: November 2, 1968
Writer: Phil Sharp
Director: Bruce Bilson
Guest cast: Leon Askin (General Burkhalter), Katherine Henryk (Hanna), Chet Stratton (Kraft), Dick Wilson (Bonner)

Carter photographs the new German tanks, but he leaves the camera in the prison yard, where Klink finds it. Where there is a camera, there must be film, and Klink wants it. Hogan must hold onto the film until his contact, Rumplestilskin, arrives to pick it up. When Klink's guards search the barracks, Hogan slips the film inside a bone, which he gives to the mutt the prisoners have been keeping as a pet. The dog naturally buries the bone. When Hogan meets Rumplestilskin, he has no film to turn over, until the dog finally appears with the missing bone.

**Highlight:** Subtlety is not Schultz's strong suit. When he instructs the prisoners to clean the prison yard so they will find the camera and admit ownership, the men see right through his poor acting. They put on a charade of their own—picking up all the litter in the yard but walking around the camera as though they don't see it.

**The heroes discuss a mission.** © Bing Crosby Productions, Inc. Reprinted with permission.

## EPISODE 99. "NEVER PLAY CARDS WITH STRANGERS"

Original airdate: November 9, 1968
Writer: Laurence Marks
Director: Marc Daniels
Guest cast: Dan Tobin (General von Treger), Arlene Martel (Olga), Jay Sheffield (Captain Moss), Walter Kightly (First Sentry), David Morick (Lieutenant Vogel)

The heroes are ordered to knock out a heavily guarded rocket fuel depot. The depot commander, General von Treger, invites Hogan to a bridge game in Klink's quarters. During the game, Hogan hears von Treger change the security codes on all trucks entering the depot. Kinch races to warn Newkirk and Carter, who are en route to sabotage the plant. The next evening, LeBeau drugs the guards and the card players, so Hogan can sneak out of camp in von Treger's car and sabotage the plant. His absence never detected, Hogan returns to the card table and rouses the others moments before the explosion.

## EPISODE 100. "COLOR THE LUFTWAFFE RED"

Original airdate: November 16, 1968
Writer: Laurence Marks
Director: Marc Daniels
Guest cast: Leon Askin (General Burkhalter), John Crawford (Gestapo Man), Arthur Hanson (German Colonel), James Vickery (Major Vogel)

The heroes volunteer for painting duty at Luftwaffe Intelligence headquarters so they can plant a bug inside the building. The job comes with another bonus: The men steal a map of German fighter deployments. Getting the map out of Luftwaffe headquarters and back to camp proves tricky, especially when Schultz insists upon stopping off for a beer at the hofbrau. The Gestapo catches up with the POWs at the hofbrau and subjects them to a search. Newkirk's sleight of hand saves the day.

## EPISODE 101. "GUESS WHO CAME TO DINNER"

Original airdate: November 23, 1968
Writer: Arthur Julian
Director: Marc Daniels
Guest cast: Milton Selzer (Otto von Krubner), Marj Dusay (Heidi Eberhardt), Ned Glass (Max), Walter Morgan (Curt)

After arranging the escape of a beautiful underground agent, Hogan learns that she is suspected as a double agent. The evidence against Heidi mounts when she shows up at camp on the arm of Otto von Krubner, a German munitions expert. She maintains her innocence and gives Hogan the location of von Krubner's munitions factory as proof of her loyalty to the Allies. The factory is bombed and von Krubner knows Heidi was the leak. Newkirk intercepts von Krubner's call to the Gestapo and sends underground agents in Gestapo uniforms to pick Heidi up and get her out of Germany.

**Familiar faces:** Marj Dusay played Blair Warner's wealthy mother on *The Facts of Life* (1979-88), and Alexandra Spaulding on the daytime drama *Guiding Light* from 1993 to 1997.

## EPISODE 102. "NO NAMES PLEASE"

Original airdate: November 30, 1968
Writer: Laurence Marks
Director: Marc Daniels

Guest cast: Howard Caine (Major Hochstetter), Richard Erdman (Walter Hobson), James B. Sikking (Private Berger)

The men save the life of an American war correspondant, who publishes a glowing account of the heroes' operation when he returns home. The newspaper does not name names, but Hochstetter immediately suspects Hogan. The major plants a spy, Private Berger, among Klink's guards. Berger's snooping jeopardizes Hogan's latest mission—delivering a radio to an underground contact. The men divert the Germans by staging an escape and inviting Klink. While Klink, Schultz, Hochstetter, and Berger are busy "capturing" three of the prisoners as they climb into a tunnel, Kinch and Carter sneak out of camp with the radio.

**Familiar faces:** James B. Sikking went on to TV fame as Lieutenant Howard Hunter on *Hill Street Blues* and the senior Dr. Howser on *Doogie Howser, M.D.* Sikking says that he remembers his experience on *Hogan's Heroes* fondly and was thrilled to be working with such a fine group of actors.

### EPISODE 103. "BAD DAY IN BERLIN"

Original airdate: December 7, 1968
Writer: Laurence Marks
Director: Richard Kinon
Guest cast: Harold J. Stone (Major Teppel), John Stephenson (Decker), Edward Knight (Major Metzger), John Hoyt (Colonel Braun), David Wiley (Agent)

Decker, a German spy operating inside Allied Intelligence in London, has fled to Germany with a briefcase full of information deadly to the Allied cause. The heroes drug the spy, but before they can escape with the briefcase, the Gestapo arrives, forcing Hogan to masquerade as Decker. Outside Decker's hotel, Hogan sets down the briefcase to light a cigarette. A Gestapo officer picks it up and leads the way to the waiting car, and is shot by underground agents who believe he is Decker. In the confusion, Hogan absconds with the briefcase. Decker is transported back to London to stand trial.

### EPISODE 104. "WILL THE BLUE BARON STRIKE AGAIN?"

Original airdate: December 14, 1968
Writer: Arthur Julian
Director: Marc Daniels

Guest cast: Leon Askin (General Burkhalter), Henry Corden (General von Richter/Blue Baron), Celeste Yarnall (Nanny), Laurie Mitchell (Honey Hornburg), Jon Cedar (Corporal Langenscheidt), Cynthia Lynn (Girl)

A flying ace known as the Blue Baron has been transferred to a fighter base near Stalag 13. In order to find out the location of the Blue Baron's base, Hogan hornswoggles the kommandant into throwing a party and inviting his "old friend," the flying ace. It requires fancy footwork (and some exotic dancers) to entice the baron to come to Klink's party. Once there, he doesn't want to leave, so Hogan pretends to be the Blue Baron and has his driver take him to the base. The heroes set a fire for Allied bombers to follow, and the base is knocked out.

**Familiar faces:** Cynthia Lynn, Helga from the first season, plays the dancer who flirts with the Blue Baron at Klink's party.

Jon Cedar appeared on *Hogan's Heroes* frequently, usually in the role of Corporal Langenscheidt, one of Klink's guards. As the series progressed, Cedar guest-starred as various German officers and returned to the role of Langenscheidt less frequently. Langenscheidt was written into this script as a substitute for Sergeant Schultz, as John Banner does not appear in the episode.

## EPISODE 105. "WILL THE REAL COLONEL KLINK PLEASE STAND UP AGAINST THE WALL?"

Original airdate: December 21, 1968
Writer: Bill Davenport
Director: Richard Kinon
Guest cast: Leon Askin (General Burkhalter), Howard Caine (Major Hochstetter), Noam Pitlik (Captain Herber)

Hochstetter and Burkhalter suspect Klink may be responsible for sabotaging three German trains. Captain Herber of the Gestapo is assigned to monitor Klink's actions. A train carrying aircraft engines is the next target for sabotage, and Carter tackles the job disguised as Klink. Herber sees "Klink" leaving camp and calls the station to warn them of the impending sabotage, but Newkirk intercepts the call. To keep Klink from the firing squad, Hogan provides him with an alibi by causing Sergeant Schultz to fall through Klink's bedroom door and awaken the kommandant. For good measure, Hogan pegs Herber as the saboteur.

## EPISODE 106. "MAN IN A BOX"

Original airdate: December 28, 1968
Writer: Laurence Marks
Director: Richard Kinon
Guest cast: Jill Donohue (Luise Mueller), John Crawford (Gestapo Major), Diana Chesney (Woman Clerk), Walter Janowitz (Oscar Schnitzer), L. E. Young (Guard)

In order to gain access to a laboratory where a new magnetic mine is being developed, LeBeau is sealed inside a box. In the guise of Gestapo soldiers, the heroes stop a supply truck headed for the lab and while Hogan speaks with the driver, the others load the box containing LeBeau on board the truck. Once inside the lab, LeBeau blows open the safe and steals the blueprints of the magnetic mine, setting fire to the place as he leaves.

**Familiar faces:** This was the first of four guest appearances for Diana Chesney, who had been a regular on Ed Feldman's series *Fair Exchange* (1962–63), and also appeared in such shows as *Bewitched*, *It Takes a Thief*, and *The Monkees*.

## EPISODE 107. "THE MISSING KLINK"

Original airdate: January 4, 1969
Writer: Bill Davenport
Director: Marc Daniels
Guest cast: Leon Askin (General Burkhalter), Howard Caine (Major Hochstetter), Chris Robinson (Karl Wagner), Ann Prentiss (Ilse), Dick Wilson (Captain Gruber)

Hogan's plans to free underground leader Hans Wagner by taking General Burkhalter hostage and offering him for trade go awry when Klink is mistakenly kidnapped instead. Burkhalter and Hochstetter refuse to consider the kidnappers' demands, claiming that Wagner is too important to trade for a nobody like Klink. To boost Klink's importance to the Germans, Hogan leads them to believe that the colonel is really Nimrod, a famous British spy. They trade Klink for Wagner, then promptly arrest Klink for treason. Once Wagner is free, Hochstetter discovers he has been fooled—Klink really is a nobody after all.

**Highlight:** An interesting twist ends the segment, when the model blueprints Hogan convinced the Germans were top secret plans of a German rocket turn out to be genuine. A note inside the plans requests that they be smuggled out of camp and is signed Nimrod, suggesting that perhaps Klink is working with the British underground. Nah!

**Familiar faces:** Soap opera fans will recognize Chris Robinson as Dr. Rick Webber from *General Hospital* (1978–86), Jason Frame from *Another World,* and Jack Hamilton from *The Bold and the Beautiful* (1992–95).

## EPISODE 108. "WHO STOLE MY COPY OF MEIN KAMPF?"

Original airdate: January 11, 1969
Writer: Phil Sharp
Director: Bruce Bilson
Guest cast: Ruta Lee (Leslie Smythe-Beddoes), Leon Askin (General Burkhalter), Alan Oppenheimer (Colonel Sitzer)

Hogan is ordered to silence British defector Leslie Smythe-Beddoes, now of the German Propaganda Ministry. Upon learning that his intended victim is a woman, Hogan decides not to kill her. Instead, he gets himself invited to appear on a propaganda broadcast and uses the opportunity to publicly discredit Beddoes. Hogan has convinced Beddoes that he has been won over by Hitler's beliefs, but when she interviews him on air, he claims to be an ex-convict and insults Adolf Hitler. Beddoes is told by her superior that her usefulness to the Third Reich has come to an end.

**Notes:** *Mein Kampf* (German for "My Struggle"), a political manifesto written by Adolf Hitler, became the bible of Nazism in Germany's Third Reich. First published in 1925, by 1939 it had sold 5.2 million copies and had been translated into eleven languages. In the book, Hitler expressed his racist ideology and outlined the political program, including terrorist methods, that the Nazis must pursue in gaining and maintaining power. Few readers at the time of its publication believed that the leader intended to carry out every phase of his stated program. Hitler's own original title for the book was "Four and a Half Years of Struggle Against Lies, Stupidity, and Cowardice."

## EPISODE 109. "OPERATION HANNIBAL"

Original airdate: January 18, 1969
Writer: Laurence Marks
Director: Bruce Bilson
Guest cast: John Hoyt (General von Behler), Louise Troy (Hedy von Behler), Dick Wilson (Captain Gruber), Jack Riley (Captain), Frank Deal (Sergeant)

Hogan's latest accomplice is Hedy von Behler, a German general's daughter who is one of the Allies best spies. She invites Hogan to a party at her father's house so that he can access top secret guerrilla warfare plans in his safe. While Hogan and Hedy distract the guards and keep the general away from his study, Carter and LeBeau photograph the plans. All is nearly lost when Colonel Klink makes a surprise appearance at the party, but Hogan does some fancy footwork to avoid him.

## EPISODE 110. "MY FAVORITE PRISONER"

Original airdate: January 25, 1969
Writer: Laurence Marks
Director: Bruce Bilson
Guest cast: Howard Caine (Major Hochstetter), Marj Dusay (Baroness von Krimm), John Orchard (Captain Sears), James Sikking (Gestapo Officer)

Colonel Klink thinks he's hatched a clever plan to pry secrets out of Colonel Hogan, using a beautiful baroness as bait. While Hogan romances the baroness, Klink listens in via a hidden microphone. Hogan easily discerns the ruse, and decides to use Klink's eavesdropping to pass phony invasion plans to the Gestapo. A British underground agent shows up on the baroness's doorstep with the phony plans, which he will pass to an underground agent. Hochstetter sends Schultz as the courier, but Schultz forgets the password! Sears gives him the phony plans, which are believed to be genuine by the Germans.

**Highlight:** Schultz would never have made it in the spy business. Not only does his approach lack subtlety, he also flubs the simple code: "The birds fly south—before the first snow." Each mangled attempt is funnier than the last.

## EPISODE 111. "WATCH THE TRAINS GO BY"

Original airdate: February 1, 1969
Writer: Laurence Marks
Director: Bruce Bilson
Guest cast: Leon Askin (General Burkhalter), Alice Ghostley (Gertrude Linkmeyer)

A German patrol hinders the heroes' attempt to blow up a munitions train. Hogan must return to the railroad tracks to finish the job, but Klink has beefed up camp security in anticipation of General Burkhalter's visit. To distract the kommandant, Hogan arranges for Burkhalter to bring his sister Gertrude along. The marriage-minded widow hopes to finally snag Klink as a husband. Klink turns to Hogan for help in avoiding such a fate. Hogan has the kommandant take Gertrude for a drive to the railroad tracks to "let her down easy." While the couple is parked, Hogan climbs out of the trunk and finishes mining the track.

**Notes:** The role of Gertrude Linkmeyer, usually portrayed by Kathleen Freeman, is played in this episode by Alice Ghostley. In the closing credits, Gertrude's last name is spelled "Linkmaier," but in other episodes, it is "Linkmeyer." Ghostley's other TV roles include Esmeralda on *Bewitched* (1969–72) and Bernice on *Designing Women* (1987–93).

## EPISODE 112. "KLINK'S OLD FLAME"

Original airdate: February 8, 1969
Writer: Arthur Julian
Director: Bruce Bilson
Guest cast: Leon Askin (General Burkhalter), Ben Wright (Count Rudolf von Heffernick), Norma Eberhardt (Marlene Schneider), Arthur Hanson (Willy), David Morick (Guard), Norbert Schiller (Farmer Hans)

Hogan must transport five shortwave radios to the French underground. Plan A, which called for LeBeau's transfer to a stalag near Paris, fails when visiting Count von Heffernick orders the prisoner sent to Stalag 14 instead. The count has come to camp to see if there are still any sparks between his girlfriend Marlene and her old flame—Colonel Klink. Klink cancels LeBeau's transfer in exchange for Hogan's assistance. To ensure Marlene's disinterest, Klink puts on a charade of drunken inefficiency. Satisfied that Marlene does not love Klink, von Heffernick proposes, and the couple travels to Paris for their honeymoon—with the shortwave radios hidden in their car.

**Highlight:** Klink's drunken charade is undoubtedly one of the series' funnies scenes, with Hogan, Schultz, and Hilda also getting in on the act. As Schultz reprimands "Willy" for his inefficiency and Hogan tries to sober up the old souse, the unshaven kommandant accosts fraulein Hilda and shows no surprise when Schultz announces that eleven prisoners—and eleven guards—have escaped.

**Notes:** LeBeau had good reason to fear being transferred to Colditz. Colditz, reserved for the most avid, troublesome escapers, was one of the most heavily guarded prisoner-of-war camps. In the early years of World War II, the number of guards usually equaled the number of prisoners. The *oflag* ("officer's camp") was the setting for a BBC television series, *Colditz* (1972–74), starring David McCallum and Robert Wagner.

## EPISODE 113. "UP IN KLINK'S ROOM"

Original airdate: February 15, 1969
Writers: Harvey Bullock and Ray S. Allen
Director: Bruce Bilson
Guest cast: Henry Corden (Doctor Klaus), Muriel Landers (Second Nurse), Forrest Compton (Major Zimmer), Victoria Carroll (Nurse Gerda)

When Hogan learns that his contact, Major Zimmer, is being transported to a German hospital, he arranges for Klink to be injured and taken to the medical facility. Unfortunately, Klink isn't badly hurt and is released before Zimmer arrives. Desperate to remain at the hospital, Hogan decides to become a patient himself. Dr. Klaus, the hospital administrator, has written a book on Eskimo diseases, and Hogan picks one to contract. When Klaus observes Hogan's strange symptoms, he declares that the POW has "polaris extremis" and admits him to the hospital. Hogan makes contact with Zimmer, who passes along vital information.

**Highlight:** Klink and Schultz's attempt to catch Hogan and Newkirk escaping from the hospital is a comedy of errors. Having tipped the kommandant off about the "escape" in advance, Hogan and Newkirk can't seem to get Klink or Schultz to capture them, despite intentionally knocking over trash cans and calling attention to themselves.

## EPISODE 114. "THE PURCHASING PLAN"

Original airdate: February 22, 1969
Writer: Laurence Marks
Director: Marc Daniels
Guest cast: Leon Askin (General Burkhalter), Howard Caine (Major Hochstetter), Walter Janowitz (Oscar Schnitzer), Inger Wegge (Heidi)

Faced with the task of delivering ammunition to four different locations, Hogan develops a plan whereby Klink purchases and distributes all the supplies for the stalags in the area. General Burkhalter agrees to implement the cost-cutting plan, which Klink claims was his own. Appointed foreman of the operation, Carter loads the ammunition on the supply truck in specially marked boxes. The underground groups employ different tactics to retrieve their ammo from the truck along the delivery route.

**Notes:** As in many series, some of the sets and buildings used on *Hogan's Heroes* were recycled for other purposes. The building used as the exterior of Burkhalter's office in Berlin was also Hochstetter's office in Episode #66 ("Sergeant Schultz Meets Mata Hari") and Gestapo headquarters in Paris in Episode #42 ("A Tiger Hunt in Paris"). In fact, watch closely and you'll see that the footage of the building is identical, with the same car pulling up and people walking by.

## EPISODE 115. "THE WITNESS"

Original airdate: March 1, 1969
Writer: Richard M. Powell
Director: Marc Daniels
Guest cast: Nita Talbot (Marya), Howard Caine (Major Hochstetter), Gavin MacLeod (General von Rauscher), Larry D. Mann (Illyich Igor Zagoskin)

Marya returns to camp on the arm of General von Rauscher, who is supervising the testing of a new rocket. At Marya's suggestion, Hogan has been selected to witness a demonstration of the rocket and report its effectiveness to the Allies. The target—a British battleship with 3,000 men aboard. The rocket's inventor, a Russian scientist, reveals he hasn't been taken in by the Germans. The rocket will take off, then return and kill everyone on site. Hogan gains access to the rocket and sabotages its controls. When tested, the rocket topples over and explodes.

## EPISODE 116. "THE BIG DISH"

Original airdate: March 8, 1969
Writer: Ben Gershman
Director: Edward H. Feldman
Guest cast: Howard Caine (Major Hochstetter), Paul Lambert (General Reicker), Karen Steele (Lady Valerie Stanford), Laurie Main (Air Marshal Woodhouse), George Cisar (General Boland), Chet Stratton (Professor Burrows), David Wiley (Radar Operator), Walter Kightly (Technician)

Hogan is ordered to destroy Germany's latest antiaircraft weapon and find its inventor, Lady Valerie Stanford, a British beauty with questionable loyalties. The radar is brought to Stalag 13 for testing. When Hogan meets Lady Valerie, she claims she is still loyal to England. But then she betrays

Hogan to the Gestapo. Rather than destroy the antiaircraft unit, the men sabotage it. When the unit is tested, it malfunctions and causes German planes to be lost. Hogan implicates Lady Stanford as the saboteur and she is arrested by the Gestapo.

## EPISODE 117. "THE RETURN OF MAJOR BONACELLI"

Original airdate: March 15, 1969
Writer: Arthur Julian
Director: Jerry London
Guest cast: Howard Caine (Major Hochstetter), Vito Scotti (MajoBonacelli), Marion Brash (Gretchen), Diana Chesney (Radio Operator)

The Gestapo is on to Major Bonacelli, Hogan's contact in Italy. Bonacelli escapes to Switzerland, stopping by Stalag 13 on his way. Hogan needs photographs of the German's new antiaircraft guns and convinces Bonacelli to obtain them before leaving Germany. Unaware that Bonacelli has defected, Klink takes his star pupil on an inspection tour of the new guns. Klink even poses for photographs in front of one of the guns! When Hochstetter arrives in pursuit of Bonacelli, Hogan, LeBeau, and Newkirk sneak out of camp to warn the Italian major.

**Highlight:** The German cuisine takes a lashing in this episode. Bonacelli is horrified at the prospect of eating sauerbraten (roasted beef marinated in vinegar and spices before cooking) and Wiener schnitzel (a thin breaded veal cutlet); when he is indisposed after the mission, he says he is suffering from an "acute case of Wiener schnitzel." Carter announces his belief that Wiener schnitzel was outlawed at the Geneva Convention along with cruel and inhuman treatment.

**Familiar faces:** Character actor Vito Scotti's most memorable TV roles include Dr. Balinkoff on *Gilligan's Island,* Sam Picasso on *The Addams Family,* and Captain Fomento on *The Flying Nun.* In this episode, he played Major Bonacelli, a character originated by Hans Conried in Episode #22, "The Pizza Parlor." According to Scotti, he was offered the role of Bonacelli first, but he was busy with another project. When the second Bonacelli script was written, he was available. In an interview prior to his death, the actor described his experience on *Hogan's Heroes* as "wonderful," and added that "the director allowed me to give my input." That director was Jerry London, who made his directorial debut with this episode.

**Behind the scenes:** London's first day directing happened to be his birthday. Howard Caine recalled, "Nobody knew it. I knew it, because we had gotten to be friends. I told Teddy, the prop man, about it, and at the end of the day, Teddy had a big sheet cake decorated as Stalag 13. The whole camp was laid out on there. It was amazing."

## EPISODE 118. "HAPPY BIRTHDAY, DEAR HOGAN"

Original airdate: March 22, 1969
Writer: Arthur Julian
Director: Marc Daniels
Guest cast: Howard Caine (Major Hochstetter), Barbara Babcock (Mama Bear)

Unaware that they are falling into a Gestapo trap, the POWs plan a sabotage mission as a surprise birthday present for Colonel Hogan. Hogan suspends all operations when he learns of the Gestapo plot. Kinch can't radio London to cancel the mission because a radio-detection truck has been brought into camp. Unable to contact the underground, the men admit their blunder. As part of Hogan's plan, the men throw a party in the compound yard. When the candles are lit on the booby-trapped birthday cake, it explodes, knocking out the radio detector. Kinch radios London and the mission is scrapped.

# FIFTH SEASON (1969-70)

Aired Fridays, 8:30–9:00 P.M.,
opposite *Mr. Deeds Goes to Town* on ABC and
*The Name of the Game* on NBC.

### Fifth Season Technical Credits

Executive Producer: Edward H. Feldman
Producer: William A. Calihan
Associate Producer: Jerry London
Theme Music: Jerry Fielding
Director of Photography: Gordon Avil
Art Director: Howard Hollander
Film Editors: Michael Kahn, Beryl Gelfond, Ken Zemke
Assistant Director: Floyd Joyer
Unit Production Manager: William A. Calihan

Set Decorator: William L. Stevens
Makeup: Armand Delmar
Costumes: Ray R. Harp, Marjorie Wahl
Post-Production Supervisor: Houseley Stevenson
Music Supervisor: Milton Lustig
Sound Editor: Bob Henderson
Production Mixer: Wallace Bearden
Re-recording Mixer: Gordon L. Day
Filmed at Cinema General Studios for Bing Crosby Productions

## EPISODE 119. "HOGAN GOES HOLLYWOOD"

Original airdate: September 26, 1969
Writer: Richard M. Powell
Story by: Tony Thomas
Director: Edward H. Feldman
Guest cast: Leon Askin (General Burkhalter), Alan Oppenheimer (Major Byron Buckles), Victoria Carroll (Actress Playing Nurse)

The arrival of a new prisoner—Hollywood star Byron Buckles—has Klink planning to make a film about Stalag 13. At first the men are opposed, but when Hogan realizes that the filming could aid them in their plan to blow up a heavily guarded bridge, they go along with it. Hogan writes and directs the film, in which Schultz plays Klink and Klink is Schultz. Even Burkhalter gets into the act, granting Hogan access to the bridge. Hogan substitutes real dynamite for the fake explosives supplied by Klink for the filming. When the cameras roll, the Germans push the detonator and blow up their own bridge!

**Highlights:** Neither Schultz nor Klink would have fared well as movie stars. Klink forgets his simple line ("Achtung!") and Schultz constantly upstages the star. Their role reversal is made more amusing by the fact that Werner Klemperer was once considered for the role of Schultz, and John Banner for the role of Klink. Seeing the characters impersonate one another gives viewers a sense of what might have been had the casting gone the other way.

## EPISODE 120. "THE WELL"

Original airdate: October 3, 1969
Writer: Laurence Marks
Director: Bruce Bilson
Guest cast: Leon Askin (General Burkhalter), Michael Fox (Captain Ritter)

Newkirk steals a German code book from Klink's safe, but when Schultz intercepts him, he drops the book into a dry well. To gain access to the well, the heroes blow up the waterworks in Hammelburg, leaving the camp without water. The heroes are allowed to dig in the well to reactivate it. They retrieve the code book, but when Schultz decides to search them, they drop the book into the well, which is slowly filling with water. They finally succeed in retrieving the code book by lowering poor Carter into ten feet of freezing water.

**Familiar faces:** British actor Michael Fox played Amos Fedders on *Falcon Crest* (1988–89) and Saul Feinberg on *The Bold and the Beautiful* (1989–96).

## EPISODE 121. "THE KLINK COMMANDOS"

Original airdate: October 10, 1969
Writer: Richard M. Powell
Director: Edward H. Feldman
Guest cast: Nita Talbot (Marya), Frank Marth (Count Von Waffenschmidt)

Marya arrives in camp with Count von Waffenschmidt, whose attaché case contains important documents. German intelligence suspects Marya of leaking military secrets to the Russians. When Hogan and Newkirk attempt to steal the attaché case, they are arrested as part of her spy ring. As part of an elaborate plan to free them, Carter masquerades as a German general and assembles a suicide squad made up of prisoners and lead by Klink. "Klink's Commandos" board the same train as Marya and the count. The heroes drug the count, steal the plans, and hijack the train back to Stalag 13.

## EPISODE 122. "THE GASOLINE WAR"

Original airdate: October 17, 1969
Writer: Laurence Marks
Director: Richard Kinon
Guest cast: Mariana Hill (Louisa/Eskimo), Eric Morris (Captain Streicker), Bruce Kirby (Franz), Richard Alden (Bartender)

A fueling pump for German convoys is erected outside of Stalag 13. Hogan is ordered to destroy the pump, as having a fueling station at Stalag 13 would shorten the Germans' traveling time to France. Hogan cannot destroy the pump without endangering prisoners' lives, so he decides to blow up the first convoy of trucks instead. As the trucks pull up to fuel, the prisoners slide underneath each one and attach dynamite charges. When all twenty-two trucks in the convoy are blown up less than twenty miles from Stalag 13, the location is deemed to be unsafe for the pump.

**Familiar faces:** Bruce Kirby's roles include Jamie Lee Curtis's father on TV's *Anything but Love*. He is the father of actor Bruno Kirby (*When Harry Met Sally...*, *City Slickers*).

## EPISODE 123. "UNFAIR EXCHANGE"

Original airdate: October 24, 1969
Writer: Laurence Marks
Director: Richard Kinon
Guest cast: Howard Caine (Major Hochstetter), Leon Askin (General Burkhalter), Kathleen Freeman (Gertrude Linkmeyer), Wendy Wilson (Maria Hoffman)

Maria Hoffman, a female underground agent who risked her life for Hogan and his men, is captured by the Gestapo. The heroes decide to kidnap General Burkhalter's sister Gertrude and arrange a trade. The men hold the blindfolded Frau Linkmeyer in the tunnel, convincing her she is in a hotel room in Düsseldorf. At first Hochstetter refuses to give in to the kidnappers' demands, but under pressure from Burkhalter, he eventually complies. Once Maria is released, Hogan brings Gertrude to an old barn where he has also sent Schultz and the Gestapo.

## EPISODE 124. "THE KOMMANDANT DIES AT DAWN"

Original airdate: October 31, 1969
Writer: Arthur Julian
Director: Richard Kinon
Guest cast: Ned Wertimer (Field Marshal Kesselring), Ben Wright (Major Feldkamp), Inger Stratton (Fraulein Ziegler), Walter Janowitz (German Vendor)

The men keep running into obstacles when they try to transport a vital piece of information to the underground. They plant the information on Klink when the kommandant goes to a cocktail party in town with Field Marshal Kesselring. But Klink blabs military secrets to impress a beautiful fraulein and is arrested for treason. To save Klink from the firing squad, Hogan convinces Kesselring that the kommandant saved the Field Marshal's life. Once freed, Klink heads off to a celebration in town—where underground agents are waiting to pick up the information.

**Highlights:** Klink's guards may not hold him in high regard (Schultz reveals that seventy-six out of Klink's eighty-two men have volunteered for his firing squad, then adds that the remaining six are either in the hospital or on furlough), but Schultz himself offers to help the kommandant escape to Switzerland. When Klink and Schultz (à la Laurel and Hardy) try to engineer Klink's escape, the results are calamitous.

**Familiar faces:** Ned Wertimer played Ralph the doorman on *The Jeffersons* (CBS, 1975–85). The German vendor is portrayed by Walter Janowitz, who usually plays the part of Schnitzer, the dogkeeper.

## EPISODE 125. "BOMBSIGHT"

Original airdate: November 7, 1969
Writers: Ray S. Allen and Harvey Bullock
Director: Richard Kinon
Guest cast: Leon Askin (General Burkhalter)

The Germans are using Stalag 13 as a testing site for "chickenhawks"—bombs with an aiming device that zeroes in on radio signals. Attempts to photograph blueprints of the bombs for the Allies are thwarted by Klink's unwitting interference. Instead of copying the plans, Hogan decides to discredit the new bomb so the Germans will halt its production. The men hide radios around camp and disconnect the transmitter leading to the test target. When the test commences, the bombs zero in on the radios planted by Hogan rather than their intended target. The chickenhawks are pronounced a complete failure.

## EPISODE 126. "THE BIG PICTURE"

Original airdate: November 14, 1969
Writer: Laurence Marks
Director: Bruce Bilson
Guest cast: Sandy Kenyon (Captain Bohrmann), Diana Chesney (Hotel Clerk)

Captain Bohrmann of the Gestapo is blackmailing Klink with a chummy photo of the kommandant with a general who was involved in a plot to assassinate Hitler. Fearful of being arrested as a conspirator, Klink dips into the stalag till to pay the blackmailer. In order to save Klink—and the camp finances—Hogan must swipe the photo and negative from Bohrmann. Hogan, Newkirk, and LeBeau go into Hammelburg and rent the hotel room next to Bohrmann's. While Newkirk and LeBeau rouse Bohrmann from his bed, Hogan sneaks into his room and steals the negative.

**Highlight:** A comic high point of this episode is the scene in which Newkirk and LeBeau stage a drunken brawl in the hotel corridor to distract Bohrmann while Hogan steals the negative.

## EPISODE 127. "THE BIG GAMBLE"

Original airdate: November 21, 1969
Writer: Laurence Marks
Director: Marc Daniels
Guest cast: Ben Wright (Major Feldkamp), Chet Stratton (Dr. Wolfgang Becker), Noam Pitlik (Captain John Mitchell), Lincoln Deyman (Dealer)

An American plane is shot down and the wreckage lands just outside Stalag 13. The pilot, Captain Mitchell, tells Hogan that the plane was equipped with a top secret directional finder, which must not fall into enemy hands. Dr. Becker, a Gestapo scientist, finds the DF box and places it in a briefcase chained to his wrist. To gain access to the briefcase, Hogan and the men exploit Becker's weakness for gambling. They set up a casino and lure Becker in. During a staged blackout, they steal the DF box in Becker's briefcase and replace it with a phony version built by Carter.

## EPISODE 128. "THE DEFECTOR"

Original airdate: November 28, 1969
Writer: Laurence Marks
Director: Jerry London
Guest cast: Howard Caine (Major Hochstetter), Harold J. Stone (Field Marshal Rudolf Richter), Arlene Martel (Gretchen)

Hogan accepts a dangerous mission: helping Field Marshal Rudolf Richter defect to England. The Gestapo suspects the field marshal of treason, and Major Hochstetter has trailed Richter to Stalag 13. Knowing that the Gestapo will never stop searching until they find Richter, the heroes make it appear that the field marshal is dead. They put a dummy dressed in Richter's uniform in the field marshal's car and send it towards the wire. Hochstetter shoots the tires just as the dynamite Hogan placed in the car explodes. Hochstetter believes he hit the gasoline tank and caused the field marshal's death.

## EPISODE 129. "THE EMPTY PARACHUTE"

Original airdate: December 5, 1969
Writer: Phil Sharp
Director: Marc Daniels
Guest cast: Howard Caine (Major Hochstetter), Parley Baer (Julius Schlager), Ronald Long (Major Blair)

A V.I.P. arrives in camp with a briefcase manacled to his wrist. Hogan convinces the V.I.P. that an enemy agent has sneaked into camp to steal the briefcase. Klink puts the case in his safe, where it is in Hogan's "back pocket." While the Germans are focusing on to Hitler's radio speech, Newkirk opens the safe and steals the briefcase from under their noses. The case contains counterfeit American money and plates, which are close to perfect. To prevent the Nazis from flooding the economy with phony money, Hogan makes a few creative adjustments to the plates before returning the briefcase to Klink's safe.

## EPISODE 130. "THE ANTIQUE"

Original airdate: December 12, 1969
Writer: Arthur Julian
Director: Bruce Bilson
Guest cast: Leon Askin (General Burkhalter), Mari Oliver (Kristina), Brenda Benet (French Girl)

The Germans have infiltrated the underground courier system, and Hogan must devise an alternate method of distributing plans to five occupied cities. Hogan comes through with a plan which calls for the unwitting aid of Colonel Klink. The kommandant has purchased a cheap cuckoo clock and Hogan offers him $100 for the "antique." Klink greedily buys fifty more clocks and goes into the antique business. Hogan inserts the secret plans in five clocks destined for the occupied cities, where agents will be waiting for their arrival.

## EPISODE 131. "IS THERE A TRAITOR IN THE HOUSE?"

Original airdate: December 19, 1969
Writer: Arthur Julian
Director: Marc Daniels
Guest cast: Antoinette Bower (Berlin Betty), Victoria Carroll (English Girl)

Kinch's radio equipment has been damaged and the heroes have no way of transmitting vital information to London. To get the message out, Newkirk turns traitor, volunteering to appear on propagandist Berlin Betty's radio program asking his countrymen to surrender. Newkirk almost backs out when Berlin Betty tells him that the Gestapo is holding her family and forcing her to do propaganda broadcasts against her will. At the heroes' urging, he delivers his speech, which contains the information in code. When the broadcast is over, Newkirk learns that Betty was only testing him and that she is a loyal German.

**Notes:** The Nazi Propoganda Ministry was created in 1933 and directed by Joseph Goebbels, Reich Minister for Public Enlightenment and Propaganda. A student of American advertising and promotion techniques, Goebbels applied them in shaping the thoughts and opinions of the German nation. Goebbels took complete control over every means of molding the minds of the German people—press, radio, books, plays, music, art, and sports—effectually becoming the dictator of the cultural life of Germany.

## EPISODE 132. "AT LAST— SCHULTZ KNOWS SOMETHING"

Original airdate: December 26, 1969
Writer: Laurence Marks
Director: Bruce Bilson
Guest cast: Leon Askin (General Burkhalter), John Myhers (Dr. Hermann Felzer), Jack Riley (Guard), Fay Spain (Carla), Dave Morick (Officer)

Klink is appointed head of security at a new atomic research laboratory. The heroes must destroy the lab, but Schultz refuses to divulge its location. Posing as a Luftwaffe doctor, Newkirk injects the sergeant with sodium pentathol (truth serum). Under the influence of the drug, Schultz talks freely— not of the laboratory, but of the food he ate while he was there! The heroes deduce that the lab is in Flenzheim. They destroy the lab by allowing the greedy guards to confiscate their baskets, which contain hollowed-out vegetables filled with dynamite.

**Highlight:** Under the influence of the truth serum, Schultz waxes poetic about the aluminum cooking utensils in the laboratory kitchen, and sings a paean to Flenzheim potatoes.

## EPISODE 133. "HOW'S THE WEATHER?"

Original airdate: January 2, 1970
Writers: Ray S. Allen and Harvey Bullock
Director: Marc Daniels
Guest cast: Leon Askin (General Burkhalter), David Morick (Radio Operator)

London is planning an attack on a hydroelectric dam near Stalag 13 and Hogan must provide daily weather reports. Hogan uses creative methods to obtain the information, including using a volleyball inflated with stove gas as a weather balloon. The men obtain additional balloons by telling Klink that they are planning a party in honor of his anniversary as camp kommandant. On the night of the raid, Hogan induces Klink to radio General Burkhalter at the dam site. The bombers are able to follow the radio signal to the dam site and knock out their target.

## EPISODE 134. "GET FIT OR GO FIGHT"

Original airdate: January 9, 1970
Writer: Bill Davenport
Director: Jerry London
Guest cast: Leon Askin (General Burkhalter), Corinne Conley (Gerda), Michael Fox (Major Kimmel)

The underground has been transporting information to the POWs in the hubcaps of Klink's car during the kommandant's visits to a barmaid in town. When Burkhalter announces that Klink must pass a physical exam or be sent to the Russian front for toughening up, the kommandant curtails his socializing. The prisoners can't persuade Klink to drive into town one last time, so Carter dons a German medical officer's uniform and gives the kommandant a clean bill of health. His mind at ease, Klink goes to see the barmaid, and the men receive the needed information.

## EPISODE 135. "FAT HERMANN, GO HOME"

Original airdate: January 16, 1970
Writer: Richard M. Powell
Director: Edward H. Feldman
Guest cast: Nita Talbot (Marya), Howard Caine (Major Hochstetter)

Russian spy Marya joins Hogan in a plan to rob Field Marshal Hermann Goering's private train of his art collection. Marya has conned Schultz into posing as Goering. She enters camp with the imposter and convinces Klink to issue orders to have Goering's train unloaded and the priceless artworks brought to Stalag 13. When Hochstetter arrives in a rage over the train robbery, Schultz masquerades as Goering long enough for the POWs to stage an attack on the camp and deliver the treasures to British planes. The Germans believe the artwork was stolen by the attackers.

**Notes:** Goering, commander of the Luftwaffe and Hitler's second-in-command, had amassed an extensive personal art collection before the war, which became even larger through expropriations in conquered countries during the War. Convicted at the Nuremburg Trial after the war, Goering committed suicide before he could be executed.

## EPISODE 136. "THE SOFTER THEY FALL"

Original airdate: January 23, 1970
Writer: Laurence Marks
Director: Richard Kinon
Guest cast: Leon Askin (General Burkhalter), John Stephenson (Major Rudel), Ralph Medina (Captain Stahl), James Savett (First Corporal), Jon Cedar (Second Corporal), Chuck Hicks (Bruno), Frankie Van (Referee)

To gain access to Luftwaffe plans to knock out the British radar network, Hogan sets up a grand scale diverson—a boxing match between prisoner Kinchloe and one of Klink's guards, "Battling Bruno." To ensure Bruno's victory, Klink puts lead weights in the boxer's gloves. The fight is broadcast over the P.A. system throughout the camp. The guards become so engrossed in the match that LeBeau easily sneaks into V.I.P. quarters and photographs the Luftwaffe plans. Though Bruno's fists of steel give him a beating, Kinch keeps the fight going long enough for LeBeau to photograph the plans and get back to the arena.

**Notes:** To impress upon Klink the importance of the German guard beating the American prisoner, Burkhalter reminds Klink of Hitler's reaction when a black American athlete, Jesse Owens, won four gold medals at the Olympic Games in Berlin in 1936. Hitler, whose racial doctrine ranked blacks along with Jews and homosexuals as inferior human beings, left the Olympic stadium before the medals were presented to the winning athletes.

## EPISODE 137. "GOWNS BY YVETTE"

Original airdate: January 30, 1970
Writer: Arthur Julian
Director: Bruce Bilson
Guest cast: Leon Askin (General Burkhalter), Muriel Landers (Frieda), Dick Wilson (Count von Hertzel), Bruce Kirby (Gestapo Man), Bruno Ve Sota (Agent)

**Schultz made an unusual bride in "Gowns by Yvette."** © Bing Crosby
Productions, Inc. Reprinted with permission.

Burkhalter's niece is to be married at the same hotel where an underground agent is being held. Hogan convinces Burkhalter that LeBeau is the famed Yvette of Paris, a French dress designer. Burkhalter commissions LeBeau to design an original wedding gown for his niece. After the wedding ceremony, the heroes stage a phony air raid. During the confusion, they detain the bride while the agent, wearing a duplicate wedding gown, walks out of the hotel on the arm of the groom, Count von Hertzel.

## YOU CAN FOOL ALL OF THE PEOPLE SOME OF THE TIME, SOME OF THE PEOPLE ALL OF THE TIME, AND COLONEL KLINK ANYTIME . . .

In order for Hogan to pull off some of his schemes, the crafty colonel had to convince Klink that his prisoners had expertise in certain fields, and therefore could be useful to the kommandant. The following are some of the phony backgrounds Hogan invented for his men.

**LeBeau:**
Before the war he was "Madame LaGrange," owner of a chain of dance schools in France. ("Six Lessons from Madame LaGrange")
He's a chemist, and was known as 'Mr. Test Tube' at the Ecole du Chimie in Paris. ("The Scientist")
He was also "Yvette of Paris," a renowned fashion designer. ("Gowns by Yvette")
He is a descendant of full-blooded gypsies. ("The Gypsy")
He was top man in the fire brigade at camp. The called him "Le Smokey." ("The Flame Grows Higher")
He's a big game hunter and expert marksman. ("Monkey Business")

**Carter:**
Was a decorator before the war. ("German Bridge Is Falling Down")
Went to business school and is therefore capable of administering the distribution of supplies to the area stalags. ("The Purchasing Plan")

**Newkirk:**
Was a successful barrister before the war. ("Klink for the Defense")
He worked as a talent scout for his uncle, a big impressario in London. ("The Big Record")
He was a fire warden in London. ("The Flame Grows Higher") ★

## EPISODE 138. "ONE ARMY AT A TIME"

Original airdate: February 13, 1970
Writer: Laurence Marks
Director: Edward H. Feldman
Guest cast: Howard Caine (Major Hochstetter), Dave Willock (Captain), Dave Morick (Sergeant)

While sabotaging a railroad bridge, the heroes are interrupted by a German patrol. The patrol spots Carter, in German uniform, and assume he is one of their soldiers. He is congratulated for finding the saboteur's dynamite and is promoted to acting corporal. When Carter finally makes it back to

Stalag 13, Hogan orders him to return to the German army long enough to recover the dynamite. Making it back in time for nightly roll calls is difficult for the double duty sergeant. He steals the dynamite, and a tank, and meets the gang at the bridge, where they complete the act of sabotage.

**Highlight:** When Carter is questioned by the German captain at the panzer division, the flustered POW can't produce his orders or recall his alias.

## EPISODE 139. "STANDING ROOM ONLY"

Original airdate: February 20, 1970
Writer: Laurence Marks
Director: Jerry London
Guest cast: Leon Askin (General Burkhalter), Noam Pitlik (Major Strauss), Forrest Compton (Captain), Eddie Firestone (POW Miller), Victoria Carroll (Sofia Lindemann)

Seven men escape from Stalag 5, and the kommandant, Major Strauss, is transferred to Stalag 13 to study Colonel Klink's methods. The major discovers discrepancies in Klink's books and threatens to turn him in, but Hogan secures his silence in exchange for the return of the seven escapees. The prisoners, who have been hiding out in Hogan's tunnel, give themselves up. A Gestapo truck arrives to transport the prisoners back to Stalag 5 and Strauss insists upon going along. The Gestapo officers are really a second group of escaping prisoners on their way to England, and Hogan tells the driver to take Strauss with them—all the way.

## EPISODE 140. "SIX LESSONS FROM MADAME LAGRANGE"

Original airdate: February 27, 1970
Writer: Arthur Julian
Director: Jerry London
Guest cast: Marlyn Mason (Lily Frankel), Leon Askin (General Burkhalter), Howard Caine (Major Hochstetter), Edward Knight (Double Agent)

Lily Frankel tells Hogan that a double agent plans to deliver a list to Major Hochstetter containing the names of several underground agents, including Hogan and his men. The heroes plan an escape, but the SS is guarding the camp. Instead, Hogan instills a rivalry between Klink and Hochstetter over Lily Frankel, which results in the major taking dance

223

lessons from LeBeau! Burkhalter arrests Hochstetter for dancing with a prisoner, and Hogan takes the major's place in the meeting with the double agent. The agent passes the list of underground members to Hogan, and the heroes' operation is saved.

**Familiar faces:** Marlyn Mason was a regular on *Ben Casey* and *Longstreet,* and starred opposite Elvis Presley in *The Trouble with Girls.* She is exceptionally fond of this episode because it gave her the chance to sing. She says that Robert Clary earned a place in her affections because he "absolutely saved me on this episode." She didn't know how to move in her singing sequences, and director Jerry London had left it up to her to come up with something. Clary had finished filming his scenes for the day and was free to go home, but stayed to help Mason. "In ten minutes he choreographed my number," she says. "He was just wonderful."

## EPISODE 141. "THE SERGEANT'S ANALYST"

Original airdate: March 6, 1970
Writer: Bill Davenport
Director: Bruce Bilson
Guest cast: Leon Askin (General Burkhalter), Bard Stevens (Guard), Norbert Schiller (Baker)

Sergeant Schultz is caught sleeping on duty and Burkhalter orders him transferred to the Russian front. This hitch comes at a bad time: The heroes have been using the sergeant to smuggle in loaves of pumpernickel containing photographs of the German West Wall fortifications. One more piece of the puzzle is needed before London has the complete picture. To save Schultz's hide, the POWs use tricks and psychology to turn him into a fierce soldier. His new attitude, along with a few bribes, convince Burkhalter to cancel Schultz's transfer. Once reinstated, the sergeant delivers a special loaf of pumpernickel to Hogan.

## EPISODE 142. "THE MERRY WIDOW"

Original airdate: March 13, 1970
Writers: Harvey Bullock and Ray S. Allen
Director: Edward H. Feldman
Guest cast: Marj Dusay (Countess Marlene), Barry O'Hara (Sergeant Meadows), Bill Henry (Florist)

Klink doubles the guards, impeding Hogan's plan to get photos of a new German land mine to London. Unable to leave camp themselves, the prisoners plant the photos in Klink's coat, and arrange a date for him with Countess Marlene, an underground agent. When he learns that he sent the wrong plans, Hogan sends Schultz as a second paramour, carrying a model of the real land mine hidden in a plant. The jealous kommandant sends Schultz back to camp, but Marlene follows. As Klink and Schultz vie for Marlene's affections, she grabs the real object of her desire—the plant.

**Highlight:** The love triangle between Marlene, Klink, and Schultz makes for some farcical moments, particularly when Marlene climbs out of Klink's window leaving Klink preparing wine and hors d'oeurves and Schultz puckered up for a kiss.

**Was ist los?** Klink pledges his devotion to Marlene 364 days a year, noting that he has to spend Christmas with his mother. But in Episode #106 he had referred to his mother as deceased.

## EPISODE 143. "CRITTENDON'S COMMANDOS"

Original airdate: March 20, 1970
Writer: Bill Davenport
Director: Edward H. Feldman
Guest cast: Bernard Fox (Colonel Crittendon), Robert Hogan (Commando Tobin)

The heroes are assigned to pick up a British commando unit and help them kidnap Field Marshal Rommel from a hospital near camp. Hogan knows the operation is doomed when he finds Colonel Crittendon leading the commando group. When Crittendon's bungling nearly ruins the operation, Hogan injects him with a sleep serum and takes over. The heroes kidnap the man from the room Crittendon claimed was Rommel's, and pass him on to London to be exchanged for a British prisoner, Admiral Toddley. They later learn that the man they kidnapped was not Rommel, but Toddley, the man London wanted in the first place.

**Notes:** Colonel Crittendon's military designation was a misnomer, as there is no rank of colonel in the Royal Air Force. The equivalent ranking to a United States air force colonel in the RAF is "group captain." The writers most likely made Crittendon a colonel because American audiences would be unfamiliar with the term group captain. The rank title was used in Episode #67, "A Funny Thing Happened on the Way to London," which introduced Hogan's old friend, Group Captain Roberts of the RAF.

## EPISODE 144. "KLINK'S ESCAPE"

Original airdate: March 27, 1970
Writers: Harvey Bullock and Ray S. Allen
Director: Bruce Bilson
Guest cast: Leon Askin (General Burkhalter), Pamela Curran (Heidi Friederich), Tom Hatten (Lieutenant), David Morick (Sentry)

In order to get out of camp to blow up a German tunnel, Hogan convinces Klink to allow the prisoners to escape, so they will lead him to the underground escape center. Klink supplies them with German uniforms and a staff car, and offers himself as a hostage. The men leave camp with their blindfolded "hostage" and drive to the tunnel to plant the explosives. Meanwhile, Schultz thinks he's following the radio signal transmitted by Klink's car, but LeBeau has moved the transmitter to Burkhalter's car. As Schultz barges in on Burkhalter (with Klink's girlfriend), the POWs return to camp, claiming they had a change of heart and decided not to escape.

# SIXTH SEASON (1970–71)

Aired Sundays, 7:30–8:00 P.M.,
opposite *The Young Rebels* on ABC and
*The Wonderful World of Disney* on NBC.

### Sixth Season Technical Credits

Executive Producer: Edward H. Feldman
Producer: William A. Calihan
Associate Producer: Jerry London
Theme Music: Jerry Fielding
Director of Photography: William Jurgenson
Art Director: Howard Hollander
Film Editors: Michael Kahn, Ken Zemke
Assistant Director: Floyd Joyer
Unit Production Manager: W. A. Calihan
Set Decorator: William L. Stevens
Makeup: Armand Delmar
Costumes: Ray R. Harp, Marjorie Wahl
Post-Production Supervisor: Houseley Stevenson
Music Supervisor: Milton Lustig

Sound Editor: James J. Klinger
Production Mixer: Wallace Bearden
Re-recording Mixer: Gordon L. Day
Produced by Bing Crosby Productions in association with Bob Crane Enterprises, Inc. and the CBS Television Network. Filmed at Cinema General Studios.

## EPISODE 145. "CUISINE À LA STALAG 13"

Original airdate: September 20, 1970
Writer: Laurence Marks
Director: Jerry London
Guest cast: Brenda Benet (Marie Bizet), John Hoyt (General Wexler), Chet Stratton (Karl), Dave Morick (Gestapo Officer), Jay Sheffield (Captain Richter)

General de Gaulle rallies all free Frenchman and LeBeau decides to go fight for his country. His announcement comes at a bad time for Hogan, who has been receiving military information from General Wexler's aide during dinners prepared by chef LeBeau. Richter has promised information on the German West Wall fortifications at the next party. When French underground agent Marie is picked up by the Gestapo, the heroes arrange her release. In exchange, LeBeau returns to prepare one last meal for Klink. Afterwards, he announces his decision to stay, as his duty lies at Stalag 13.

**Notes:** After the fall of France in June 1940, General de Gaulle and others escaped into England and formed "The Free French" (later changed to "The Fighting French"). The Free French supported the Allies in their war against the Axis powers.

Since portraying gourmet chef LeBeau for six years, Robert Clary is often asked by fans if he possesses similar culinary skills. He responds, "No, not at all. My wife usually does the cooking. I can cook if I have to, but I'm not a trained chef. I'm just a good actor, that's all!"

**Was ist los?** When the series returned for its sixth season, Ivan Dixon (Kinch) had left the cast and was replaced by Kenneth Washington as Sergeant Baker. Nothing was ever mentioned on screen about Kinch's departure or Baker's arrival. This created some confusion due to the fact that "no one ever escapes from Stalag 13." Not officially, anyway. If Kinch had escaped and was replaced by Baker, then Baker would still be known as Kinchloe to the Germans. Perhaps Kinch was transferred to another prison camp and no longer had contact with the heroes?

## EPISODE 146. "THE EXPERTS"

Original airdate: September 27, 1970
Writer: Laurence Marks
Director: Marc Daniels
Guest cast: Noam Pitlik (Captain Karl Metzler), Sabrina Scharf (Luisa), Barbara Babcock (Maria), Edward Knight (Major Stern), Walter Janowitz (Oscar Schnitzer)

When Captain Metzler, one of Klink's guards, is ordered to be executed, Hogan intervenes to save the man's life. Hogan tracks Metzler to his girlfriend's apartment and informs him that his life is in danger. At first dubious, the captain eventually agrees to accept Hogan's aid. The heroes bring Metzler and his girlfriend back to camp and arrange for them to escape from Germany. In exchange, Metzler gives Hogan the communications information the Gestapo was ready to kill him for.

## EPISODE 147. "KLINK'S MASTERPIECE"

Original airdate: October 4, 1970
Writer: Phil Sharp
Director: Richard Kinon
Guest cast: Victoria Carroll (Rhona), Jon Cedar (Corporal Langenscheidt), David Frank (Underground Agent #1), Bard Stevens (Underground Agent #2), Karl Bruck (Underground Agent #3)

Hogan must get maps of a German convoy route to three different underground units, but the escape tunnel has caved in. Banking on Klink's visions of greatness, Hogan convinces the kommandant that his doodling is art! Klink paints up a storm, and brings his terrible paintings to an art gallery in town. Three underground agents pose as art buyers and purchase Klink's paintings. Hogan has hidden the secret maps behind the canvases.

## EPISODE 148. "LADY CHITTERLY'S LOVER, PART 1"

Original airdate: October 11, 1970
Writer: Richard M. Powell
Director: Edward H. Feldman
Guest cast: Bernard Fox (Colonel Crittendon/Sir Charles Chitterly), Anne Rogers (Lady Leslie Chitterly), Harold Gould (General von Schlomm)

Sir Charles Chitterly, a British traitor, parachutes into Stalag 13 when his plane is shot down. Hitler sends General von Schlomm to help Chitterly carry out his mission. Since Chitterly bears a remarkable to Colonel Crittendon, Hogan enlists the help of that bungler in countermanding Chitterly's mission—whatever it is. The heroes abduct Chitterly and Crittendon takes his place. Chitterly's wife arrives and tries to stab her traitorous husband in the back. When she learns he's an imposter, she agrees to work with Hogan to stop Chitterly's mission: orchestrating England's surrender to Germany.

**Was ist los?** Crittendon is upset when the prisoners tell him they must shave off his mustache for the ruse, but Chitterly has a mustache too.

## EPISODE 149. "LADY CHITTERLY'S LOVER, PART 2"

Original airdate: October 18, 1970
Writer: Richard M. Powell
Director: Edward H. Feldman
Guest cast: Howard Caine (Major Hochstetter), Bernard Fox (Crittendon/Chitterly), Anne Rogers (Lady Leslie Chitterly), Harold Gould (General von Schlomm)

Von Schlomm insists the Chitterlys leave for Berlin immediately, but Lady Chitterly stalls by concocting a story about her past relationship with Colonel Hogan. Meanwhile, the real Sir Charles escapes and causes much confusion before he is recaptured by the prisoners. Lady Chitterly persuades Hitler to send troops across the English Channel. With Allied bombers lying in wait, the German vessels are knocked out. Lady Chitterly gets out of camp before the Germans learn they've been duped. Hogan lets Chitterly free, and he is arrested for orchestrating the attack in the English Channel.

**Notes:** Bernard Fox came up with the idea for this two-part episode, in which he played a dual role. Chitterly's speech impediment not only made for some amusing moments—"By all the wules of warfare I have evwy wight . . ."— it also helped him to keep the two characters distinct. He says, "I was the one who decided to play the one character with the 'wees and wobble-U's.' And once I'd latched on that, the change was so enormous there was no other problem."

## EPISODE 150. "THE GESTAPO TAKEOVER"

Original airdate: October 25, 1970
Writer: Laurence Marks
Director: Irving J. Moore

Guest cast: Leon Askin (General Burkhalter), Joseph Ruskin (Major Strauss), Bruce Kirby (Otto Baum), Martin Kosleck (General Mueller), Forrest Compton (Captain Geissler), Milli Schuber (Fraulein), Richard Alden (Bartender)

Major Strauss of the Gestapo plans to take over Stalag 13 and send Klink and Schultz to the Russian front. Klink and Schultz team up with the prisoners in a scheme to rid Stalag 13 of the Gestapo for their mutual benefit. Hogan drafts a document outlining a plan to arrest Hitler. Two underground agents convince Major Strauss to sign the document in the name of his superior, General Mueller. Strauss calls Mueller to confirm his wishes, and Newkirk intercepts the call. Burkhalter uses the document to blackmail Mueller into restoring Stalag 13 to Klink.

## EPISODE 151. "KOMMANDANT SCHULTZ"

Original airdate: November 1, 1970
Writer: Laurence Marks
Director: Marc Daniels
Guest cast: Leon Askin (General Burkhalter), Eric Morris (Hercules), Jon Cedar (Corporal Langenscheidt), Norbert Schiller (Farmer), Walter Janowitz (Oscar Schnitzer), Richard Alden (Bartender), Walter Smith (American POW)

An order from Hitler elevates Schultz to camp kommandant and forces Klink to train for active combat. Nervous at first, Kommandant Schultz soon becomes power mad, doubling the guards and jeopardizing Hogan's plan to get underground courier Hercules out of camp with some uranium blocks. Hogan gains Klink's cooperation in arranging an escape, during which an Allied plane picks up Hercules and the uranium. When Schultz cannot recapture the prisoners, Klink is called in. Once Klink regains control of Stalag 13, Hogan arranges the surrender of the escapees.

**Familiar faces:** Eric Morris is a famed acting coach and the author of several books on the craft, including *Being and Doing* and *Acting from the Ultimate Consciousness*.

## EPISODE 152. "EIGHT O'CLOCK AND ALL IS WELL"

Original airdate: November 8, 1970
Writer: Laurence Marks
Director: Richard Kinon

Guest cast: Howard Caine (Major Hochstetter), Monte Markham (Captain James Martin/Seifert), Dick Wilson (Karl)

The new prisoner in Hogan's barracks passes the heroes' usual investigation procedure. Confident he's not a spy, the heroes fill Captain Martin in on their entire operation, and the details of an upcoming train sabotage job. When one of Hochstetter's men salutes the captain out of habit, Hogan discerns the truth: Martin is a Gestapo spy. The men abduct Martin and send him to England for interrogation. The heroes plant explosives on the railroad track and leave the spy's scorched jacket near the site. The munitions train explodes, and the spy is presumed dead.

**Familiar faces:** As Captain Don Thorpe, Monte Markham was David Hasselhoff's boss on *Baywatch* from 1989 to 1992. He starred in several other series, including *The New Perry Mason* (1973–74), in which he tried to fill Raymond Burr's shoes as the famous defense attorney.

## EPISODE 153. "THE BIG RECORD"

Original airdate: November 15, 1970
Writers: Ray S. Allen and Harvey Bullock
Director: Richard Kinon
Guest cast: Leon Askin (General Burkhalter), John Myhers (Colonel Schneider), Jack Riley (SS Man)

The heroes capitalize on Schultz's dreams of stardom to get the sergeant to let them into the meeting hall where a top secret SS meeting will be held. Once inside, the men hide the recorder and wire it to the light switch, while pretending to record Schultz's singing voice. Klink almost ruins the plan when he insists that *his* violin playing be recorded instead. Hogan leaves the recorder in place and brings the empty box to Klink's impromptu recital. The record of the meeting is sent to London and the Allies successfully ward off a German attack.

**Familiar faces:** Jack Riley played Bob's neurotic patient Mr. Carlin on *The Bob Newhart Show* (1972–78).

## EPISODE 154. "IT'S DYNAMITE"

Original airdate: November 22, 1970
Writer: Laurence Marks
Director: Bob Sweeney
Guest cast: Howard Caine (Major Hochstetter), Michael Fox (Berger), Lyn Peters (Elsa)

Major Hochstetter is using Stalag 13's cooler as a storage facility for dynamite, which is transported nightly to another location by truck. The heroes attempt to hijack the dynamite truck, but it keeps vanishing from its prearranged route. An underground agent discovers that the Germans have been hiding the dynamite in the woods for use in case of an Allied invasion. Hogan plans a diversion so he can steal Hochstetter's map of the hiding places. Carter, disguised as a fire marshall, sets off smoke bombs in the cooler. The prisoners pull Hochstetter out of the building and swipe the maps.

## EPISODE 155. "OPERATION TIGER"

Original airdate: November 29, 1970
Writer: Laurence Marks
. Director: Jerry London
Guest cast: Arlene Martel (Tiger), Dick Wilson (Karl), Frank Marth (Captain Steiger), Walter Janowitz (Oscar Schnitzer), David Morick (Guard One), David Frank (Guard Two)

London denies Hogan's request for permission to rescue underground agent Tiger from the Gestapo. Disobeying orders, Hogan and his men stop the train which is transporting Tiger to Berlin. Carter and LeBeau persuade the Gestapo chief, Colonel Steiger, to bring Tiger to Stalag 13 for safe holding until the train can resume its journey. When the train is reboarded, there are two new Gestapo men—Hogan and Newkirk. They overpower Tiger's guards and place dynamite charges on the train, timed to go off after they flee with Tiger. Tiger is presumed dead in the explosion, and Hogan arranges for her safe passage to London.

**Notes:** Jerry London, who started as an editor on the *Hogan's Heroes* pilot before moving up to associate producer and eventually directing ten episodes of the series, names "Operation Tiger" as his favorite of the episodes he directed.

## EPISODE 156. "THE BIG BROADCAST"

Original airdate: December 6, 1970
Writer: William Davenport
Director: Jerry London
Guest cast: Howard Caine (Major Hochstetter), James B. Sikking (Hercules), Yvonne E. Dardenne (Bertha), Willard Sage (First Officer), John Crawford (Second Officer), Jay Sheffield (SS Man), Buck Young (Guard)

Baker's radio signal is detected by the Gestapo just as they receive a vital message from the underground. The heroes must find an alternate way to get in touch with the underground. They keep Klink's car in the motor pool so they can install a radio transmitter in it. Hogan meets with underground agent Hercules, who gives him information about a rocket factory that has to be bombed. Hogan poses as a German officer and sends the message from the Gestapo's own radio detector unit.

## EPISODE 157. "THE GYPSY"

Original airdate: December 13, 1970
Writer: Laurence Marks
Director: Richard Kinon
Guest cast: Mat Reitz (Captain Gruber)

When they can't identify a strange object being held in the camp, the men con Schultz into posing for a picture with it. Headquarters determines that it is an antiradar device and orders Hogan to smuggle it to London. Hogan exploits Klink's belief in fortune tellers to pull off his outrageous scheme. He convinces the kommandant that LeBeau has psychic powers. LeBeau warns the kommandant of an impending attack on the camp, and Klink orders all his guards to defend the front gate, leaving the device unguarded. The men smuggle it into the tunnel, and leave a bomb in its place.

## EPISODE 158. "THE DROPOUTS"

Original airdate: December 27, 1970
Writer: Laurence Marks
Director: Marc Daniels
Guest cast: Howard Caine (Major Hochstetter), Gordon Pinsent (Captain Steiner), John Stephenson (Professor Bauer), Ben Wright (Dr. Reimann), Chris Anders (Guard)

When three Gestapo officers whom Carter and Hogan encountered in town turn up at Stalag 13, the heroes assume their operation has been discovered and they make frantic plans for escape. The trio comes to Hogan announcing their desire to defect. Hogan agrees to help them get to London, but Hochstetter arrives at camp looking for them. The defectors dress as prisoners and hide among the other POWs while Klink searches the compound. Major Hochstetter's frequent visits to camp provide the three men with the means for escape. One by one, they leave camp in the trunk of Hochstetter's car.

# EPISODE 159. "EASY COME, EASY GO"

Original airdate: January 10, 1971
Writer: Laurence Marks
Director: Edward H. Feldman
Guest cast: Leon Askin (General Burkhalter), Paul Lambert (Colonel Forbes), Brett Parker (Lieutenant), Jocelyn Peters (Greta), Cynthia Lynn (Eva), Tom Hatten (Air Force Captain), Stewart Moss (Lieutenant Mills), George Gaynes (General), Judson Morgan (Brewster), William Beckley (RAF Intelligence Man)

Burkhalter plies Hogan with wine, women—and one million dollars—to convince the POW to steal an American P-51 fighter plan from England and fly it back to Germany. Hogan agrees so that he can ferret out a German spy ring operating in London. Klink goes along to guard Hogan. Unbeknownst to Klink, their "theft" of a P-51 was arranged by the RAF. The engine dies out over Hammelburg and Hogan and Klink bail out. The plane crashes and the wreckage is useless to the Germans—its engine came from a captured German Messerschmidt!

# EPISODE 160. "THE MEISTER SPY"

Original airdate: January 17, 1971
Writers: Ray S. Allen and Harvey Bullock
Director: Bruce Bilson
Guest cast: Alan Bergmann (Major MartinHans Strasser), Dave Morick (Lieutenant J. B. Miller), Oscar Beregi (Herr Schneer), Ray Hastings (Herr Mayerink), Eva von Felitz (Fraulein Kissinger)

Major Martin, a captured American flier, informs Klink that he is really Hans Strasser, a German spy. Hogan discredits the spy's story and Strasser is sent to the cooler for attempting escape. In order to learn the identity of Strasser's Allied contact, Hogan convinces the spy he has been brought to Berlin. Klink's office is rearranged to pass as Hitler's, and Carter once again dons his Führer disguise. Faced with Hitler's fury and the threat of execution, Strasser reveals the name of his contact. Moments later, Schultz barges into Klink's office to retrieve the prisoner Strasser, who realizes he's been fooled.

**Familiar faces:** Dave Morick played small roles in several episodes of *Hogan's Heroes*. He says that staying in the background had its advantages. "Always the parts I played were small, but Mr. Feldman asked me one day if I wanted a larger part and not be brought back to film other episodes or was I satisfied with the small parts, and if I was he could keep bringing me back more often. Knowing that the more I worked the more residual payments I received, I opted for the latter." With the series nearing its end, Feldman gave Morick a costarring role as an American flier in this episode. "He was that kind of person," reflects the actor. Feldman also cast Morick in a regular role in his short-lived 1969 series, *The Queen and I*.

## EPISODE 161. "THAT'S NO LADY, THAT'S MY SPY"

Original airdate: January 24, 1971
Writer: Arthur Julian
Director: Jerry London
Guest cast: Leon Askin (General Burkhalter), Alice Ghostley (Mrs. Mannheim), Diana Chesney (Berta Burkhalter), Wendy Wilson (Red Riding Hood), Jon Cedar (Oskar Danzig), Dave Morick (Patrol Leader)

Underground leader Oscar Danzig is injured and his unit radios Hogan with a request for penicillin. London drops the penicillin to the heroes by parachute, but the woods around Stalag 13 are thick with Gestapo guards searching for Danzig. A man must leave camp to make the delivery, but Hogan cannot divine how—until Klink announces that a tea party for German officers' wives will be held at Stalag 13. Dressed as a woman, Newkirk crashes the tea party so he can leave camp with the other women and deliver the penicillin.

**Highlight:** Burkhalter realizes that there is an extra woman present and he and Klink try to ferret out the spy. Noting that one of the women is wearing a wig, Klink yanks it off. But instead of unveiling a spy, the kommandant has de-wigged Field Marshal Manheim's wife. Mrs. Mannheim is played by Alice Ghostley, who portrayed Gertrude Linkmeyer in Episode #111, "Watch the Trains Go By."

## EPISODE 162. "TO RUSSIA WITHOUT LOVE"

Original airdate: January 31, 1971
Writer: Arthur Julian
Director: Bruce Bilson
Guest cast: Leon Askin (General Burkhalter), Ruta Lee (Olga), H. M. Wynant (Colonel Becker)

Colonel Becker, weary of life on the Russian front, is jealous of Klink's easy post at Stalag 13 and wants to trade assignments. He offers Hogan a peek at the secret papers he is carrying if he can pull off the trade. With the aid of a beautiful Russian woman, Hogan convinces the kommandant that the good life at the Russian front is one of Germany's best-kept secrets. Klink pleads for a transfer and Becker is assigned the new kommandant. But when Becker double-crosses Hogan, the heroes shanghai the traitor and send him to England.

## EPISODE 163. "KLINK FOR THE DEFENSE"

Original airdate: February 7, 1971
Writer: William Davenport
Director: Jerry London
Guest cast: Howard Caine (Major Hochstetter), Leon Askin (General Burkhalter), Sandy Kenyon (Colonel Hugo Hauptmann), Karl Bruck (President of Court), Lynnette Mettey (Fraulein Hibbler)
    Colonel Hauptmann, a German traitor, offers Hogan a map of the German submarine pens in exchange for safe passage out of Germany. The Gestapo arrests Hauptmann and holds him at Stalag 13 pending court martial. General Burkhalter is prosecuting the case, and to ensure that Hauptmann is found guilty, he appoints Klink as Hauptmann's defense attorney. With the evidence stacked against him, Hauptmann's fate seems certain—death by firing squad. But Hogan and his men tamper with the evidence to make it appear that Hauptmann was framed by his secretary, whom they implicate as a British agent.

## EPISODE 164. "THE KAMIKAZES ARE COMING"

Original airdate: February 21, 1971
Writer: Richard M. Powell
Director: Edward H. Feldman
Guest cast: Howard Caine (Major Hochstetter), Nita Talbot (Marya), Henry Corden (Dr. Otto von Bornemann), Richard Alden (Assistant), Chris Anders (Guard), Erik Stern (German Partisan)
    Russian spy Marya shows up at camp with Dr. von Bornemann, a German rocket scientist whose rocket went off course and is missing. Hogan has found the rocket but doesn't know what to do with it—it's too large to dissemble and bring back to camp. Marya and Hogan team up to steal the rocket, but they can't agree on where to send it—London or Moscow! As

**MAD magazine parodied *Hogan's Heroes* in a 1966 issue.** Reprinted with permission of *MAD Magazine*, E.C. Publications, Inc. © 1966

Marya leads the Germans on a wild goose chase in search of the missing rocket, Hogan reprograms the course of the rocket and it is launched toward London.

## EPISODE 165. "KOMMANDANT GERTRUDE"

Original airdate: February 28, 1971
Writer: Laurence Marks
Director: Bruce Bilson
Guest cast: Leon Askin (General Burkhalter), Kathleen Freeman (Gertrude Linkmeyer*), Lee Bergere (Major Wolfgang Karp), Leslie Parrish (Karen Richter), Johnny Haymer (General Sharp)
*misspelled "Linkmeier" in the end credits

Burkhalter's sister Gertrude is back, and engaged to a slow-witted major, whom she gets appointed as Klink's adjutant. Hoping to gain her fiancé a promotion, Gertrude influences him to tighten camp security. With the added security, Hogan and his men can't smuggle an American general to London. Hogan arranges for Major Karp to be caught in a compromising position with a beautiful young woman. Karp is sent packing to the Russian front. With security relaxed, the American general is moved out safely. And with Major Karp out of the picture, Klink is once again the unwilling object of Gertrude's affections.

**Familiar faces:** The ornery general is played by Johnny Haymer, better known as Sergeant Zale on *M\*A\*S\*H* (1977–79).

## EPISODE 166. "HOGAN'S DOUBLE LIFE"

Original airdate: March 7, 1971
Writer: Phil Sharp
Director: Bruce Bilson
Guest cast: Malachi Throne (Major Pruhst), John Hoyt (Field Marshal von Leiter), David Frank (Underground Agent Albert), Dick Wilson (Underground Agent Bruner)

Major Pruhst of the Gestapo arrives at Stalag 13 with an outlandish claim: POW Hogan is responsible for all the sabotage in the area! A man who witnessed Hogan blowing up a bridge identifies him from a photograph. To free himself from suspicion, Hogan convinces his accusers that he has an exact double, a German traitor named Erik Scarfstein, who has been committing the sabotage.

**Familiar faces:** Malachi Throne portrayed Noah Bain, Alexander Mundy's (Robert Wagner) spy agency boss on *It Takes a Thief* (1968–69).

## EPISODE 167. "LOOK AT THE PRETTY SNOWFLAKES"

Original airdate: March 21, 1971
Writer: Arthur Julian
Director: Irving J. Moore
Guest cast: Harold J. Stone (General Strommberger), Edward Knight (Corporal Dietrich)

The heroes must prevent General Strommberger's Third Panzer Division from reaching its destination. They accept the task of clearing the snow-covered roads for the panzer division so that they can blow up the lead tank and delay the entire division. The plan is thwarted when a guard confiscates the dynamite. Next, the men attempt to cause an avalanche, which would block the road. The men aren't able to create enough noise to trigger the snowslide, but a sneeze from Klink does the trick.

**Highlight:** This episode gave Bob Crane the opportunity to display his skills as a drummer. The prisoners' jam session, with Carter on trumpet, Baker on base, LeBeau on piano, and Newkirk playing bandleader, is superb.

**Notes:** This was the last episode of the series to be filmed.

## EPISODE 168. "ROCKETS OR ROMANCE"

Original airdate: April 4, 1971
Writer: Arthur Julian
Director: Marc Daniels
Guest cast: Leon Askin (General Burkhalter), Marlyn Mason (Lily Frankel), Norman Alden (Major Heintzen), Kenneth DuMain (Guard), James Savett (Radio Operator)

Hogan and underground agent Lily Frankel team up to locate three mobile rocket launchers. One is planted right in Stalag 13, and the heroes are ordered to disarm it. Hogan and Lily locate the other two and radio the information to England, but it's a close call when a radio-detector truck picks up their signal. Newkirk and Baker divert the detector and the mobile launchers are bombed. Carter and LeBeau use a high-powered magnet to throw the rocket launcher in camp off course, and when Klink fires the rocket at England, it heads towards Burkhalter's house instead.

**Was ist los?** Marlyn Mason reprised her role as Lily Frankel from Episode #140, "Six Lessons from Madame LaGrange." In "Six Lessons," Hogan and Lily were quite amorous with one another, but when they meet in

**Klink, Hogan, Newkirk, and LeBeau in "Look at the Pretty Snowflakes."**
© Bing Crosby Productions, Inc. Reprinted with permission.

this episode, they are strangers. However, it doesn't take them long to ignite—or reignite—the attraction between them.

Marlyn Mason recalls that working on *Hogan's Heroes* was especially nice because of the happy and relaxed mood evoked by Bob Crane's drumming to big band music between sets. "It was a great deal of fun," she says.

**Familiar faces:** Among Norman Alden's many memorable roles was the part of Frank Heflin, the head of CrimeScope, on the Saturday morning *Krofft Supershow* serial, "ElectraWoman and DynaGirl" (1976–77).

## Alphabetical List of Episodes

| Episode Title | Number | Airdate |
|---|---|---|
| "Anchors Aweigh, Men of Stalag 13" | 16 | 12/31/65 |
| "The Antique" | 130 | 12/12/69 |
| "Art for Hogan's Sake" | 48 | 12/30/66 |
| "The Assassin" | 29 | 4/8/66 |
| "At Last—Schultz Knows Something" | 132 | 12/26/69 |
| "Axis Annie" | 85 | 2/10/68 |
| "Bad Day in Berlin" | 103 | 12/7/68 |
| "The Battle of Stalag 13" | 37 | 10/14/66 |
| "The Big Broadcast" | 156 | 12/6/70 |
| "The Big Dish" | 116 | 3/8/69 |
| "The Big Gamble" | 127 | 11/21/69 |
| "The Big Picture" | 126 | 11/14/69 |
| "The Big Record" | 153 | 11/15/70 |
| "Bombsight" | 125 | 11/7/69 |
| "Carter Turns Traitor" | 78 | 12/23/67 |
| "Casanova Klink" | 68 | 10/14/67 |
| "Clearance Sale at the Black Market" | 93 | 9/28/68 |
| "The Collector General" | 89 | 3/9/68 |
| "Colonel Klink's Secret Weapon" | 60 | 3/24/67 |
| "Color the Luftwaffe Red" | 100 | 11/16/68 |
| "The Crittendon Plan" | 63 | 9/9/67 |
| "Crittendon's Commandos" | 143 | 3/20/70 |
| "Cuisine à la Stalag 13" | 145 | 9/20/70 |
| "Cupid Comes to Stalag 13" | 30 | 4/15/66 |
| "D-Day at Stalag 13" | 65 | 9/23/67 |
| "The Defector" | 128 | 11/28/69 |
| "Diamonds in the Rough" | 35 | 9/30/66 |
| "Don't Forget to Write" | 45 | 12/9/66 |
| "The Dropouts" | 158 | 12/27/70 |
| "Drums Along the Düsseldorf" | 92 | 3/30/68 |
| "Duel of Honor" | 84 | 2/3/68 |
| "Easy Come, Easy Go" | 159 | 1/10/71 |
| "Eight O'Clock and All Is Well" | 152 | 11/8/70 |
| "The Empty Parachute" | 129 | 12/5/69 |
| "An Evening of Generals" | 75 | 12/2/67 |
| "Everybody Loves a Snowman" | 761 | 2/9/67 |
| "Everyone Has a Brother-In-Law" | 55 | 2/17/67 |

| | | |
|---|---|---|
| "Never Play Cards with Strangers" | 99 | 11/9/68 |
| "Nights in Shining Armor" | 70 | 10/28/67 |
| "No Names Please" | 102 | 11/30/68 |
| "Oil for the Lamps of Hogan" | 14 | 12/17/65 |
| "One Army at a Time" | 138 | 2/13/70 |
| "One in Every Crowd" | 72 | 11/11/67 |
| "Operation Briefcase" | 36 | 10/7/66 |
| "Operation Hannibal" | 109 | 1/18/69 |
| "Operation Tiger" | 155 | 11/29/70 |
| "The Pizza Parlor" | 22 | 2/11/66 |
| "Praise the Führer and Pass the Ammunition" | 51 | 1/20/67 |
| "The Prince from the Phone Company" | 26 | 3/18/66 |
| "The Prisoner's Prisoner" | 6 | 10/22/65 |
| "Psychic Kommandant" | 25 | 3/11/66 |
| "The Purchasing Plan" | 114 | 2/22/69 |
| "The Reluctant Target" | 62 | 4/7/67 |
| "Request Permission to Escape" | 32 | 4/29/66 |
| "Reservations Are Required" | 15 | 12/24/65 |
| "The Return of Major Bonacelli" | 117 | 3/15/69 |
| "Reverend Kommandant Klink" | 57 | 3/3/67 |
| "The Rise and Fall of Sergeant Schultz" | 38 | 10/21/66 |
| "Rockets or Romance" | 168 | 4/4/71 |
| "A Russian Is Coming" | 74 | 11/25/67 |
| "The Safecracker Suite" | 27 | 3/25/66 |
| "The Schultz Brigade" | 34 | 9/23/66 |
| "The Scientist" | 12 | 12/3/65 |
| "Sergeant Schultz Meets Mata Hari" | 66 | 9/30/67 |
| "The Sergeant's Analyst" | 141 | 3/6/70 |
| "Six Lessons from Madame LaGrange" | 140 | 2/27/70 |
| "The Softer They Fall" | 136 | 1/23/70 |
| "Some of their Planes Are Missing" | 64 | 9/16/67 |
| "Standing Room Only" | 139 | 2/20/70 |
| "Sticky Wicket Newkirk" | 82 | 1/20/68 |
| "The Swing Shift" | 53 | 2/3/67 |
| "Tanks for the Memory" | 41 | 11/11/66 |
| "That's No Lady, That's My Spy" | 161 | 1/24/71 |
| "A Tiger Hunt in Paris" (Part 1) | 42 | 11/18/66 |
| "A Tiger Hunt in Paris" (Part 2) | 43 | 11/25/66 |
| "To Russia without Love" | 162 | 1/31/71 |

| | | |
|---|---|---|
| "To the Gestapo with Love" | 97 | 10/26/68 |
| "Top Hat, White Tie and Bomb Sight" | 10 | 11/19/65 |
| "The Top Secret Top Coat" | 61 | 3/31/67 |
| "The Tower" | 59 | 3/17/67 |
| "Two Nazis for the Price of One" | 79 | 12/30/67 |
| "The Ultimate Weapon" | 90 | 3/16/68 |
| "Unfair Exchange" | 123 | 10/24/69 |
| "Up in Klink's Room" | 113 | 2/15/69 |
| "War Takes a Holiday" | 83 | 1/27/68 |
| "Watch the Trains Go By" | 111 | 2/1/69 |
| "The Well" | 120 | 10/3/69 |
| "What Time Does the Balloon Go Up?" | 86 | 2/17/68 |
| "Who Stole My Copy of Mein Kampf?" | 108 | 1/11/69 |
| "Will the Blue Baron Strike Again?" | 104 | 12/14/68 |
| "Will the Real Adolf Please Stand Up?" | 44 | 12/2/66 |
| "Will the Real Colonel Klink Please Stand Up Against the Wall?" | 105 | 12/21/68 |
| "The Witness" | 115 | 3/1/69 |

In the episode guide, episodes are listed in the order in which they aired. The following is a listing of episodes by production number, which is the order in which they were filmed.

| | |
|---|---|
| 5784-01 | "The Informer" (Pilot) |
| 5784-02 | "The Late Inspector General" |
| 5784-03 | "Hold That Tiger" |
| 5784-04 | "Kommandant of the Year" |
| 5784-05 | "Happy Birthday, Adolf" |
| 5784-06 | "The Prisoner's Prisoner" |
| 5784-07 | "German Bridge Is Falling Down" |
| 5784-08 | "Reservations Are Required" |
| 5784-09 | "The Flight of the Valkyrie" |
| 5784-10 | "Go Light on the Heavy Water" |
| 5784-11 | "Anchors Aweigh, Men of Stalag 13" |
| 5784-12 | "Movies Are Your Best Escape" |
| 5784-13 | "The Scientist" |
| 5784-14 | "Top Hat, White Tie and Bomb Sight" |
| 5784-15 | "Happiness Is a Warm Sergeant" |
| 5784-16 | "Hogan's Hofbrau" |

5784-17   "Hello, Zolle"
5784-18   "Oil for the Lamps of Hogan"
5784-19   "The Gold Rush"
5784-20   "It Takes a Thief...Sometimes"
5784-21   "The 43rd, A Moving Story"
5784-22   "The Great Impersonation"
5784-23   "How to Cook a German Goose by Radar"
5784-24   "The Pizza Parlor"
5784-25   "The Prince from the Phone Company"
5784-26   "Psychic Kommandant"
5784-27   "I Look Better in Basic Black"
5784-28   "The Safecracker Suite"
5784-29   "Cupid Comes to Stalag 13"
5784-30   "The Flame Grows Higher"
5784-31   "The Assassin"
5784-32   "Request Permission to Escape"
5784-33   "The Schultz Brigade"
5784-34   "Diamonds in the Rough"
5784-35   "Operation Briefcase"
5784-36   "Hogan Gives a Birthday Party"
5784-37   "Information Please"
5784-38   "A Klink, a Bomb and a Short Fuse"
5784-39   "The Battle of Stalag 13"
5784-40   "The Rise and Fall of Sergeant Schultz"
5784-41   "Hogan Springs"
5784-42   "Tanks for the Memory"
5784-43   "Art for Hogan's Sake"
5784-44   "A Tiger Hunt in Paris" (Part 1)
5784-45   "A Tiger Hunt in Paris" (Part 2)
5784-46   "Don't Forget to Write"
5784-47   "Will the Real Adolf Please Stand Up?"
5784-48   "The General Swap"
5784-49   "Hogan and the Lady Doctor"
5784-50   "Klink's Rocket"
5784-51   "Praise the Führer and Pass the Ammunition"
5784-52   "The Great Brinksmeyer Robbery"
5784-53   "Killer Klink"
5784-54   "The Swing Shift"
5784-55   "Heil Klink"

| | |
|---|---|
| 5784-56 | "Everyone Has a Brother-In-Law" |
| 5784-57 | "The Most Escape-Proof Camp I've Ever Escaped From" |
| 5784-58 | "Colonel Klink's Secret Weapon" |
| 5784-59 | "Reverend Kommandant Klink" |
| 5784-60 | "The Tower" |
| 5784-61 | "The Top Secret Top Coat" |
| 5784-62 | "Carter Turns Traitor" |
| 5784-63 | "The Reluctant Target" |
| 5784-64 | "Hot Money" |
| 5784-65 | "The Crittendon Plan" |
| 5784-66 | "Some of Their Planes Are Missing" |
| 5784-67 | "D-Day at Stalag 13" |
| 5784-68 | "Casanova Klink" |
| 5784-69 | "Funny Thing Happened on the Way to London" |
| 5784-70 | "Sergeant Schultz Meets Mata Hari" |
| 5784-71 | "Nights in Shining Armor" |
| 5784-72 | "Is General Hammerschlag Burning?" |
| 5784-73 | "Drums Along the Dusseldorf" |
| 5784-74 | "How to Win Friends and Influence Nazis" |
| 5784-75 | "Is There a Doctor in the House?" |
| 5784-76 | "One in Every Crowd" |
| 5784-77 | "Monkey Business" |
| 5784-78 | "Everybody Loves a Snowman" |
| 5784-79 | "A Russian Is Coming" |
| 5784-80 | "An Evening of Generals" |
| 5784-81 | "The Hostage" |
| 5784-82 | "Two Nazis for the Price of One" |
| 5784-83 | "Hogan, Go Home" |
| 5784-84 | "War Takes a Holiday" |
| 5784-85 | "Axis Annie" |
| 5784-86 | "Sticky Wicket Newkirk" |
| 5784-87 | "What Time Does the Balloon Go Up?" |
| 5784-88 | "The Ultimate Weapon" |
| 5784-89 | "Duel of Honor" |
| 5784-90 | "The Collector General" |
| 5784-91 | "LeBeau and the Little Old Lady" |
| 5784-92 | "How to Escape from a Prison Camp Without Really Trying" |
| 5784-93 | "Hogan's Trucking Service . . . We Deliver the Factory to You" |
| 5784-94 | "Klink vs. the Gonculator" |

| | |
|---|---|
| 5784-95 | "Man's Best Friend Is Not His Dog" |
| 5784-96 | "Clearance Sale at the Black Market" |
| 5784-97 | "To the Gestapo with Love" |
| 5784-98 | "How to Catch a Papa Bear" |
| 5784-99 | "Color the Luftwaffe Red" |
| 5784-100 | "Will the Blue Baron Strike Again?" |
| 5784-101 | "Guess Who Came to Dinner" |
| 5784-102 | "Never Play Cards with Strangers" |
| 5784-103 | "No Names Please" |
| 5784-104 | "The Missing Klink" |
| 5784-105 | "Bad Day in Berlin" |
| 5784-106 | "Man in a Box" |
| 5784-107 | "Will the Real Colonel Klink Please Stand Up Against the Wall?" |
| 5784-108 | "Klink's Old Flame" |
| 5784-109 | "Who Stole My Copy of Mein Kampf?" |
| 5784-110 | "Operation Hannibal" |
| 5784-111 | "Watch the Trains Go By" |
| 5784-112 | "My Favorite Prisoner" |
| 5784-113 | "Up in Klink's Room" |
| 5784-114 | "The Big Dish" |
| 5784-115 | "Happy Birthday, Dear Hogan" |
| 5784-116 | "The Purchasing Plan" |
| 5784-117 | "The Witness" |
| 5784-118 | "The Return of Major Bonacelli" |
| 5784-119 | "Klink's Escape" |
| 5784-120 | "The Big Picture" |
| 5784-121 | "Hogan Goes Hollywood" |
| 5784-122 | "The Well" |
| 5784-123 | "The Antique" |
| 5784-124 | "Unfair Exchange" |
| 5784-125 | "The Gasoline War" |
| 5784-126 | "The Klink Commandos" |
| 5784-127 | "The Kommandant Dies at Dawn" |
| 5784-128 | "Bombsight" |
| 5784-129 | "The Big Gamble" |
| 5784-130 | "How's the Weather?" |
| 5784-131 | "The Defector" |
| 5784-132 | "The Empty Parachute" |

| 5784-133 | "Is There a Traitor in the House?" |
| 5784-134 | "At Last—Schultz Knows Something?" |
| 5784-135 | "Gowns by Yvette" |
| 5784-136 | "Fat Hermann, Go Home" |
| 5784-137 | "The Softer They Fall" |
| 5784-138 | "Get Fit or Go Fight" |
| 5784-139 | "One Army at a Time" |
| 5784-140 | "The Sergeant's Analyst" |
| 5784-141 | "Standing Room Only" |
| 5784-142 | "The Merry Widow" |
| 5784-143 | "Six Lessons from Madame LaGrange" |
| 5784-144 | "Crittendon's Commandos" |
| 37784-145 | "The Experts" |
| 37784-146 | "Cuisine à la Stalag 13" |
| 37784-147 | "Klink's Masterpiece" |
| 37784-148 | "The Gypsy" |
| 37784-149 | "Kommandant Schultz" |
| 37784-150 | "The Gestapo Takeover" |
| 37784-151 | "Lady Chitterly's Lover, Part 1" |
| 37784-152 | "Lady Chitterly's Lover, Part 2" |
| 37784-153 | "It's Dynamite" |
| 37784-154 | "The Big Record" |
| 37784-155 | "Eight O'Clock and All Is Well" |
| 37784-156 | "Rockets or Romance" |
| 37784-157 | "The Dropouts" |
| 37784-158 | "Operation Tiger" |
| 37784-159 | "Easy Come, Easy Go" |
| 37784-160 | "The Big Broadcast" |
| 37784-161 | "Kommandant Gertrude" |
| 37784-162 | "That's No Lady, That's My Spy" |
| 37784-163 | "To Russia without Love" |
| 37784-164 | "The Meister Spy" |
| 37784-165 | "Hogan's Double Life" |
| 37784-166 | "The Kamikazes Are Coming" |
| 37784-167 | "Klink for the Defense" |
| 37784-168 | "Look at the Pretty Snowflakes" |

# TRIVIA QUIZ

Your mission: Test your expertise with this *Hogan's Heroes* trivia quiz. Answers on page 254.

1. What was Klink's occupation before the war?

2. What was Schultz's occupation before the war?

3. What is Hogan's barracks number?

4. What is Hogan's code name?

5. What unit was Hogan with before he was shot down?

6. Where is the listening device hidden in Klink's office?

7. What is the heroes' radio receiver disguised as?

8. Recite the poem Carter writes for the prisoners' get well card to Klink when the kommandant gets the flu.

9. When Hogan gives Klink the nickname "Klink the Fink," what does he tell him F.I.N.K. stands for?

10. What town is Stalag 13 located in?

11. Where would Carter most like to go to in town?

12. What Shakespearean play does Crittendon attempt to quote in two episodes?

13. Where was Klink born?

14. Where did Klink get his military training?

15. When the prisoners overhear Schultz singing in the shower, what song is he crooning?

16. What song do the POWs play when they try to start an avalanche?

17. According to Klink, what musical instrument does Burkhalter play (and badly)?

18. According to Kinch, how does Hogan physically react to a tough assignment?

19. What was Gertrude Linkmeyer's first husband's name?

20. Who was Carter's childhood sweetheart?

21. What honorary Indian name does Hogan give to Schultz?

22. Who is the Klink of Capezio?

23. What was Carter's name when he was a corporal in the German army?

24. Which agent is Hogan *not* interested in romantically?:
    A. Tiger
    B. Eskimo
    C. Freddy
    D. Mama Bear

25. Which is *not* an alias used by Colonel Hogan:
    A. Frank Dirken
    B. Major Hoganborg
    C. Major Hogan Hoople
    D. Colonel Klink
    E. Lieutenant Hoganheffer
    F. Erik Scharfstein
    G. Captain Gruber

26. Which is *not* given as one of the guard dogs' names?
    A. Heidi
    B. Bruno
    C. Wolfgang
    D. Oscar
    E. Hans

27. Newkirk is a master at impressions. Which of the following voices does he *not* impersonate in the series?
    A. Humphrey Bogart
    B. Winston Churchill
    C. Colonel Klink
    D. Adolf Hitler
    E. Bette Davis

28. Match the hero with the woman who captured his heart.
    A. LeBeau      1. Yawanda
    B. Kinch       2. Gretel
    C. Carter      3. Mady
    D. Newkirk     4. Wilhelmina

29. Name the four actors who played dual roles on separate *Hogan's Heroes* episodes.

30. Name the character that says each of these running lines:
    A. "What is this remarkable attraction I have for women?"
    B. "What is this man doing here?"
    C. "I see nothing, I know nothing!"
    D. "You got it boy. I mean, Sir."

31. Which character:
    A. fought in the Golden Gloves
    B. once played Peter Pan
    C. has a nephew named Wolfie
    D. has a niece named Lotte
    E. is nicknamed "Cockroach"
    F. was the top man in his cryptology course
    G. has a sister named Mavis
    H. ran a drug store in Muncie, Indiana
    I. has a touch of night blindness
    J. was voted "Most Likely to Be a Troublemaker" in school
    K. would Klink "trust to shave the Fuhrer"

Answers (Score 2 points for each correct answer):

1. bookkeeper

2. owner of a toy company

3. 2

4. Score 1 point if you answered Papa Bear.
   Score 1 point if you answered Goldilocks.
   Score 2 points if you knew that in earlier episodes, Hogan was Goldilocks, the submarine was Mama Bear and London was Papa Bear, and in later episodes, Hogan's code name was Papa Bear and London was either Mama Bear or Goldilocks.

5. the 504th Bomber Squadron

6. in the microphone on the picture of Hitler hanging on the wall

7. a coffee pot

8. To the heavens we all shout,
   Get well soon to our favorite Kraut

9. Firm, Impartial, Nazi Kommandant

10. Hammelburg

11. the zoo

12. *The Merchant of Venice*

13. Leipzig (in the German-dubbed version of the series, he is from Dresden, Saxony)

14. Potsdam

15. "Swanee"

16. "Cherokee"

17. the mandolin

18. his left eyebrow goes up

19. Otto

20. Mary Jane

21. Big Chief Running Bear Who Goes Swift and Sure to Beer Garden

22. Major Bonacelli

23. Hans Wagner

24. (C) Tiger, Eskimo, and Mama Bear were all beautiful underground agents, Freddy was a chimpanzee.

25. (E) Hogan masqueraded as Klink on a few different occasions, and used all of these names, except E.

26. (D) Oscar Schnitzer is the dogkeeper. The others are dogs.

27. (E) Carter did a Bette Davis impersonation.

28. A–4; B–1; C–3; D–2 (2 points each)

29. John Banner, Ivan Dixon, Bernard Fox, and Lloyd Bochner (2 points each)

30. For 2 points each:
    A. Klink
    B. Hochstetter
    C. Schultz
    D. Carter

31. For 2 points each:
    A. Kinch
    B. Klink
    C. Schultz
    D. Burkhalter
    E. LeBeau
    F. Hochstetter
    G. Newkirk
    H. Carter
    I. Crittendon
    J. Hogan
    K. Hilda

Scoring:
| | |
|---|---|
| 0–50 points | Dummkopf! |
| 51–70 points | Whose side are you on? |
| 71–90 points | You're one of the Allies. |
| 91–100 points | You're an honorary hero! |

# BIBLIOGRAPHY

"Actor, Activist Caine Dies at 67." *Hollywood Reporter,* December 30, 1993, p. 4.

"Actor Bob Crane Discovered Slain." *Dallas Morning News,* June 30, 1978, p. 1A.

"Actor Calls the Tune (Werner Klemperer)." *New York Times,* May 13, 1980, p. B6.

"Actor's Moves Before Death Probed." *Dallas Morning News,* July 1, 1978, p. 3A.

Adler, Renata. *Wicked Dreams of Paula Schultz.* Review. *New York Times,* January 4, 1968, p. 28.

Allman, Kevin. *TV Turkeys: An Outrageous Look at the Most Preposterous Shows Ever on Television.* New York: Perigree Books, 1987.

Alpert, Don. "Bob Crane Ired Over Anti-TV Snobs." *Los Angeles Times,* Calendar Section, January 21, 1968.

Andrews, Bart with Brad Dunning. *The Worst TV Shows Ever.* New York: E.P. Dutton, 1980.

Arcella, Lisa. "*Hogan's Heroes* Beauty: Brando Is Father of My Lovechild." *Star,* February 24, 1998, p. 27.

Arkush, Michael. "Survivors of the Holocaust Take Look Back." *Los Angeles Times,* May 4, 1995.

Askin, Leon. *Quietude and Quest: Protagonists and Antagonists in the Theater, On and Off Stage, as Seen Through the Eyes of Leon Askin.* Riverside, Calif: Ariadne Press, 1989.

Atkinson, Brooks. " 'Dear Charles' Arrives at the Morosco." *New York Times,* September 16, 1954, p. 37.

———. *New Faces of 1952.* Review. *New York Times,* May 17, 1952, p. 23.

Babbin, Arnold. "Elke Sommer Stars in Cold War Comedy." *Hollywood Citizen-News,* January 24, 1968.

Bacon, James. "Bob Crane's Costar Astounded by Police Reports." *Los Angeles Herald-Examiner,* July 27, 1978, p. B4.

Baessler, Paul. "The Cook Sings." *Los Angeles Herald-Examiner TV Weekly,* November 19–25, 1967, pp. 6–7.

Bates, Hal. "Klemperer Cracks His Klink Image Through Musical Shows." *Hollywood Reporter,* July 10, 1972.

Berger, Leslie and Laura Laughlin. "Suspect Charged in 1978 Death of Actor Bob Crane." *Los Angeles Times,* June 2, 1992, pp. A1–3.

Berman, Janice. "The Sound, and Spirit, of Music." *New York Newsday,* March 9, 1990.

"Bernard Fox's Career Spans TV, Film, Stage." *Los Angeles Times,* July 31, 1983.

"Bob Crane Buried in Chatsworth." *Los Angeles Herald-Examiner,* July 6, 1978.

"Bob Crane, *Hogan's Heroes* Star, Found Slain at Home in Arizona." *New York Times,* June 30, 1978.

"Bob Crane's Ghost Is Haunting Me!" *The Globe,* June 3, 1997.

Bogle, Donald. "Ivan Dixon." *Blacks in American Films and Television: An Illustrated Encyclopedia.* New York: Garland Publishing, Inc., 1988.

Bond, Ed. "Actor Who Survived Holocaust Speaks." *Los Angeles Times,* April 7, 1995.

Bornfeld, Steve. "OK to Call Klemperer 'Colonel.' " *New York Post,* December 2, 1993, p. 67.

Brooks, Tim and Earle Marsh. *The Complete Directory to Prime Time Network and Cable TV Shows, 1946–Present.* New York: Ballantine Books, 1995.

Buckley, Michael. "Curtain Calls: Werner Klemperer." *Theater Week,* April 23, 1990.

Burden, Martin. "Robert Clary, Survivor: His Life Rivals His TV Role." *New York Post,* December 6, 1982, p. 8.

*Campo 44.* Review. *Variety,* September 13, 1967.

Canby, Vincent. *The Running Man*. Review. *New York Times,* November 13, 1987, p. 10.

Carroll, Harrison. "Crane in Plumage." *Los Angeles Herald-Examiner,* April 9, 1967.

Champlin, Charles. "Klemperer's Klink Made of Solid Stuff." *Los Angeles Times,* March 6, 1967, part IV, p. 26.

"Cheeky King Richard." *Newsweek,* June 25, 1979, pp. 92–93.

Clark, Jim. "Bernard Fox Makes Fans Merry Whether He's in Mayberry or Elsewhere!" *The Bullet* (Andy Griffith Show Rerun Watchers Club Newsletter), volume 13, issue 1, August 19, 1996.

Clary, Robert. "Why I Gave Up Night Life for Day Life." *Hollywood Citizen-News,* December 17, 1966, p. 23.

Coates, Bill. "After One Year, Crane Murder Still Unsolved; Police Get Plenty of Free Advice." *Scottsdale Daily Progress,* June 23, 1979.

"Cover Close-Up: *Hogan's Heroes.*" *TV Week,* January 30, 1966, p. 9.

Cowell, Alan. "Hogan! Germans Need You." *New York Times,* July 20, 1997, p. E1.

Crane, Bob. "How I Avoid Trouble." *Guideposts,* February 1968, pp. 22–23.

———. "No Laughing Matter." *Los Angeles Herald-Examiner,* August 14, 1969.

"Crane Pal Found Not Guilty of Killing Actor in '78." *Hollywood Reporter,* November 1, 1994, p. 6.

"Crane Waiting for *Hogan's Heroes* to Pay Off." *Los Angeles Herald-Examiner,* November 29, 1972.

"Crane's Kin, Friends Quizzed." *Dallas Morning News,* July 4, 1978, p. 22A.

Dern, Marian. "Man in Pursuit of Himself." *TV Guide,* February 27, 1965, pp. 15–17.

Dumas, Lynne S. "Werner Klemperer Can Play All Parts." *Spotlight,* October 1988, pp. 24–27+.

Dutton, Walt. "Clary at Home on the Range as Cook for *Hogan's Heroes.*" *Los Angeles Times,* February 2, 1966.

"Edward Feldman—Producer of 'The Brothers.' " CBS Television Network, Studio Biography, July 3, 1956.

Efron, Edith. "Think John Wayne!: Hip, Flip, Cocky Bob Crane Reveals His Secret of Playing a Hero's Role." *TV Guide,* August 3, 1968, pp. 25–27.

Egan, Cy. "Slaying of TV's Col. Hogan Stumps Arizona Police." *New York Post,* June 30, 1978, p. 3.

Eisner, Joel and David Krinsky. *Television Comedy Series: An Episode Guide to 153 TV Sitcoms in Syndication.* Jefferson, N.C.: McFarland and Co., 1984.

"Family Feud." Review. *Variety,* September 28, 1977.

Feeney, Mark Goodman F.X. "Top of His Game: Richard Dawson Is Back on Family Feud—and a Family Man—Again," *People,* November 14, 1994, p. 67.

Fessier, Michael Jr. "A War Ivan Dixon Is Winning." *New York Times,* January 29, 1967, p. D19.

Foster, Barbara. "Celebrity Update: The Many Facets of a One-time German Colonel, Werner Klemperer." *Orange Coast,* November 1983.

"Fun With the Nazis." *Newsweek,* November 11, 1969, p. 64.

Gardella, Kay. "Mozart Is Klemperer's Hero." *New York Daily News,* July 10, 1990, p. 63.

———. "Who Is Bob Crane? TV's Next Sgt. Bilko." *New York Daily News,* August 29, 1965.

Geitner, Paul. "Revamped *Hogan's Heroes* Has Germans in Stitches." Associated Press, August 1, 1997.

Grant, Hank. "On The Air." *Hollywood Reporter,* December 22, 1964.

———. "On The Air." *Hollywood Reporter,* March 1, 1965.

Gratz, Roberta Brandes. "Ivan Dixon: A Choice of Heroes." *New York Post,* June 17, 1967, section 3, p. 1.

Graysmith, Robert. *The Murder of Bob Crane.* New York: Berkeley Books, 1994.

Gross, Ben. "A TV Nazi Who Hates Nazis." *New York Daily News,* March 10, 1968.

———. "War's Not Hell; It's Really Fun." *New York Daily News,* July 10, 1966, p. S23+.

Guarino, Ann. "Comic Adventure for Elke." *New York Daily News,* January 4, 1968.

———. "Off Camera: Bob Crane." *New York Daily News,* February 10, 1974.

Hall, Bob. "Banner Year of John." *Los Angeles Herald-Examiner,* June 16, 1967.

Hanta, Karin. "A New Beginning in Vienna (Leon Askin)." *Austria Kultur,* January/February 1996.

Heffley, Lynne. "A New Hero for Werner Klemperer: Dr. Seuss' Gerald McBoing Boing." *Los Angeles Times,* June 8, 1991.

Hellman, Jack. "Light and Airy." *Variety,* March 25, 1968.

Herbstman, Mandel. *Wicked Dreams of Paula Schultz.* Review. *Film Daily,* January 3, 1968.

"A Hero with Many Talents: Larry Hovis." *Los Angeles Herald-Examiner,* January 9, 1969, p. D8.

Hersch, Linda T. "Robert Clary: He's Not Singing the Blues." *Soap Opera Digest,* May 26, 1981, pp. 21–27.

Hobson, Dick. "Achtung!... Please: John Banner Plays the Most Huggable Nazi on TV." *TV Guide,* May 6, 1967, pp. 16–17.

———. "Invisible Actor: Larry Hovis Even Got Left Out of His High School Yearbook." *TV Guide,* August 8, 1970, pp. 12–13.

———. "The Strange History of A-5714: He's Robert Clary, Who Has Moved from Buchenwald (in Germany) to Stalag 13 (in Hollywood)." *TV Guide,* November 19, 1966, pp. 23–26.

*Hogan's Heroes.* Review. *Variety,* September 22, 1965.

*Hogan's Heroes.* Review. *Variety,* October 13, 1965.

*Hogan's Heroes.* Review. *Variety,* September 21, 1966.

*Hogan's Heroes.* Review. *Variety,* September 20, 1967.

*Hogan's Heroes.* Review. *Variety,* October 2, 1968.

*Hogan's Heroes.* Review. *Variety,* October 1, 1969.

*Hogan's Heroes.* Review. *Variety,* September 30, 1970.

"*Hogan's Heroes* Fun-bound In TV Series on POW Camps." *New York Morning-Telegraph,* September 9, 1965.

Holms, John P. and Ernest Wood. *The TV Game Show Almanac.* Radnor, Pa.: Chilton Book Company, 1995.

Horn, John. "*The General* Stars Keaton in '27 Silent." *New York Tribune,* December 30, 1965, p. 15.

Humphrey, Hal. "Banner Sticks to Stars and Stripes." *Los Angeles Times,* September 28, 1965.

———. "Hogan's a Hero in Other Countries." *Los Angeles Times,* June 12, 1968, part V, p. 22.

———. "*Hogan's Heroes*: A Real Camp." *Los Angeles Times TV Times,* July 21–27, 1968.

"Hunting for the Brass Ring: For Sigrid Valdis, it's a husband who'll buy her a carousel." *TV Guide,* August 5, 1967, pp. 24–25.

Japenga, Ann. "Old Murders That Won't Die." *Los Angeles Times,* February 6, 1990, pp. E1–3.

Jarlett, Franklin. "Tragedy in Tinseltown." *Movie Collector's World,* December 22, 1989, p. 56+.

"John Banner, the Sgt. Schultz of *Hogan's Heroes*, Dies at 63." *New York Times,* February 2, 1973, p. L34.

Johnson, Erskine. "Meet Leon Askin: Who's a Bad Guy?" *TV Scout,* January 19, 1967.

Klein, Doris. "Bob Crane Has Hectic Hiatus." *Hollywood Reporter,* April 24, 1968, p. 16.

Klemperer, Werner. "Monocled Klink: No Fiercer Than a Dachshund." CBS Television Network press release, August 10, 1967.

"Klink Clicks: *Hogan's Heroes* and Werner Klemperer Find a New Generation of Fans Overseas." *People,* September 9, 1996, p. 66.

"Lack of Clues Stalls Crane Murder Probe." *Scottsdale Daily Progress,* July 26, 1978.

"Larry Hovis, of Original Cast of *Rowan and Martin's Laugh-In,* to Return When Series Starts Fifth Season on NBC-TV." NBC-TV Press Release, June 2, 1971.

Leslie, Kyra and Marc Cetner. "Bittersweet Life of the Spy from *Hogan's Heroes* (Robert Clary)." *National Enquirer,* September 24, 1996.

Liefgreen, Dan. "Police Sure of 'No. 1' Crane Case Suspect." *Scottsdale Daily Progress,* February 8, 1980.

———. "Unsolved Crane Case Still Hounds Police." *Scottsdale Daily Progress,* June 27, 1980.

Lipton, Michael A., Michael Haederle, Danelle Morton, and Joan DeClaire. "Sex, Murder and Videotape." *People,* September 12, 1994, pp. 44–49.

Lovece, Frank. "London Forfeits Film for Quality Television (Jerry London)." *TV Scene,* March 15, 1986, p. 12.

Lowry, Cynthia. "Klemperer's 'Colonel Klink' Is a Fine-Line Portrayal." *Los Angeles Herald-Examiner TV Weekly,* July 10–16, 1966, pp. 10–12.

Ludvigson, Evelyn. "'Col. Klink' Very Busy with Career." King Features Weekly Syndicate, June 20, 1990.

Mackin, Tom. "Briton Docs Anything for Big Laugh on TV." *Newark Sunday News,* May 17, 1970, section 6, p. E7.

Mahoney, John. *The Wicked Dreams of Paula Schultz.* Review. *Hollywood Reporter,* January 3, 1968.

Maksian, George. "Crane's Jokes on Death Shelve Show." *New York Daily News,* July 1, 1978, p. 35.

Maples, Tina. "The Musical Side of Werner Klemperer." *Milwaukee Journal,* January 18, 1991.

Marshall, Steve. "Suspect Arrested in '78 Death of Actor." *USA Today,* June 2, 1992, p. 3A.

Martindale, David. "Where Are They Now?: Werner Klemperer." *Biography,* February 1998, p. 22.

Martinez, Julio. "Enjoying Life in Cabaret." *Drama-Logue,* July 30–August 5, 1987, p. 5.

McMillan, Penelope. "Funeral Services Held for Actor Bob Crane." *Los Angeles Times,* July 6, 1978.

Mirkin, Steven. "Spielberg's Heroes." *Spy,* July/August 1994, pp. 50–55.

Morrison, Patt. "Bob Crane's Friend Acquitted in Death." *Los Angeles Times,* November 1, 1994, p. A3.

Moss, Morton. "Singin' in the Shower (Robert Clary)." *Los Angeles Herald-Examiner,* July 8, 1970.

Murphy, Mary. "The Prizes... The Applause... The Pain (Richard Dawson)." *TV Guide,* January 21, 1984, pp. 35–42.

Norbom, Mary Ann. *Richard Dawson and Family Feud.* New York: New American Library, 1981.

Novak, Ralph. *The Running Man.* Review. *People,* November 30, 1987, p. 18.

Oppel, Pete. "Associate Calls Crane 'the Best.' " *Dallas Morning News,* June 30, 1978.

"Our Guest Today (Bernard Fox)." *TV Collector,* July August 1986, pp. 22–28.

Owen, Elizabeth. "Werner Klemperer: Klink's Not His Only Claim to Fame." *VCR,* August 1986, pp. 44–46.

Page, Don. "Crane to Fill in for Whittinghill." *Los Angeles Times,* July 5, 1972.

———. "Ivan Dixon's Curious Career." *Los Angeles Times,* June 22, 1967, part V, p. 14.

Parish, James Robert. *Actor's Television Credits, 1950–1972.* Metuchen, N.J.: Scarecrow Press, 1973. Also Supplements I (1978) and II (1982).

Paulsen-Nalle, Amy. "Werner Klemperer: From Stalag 13 to the Broadway Stage." *Us,* December 14, 1987.

Petryni, Mike. "Bob Crane Whole Show." *Arizona Republic,* June 8, 1978, p. F7.

"The Phony Baloney Awards." *TV Guide,* January 6, 1990, p. 5.

Prelutsky, Burt. "Have Jokes, Will Travel (Richard Dawson)." *Los Angeles Times,* July 17, 1977.

"Probe of Actor's Death Hits Snag Amid Criticism." *Arizona Republic,* July 23, 1978, pp. A1–2.

Raddatz, Leslie. "World War II With a Laugh Track." *TV Guide,* November 27, 1965, pp. 22–24.

Reed, Jon-Michael. "Clary Can't Kick the Losing Habit." *Los Angeles Times,* June 10, 1977, pt. IV, p. 30.

Reilly, Sue. "Richard Dawson: TV's King Con Swings for Prime Time." *People,* November 21, 1977, pp. 67–68.

Rich, Allen. "Col. Klink, No Clunk; Eyes Emmy Chances." *Hollywood Citizen-News,* May 14, 1968, p. A6.

————. Profile of Bernie Fein. *Hollywood Citizen-News,* October 14, 1965, p. B12.

Robbins, Fred. "Fred Robbins Interviews Bob Crane." *Photoplay,* December 1968.

Rockwell, John. "*Sound of Music* Takes on the Icons of a Heroic Past." *New York Times,* March 9, 1990.

Ronnie, Art. "Radio Sends a Message." *Los Angeles Herald-Examiner TV Weekly,* March 31, 1963, pp. 10–11.

Scheur, Philip K. "Return Celebrated by Our Gang 'Kid' (Howard Caine)." *Los Angeles Times,* February 25, 1960.

Scott, Vernon. "Klink Forerunner of New Fashions." *Hollywood Citizen-News,* July 31, 1970.

"The Sergeant's Hard Climb from the Ranks: How Ivan Dixon Made it from Harlem to *Hogan's Heroes.*" *TV Guide,* September 16, 1967, pp. 35–36.

Shaw, Jim. "The 'Perfect' Marriage that Cracked Apart at the Seams." *TV Radio Mirror,* August 1969, p. 74+.

Siegel, Joel. "*Cabaret* Review." WABC–TV, October 22, 1987.

Smith, Cecil. "Bob Crane's 3rd Season." *Los Angeles Times,* March 6, 1975.

" 'Stalag' Authors File 'Hogan' Suit." *Hollywood Reporter,* January 18, 1967.

Stang, Joanne. "Bob Crane–Con Man to the Wehrmacht." *New York Times,* October 31, 1965, p. 19.

Stearns, David Patrick. "Stage Is Anything but Alive with *The Sound of Music.*" *USA Today,* March 12, 1990.

Steinmetz, Greg. "In Germany Now, Col. Klink's Maid Cleans in the Nude." *Wall Street Journal,* May 31, 1996.

*Superdad.* Review. *Variety,* January 16, 1974.

Swanson, Jack. "2 Bottles of Liquor and a Black Bag—Crane Case Riddles." *Arizona Republic* July 9, 1978, p. B1+.

Terry, Polly. "Bob Crane: I Struck Out on My Honeymoon!" *TV Radio Mirror,* February 1966, p. 42+.

Thomas, Kevin. " 'Wicked Dreams' to Open Multiple Run." *Los Angeles Times,* January 24, 1968.

Thompson, Howard. *Operation Eichmann.* Review. *New York Times,* May 4, 1961, p. 40.

————. "*Superdad* Is Typical Exercise by Disney." *New York Times,* February 3, 1974, p. 46.

"Those Cool War Heroes." *Newsweek,* December 19, 1966, p. 77.

"Transition." (John Banner obituary) *Newsweek,* February 12, 1973, p. 45.

"Transition." (Bob Crane obituary) *Newsweek,* July 10, 1978, p. 83.

Tuck, Lon. "Following His Father: The Music in Actor Werner Klemperer." *Washington Post,* July 12, 1985.

"War on Television." *Wall Street Journal,* July 25, 1966, p. 14.

Warnagieris, Greg. "Actor, Rabbi Tell Horrors of Holocaust." *Los Angeles Times,* June 21, 1981, Westside section, p. 1.

Weingrad, Jeff. "The Last Bob Crane Show." *New York Post,* July 6, 1978, p. 30.

"Weisenthal Center Pays Tribute to Robert Clary." *Variety,* March 30, 1982.

Whitney, Dwight. "His Podium Is a Prison Camp." *TV Guide,* January 22, 1966, pp. 22–25.

*Wicked Dreams of Paula Schultz.* Review. *Box Office,* January 15, 1968.

Williams, Bob. "On the Air (Bob Crane)." *New York Post,* June 17, 1974, p. 66.

Winsten, Archer. " 'Wicked Dreams' at Astor." *New York Post,* January 4, 1968.

Witbeck, Charles. "Playful 'Chicago Teddy Bears.' " *New York Daily News,* October 21, 1971.

Zakariasen, Bill. "Colonel Klink Vill Give the Orderss!" *New York Daily News,* March 12, 1985, p. 37.

# INDEX

Also available from
RENAISSANCE BOOKS

Party of Five: The Unofficial Companion
by Brenda Scott Royce
ISBN: 1-58063-000-6 • $14.95

Hercules & Xena: The Unofficial Companion
by James Van Hise
ISBN: 1-58063-001-4 • $15.95

Alien Nation: The Unofficial Companion
by Ed Gross
ISBN: 1-58063-002-2 • $14.95

Pufnstuf & Other Stuff
The Weird and Wonderful World of Sid & Marty Krofft
by David Martindale, Foreword by Marty Krofft & Afterword by Sid Krofft
ISBN: 1-58063-007-3 • $16.95

The Ultimate Marilyn
by Ernest W. Cunningham
ISBN: 1-58063-003-0 • $16.95

Rock Stars Do the Dumbest Things
by Margaret Moser & Bill Crawford
ISBN: 1-58063-023-5 • $12.95

Law and Order: The Unofficial Companion
by Kevin Courrier & Susan Green
ISBN: 1-58063-022-7 • $16.95

Reel Gags
by Bill Givens
ISBN: 1-58063-042-1 • $9.95

The Girl's Got Bite: An Unofficial Guide to Buffy's World
by Kathleen Tracy
ISBN: 1-58063-035-9 • $14.95

The Dukes of Hazzard: The Unofficial Companion
by David Hofstede
ISBN: 1-58063-038-3 • $14.95

To order please call
1-800-452-5589